Helion & Company Limited
Unit 8 Amherst Business Centre
Budbrooke Road
Warwick
CV34 5WE
England
Tel. 01926 499 619
Email: info@helion.co.uk
Website: www.helion.co.uk
Twitter: @helionbooks
https://helionbooks.wordpress.com/

Cover image: At around 04.30 hours on
   25 February 2022, the sky over Kyiv
   was brightly lit by a giant explosion.
   According to US sources, the Russian
   Aerospace Forces had forward-deployed
   one of its S-400 SAM sites right up
   to the border with Ukraine, and then
   opened fire. After travelling over some
   120 kilometres, the Russian SAM hit
   the Su-27P Bort 100, piloted by Colonel
   Aleksander Oksanchenko, one of the
   most famous Ukrainian aerobatic
   pilots and deputy commander of the
   831st Brigade. Oksanchenko, who had
   been decorated for his actions against
   the separatists and Russians in 2014,
   was killed. (Artwork by Pablo Patricio
   Albornoz © Helion & Company 2024)

Designed and typeset by Mach 3 Solutions
   (www.mach3solutions.co.uk)
Cover design Paul Hewitt, Battlefield Design
   (www.battlefield-design.co.uk)

ISBN: 978-1-804515-78-5

British Library Cataloguing-in-Publication
   Data
A catalogue record for this book is available
   from the British Library

We always welcome receiving book
proposals from prospective authors.

CONTENTS

Abbreviations and Acronyms		2
Introduction		2
1	Think Russian	3
2	Guerrilla Air Force	25
3	Coup Attempt	37
4	From a Coup to a War	52
5	The Flying Fire Brigade	57
6	Battle of Kharkiv	63
7	The Siege of Mariupol	66
8	Southern Ukraine	73
Bibliography		84
Notes		85

MAP OF EUROPE SINCE 1992

Note: In order to simplify the use of this book, all names, locations and geographic designations are as provided in *The Times World Atlas*, or other traditionally accepted major sources of reference, as of the time of described events.

ABBREVIATIONS AND ACRONYMS

ARH	active radar homing
ATGM	anti tank guided missile
ATMS	automated tactical management system
AWACS	airborne early warning and control system
BMD	*Boyevaya Mashina Desanta* (airborne combat vehicle)
BMP	*Boyevaya Mashina Pyekhoty* (infantry combat vehicle)
BTG	*batalonnaja takticheskaja gruppa* (battalion tactical group) (Russia and Ukraine)
BTR	*bronyetransportyor* (armoured personnel carrier)
CAA	Combined Arms Army (Russia)
CM	contour matching
COMINT	communications intelligence
ELINT	electronic intelligence
EO	electro-optical (or TV) guidance
EW	electronic warfare
FSB	*Federalnaya Sluzhba Bezopasnosti* (Federal Security Service) (Russia)
GAI	ground aided inertial guidance
GenStab	*Generalnyi shtab* (General Staff) (Russia and Ukraine)
GPS/GLONASS	global satellite positioning system
GRU	*Glavnoye Razvedyatelnoye Upravleniye* (Main Intelligence Directorate) (Russia)
IADS	integrated air defence system
IAP	International Airport
INS	inertial navigation system
IR	infrared
LDARZ	Lviv State Aircraft Repair Plant (also known as also LSARP) (Ukraine)
MANPADS	man portable air defence system
NARP	Nikolayev Aircraft Repair Plant (Ukraine)
NATO	North Atlantic Treaty Organization
NTsUO	National Defence Management Centre (Russia)

OAK	*Obyedinyonnaya Aviastoritelnaya Korporaciya* (United Aircraft Corporation) (Russia)
OBrAA	Separate Army Aviation Brigade (Ukraine)
OSK	*Ob'edinyonnoye strategicheskoe komandovanie* (Strategic Operational Command) (Russia)
PRH	passive radar homing
PSZSU	*Povitriyani syly Zbroiynyh syl Ukrayini* (Air Force of the Armed Forces of Ukraine)
PVO	*Protivovozdushnaya Oborona* (Air Defence Force) (USSR)
RUK	*razveyvatelno-udarnnyy komplekx* (Reconnaissance-Strike Complex) (VSRF)
SAGG	seeker-aided ground guidance
SARH	semi-active radar homing
SBU	*Sluzhba Bezpeky Ukrayiny* (Ukraine Security Service)
SIGINT	signals intelligence
SMG	scene matching guidance
SSO	*Syly spetsialnykh operatsii* (Special Operations Forces) (Ukraine)
TCM	terrain contour matching/mapping
TVM	track-via-missile
UAV	Unmanned Aerial Vehicle
USSR	Union of Soviet Socialist Republics
VDV	*Vozdushno-desantnye voyska* (airborne troops) (Russia)
VKS	*Vozdushno-kosmicheskiye sily* (Aerospace Forces) (Russia)
VSRF	*Vooruzhonnije Síly Rossíyskoj Federátsii* (Armed Forces of the Russian Federation)
VVS	*Voyenno-vozdushnye sily Rossii* (Russian Air Force) (Since 2015 a branch of the VKS)
ZDARZ	Zaproizhzhya State Aircraft Repair Plant (Ukraine; also known as 'MiGremont')
ZSU	*Zbroiynyh syl Ukrayiny* (Armed Forces of Ukraine)

INTRODUCTION

Whenever one attempts to shed light on *ongoing* conflicts, the infamous 'fog of war' stands in the way, obscuring countless facts behind a veil of secrecy. Particularly within the realm of aerial warfare, this fog is 'dense' due to its intricacy, the inaccessibility of information, and the fact that aerial warfare is the military discipline that is the hardest to explain. With the war in Ukraine very much going on and unlikely to be over any time soon, it is certain to remain this way for a few years longer. Therefore, our aim with this book is not to 'fix' any kind of 'ultimate truth' but to guide the reader through at least some of that fog: to do so through elucidating the strategic and tactical decisions made, and though describing the technology used and the resulting air warfare, while ensuring the complex technical concepts are presented in a manner accessible to all readers.

The methodology used in the research for this book was relatively simple: we have used a mix of information obtained from first-hand sources in Ukraine and the Russian Federation, and so-called open-source intelligence – where the latter includes extensive cross-examination of all available reporting by mainstream and social media. Indeed, the sheer volume of open sources of reference has reached such proportions that in the case of well-established fact we have decided to leave out most of the related references and focus on those that are most important and relevant to aerial warfare.

Finally, we have almost entirely left out discussion of socioeconomic and geostrategic background and context: these have been discussed in-depth in earlier volumes of this mini-series – especially Volume 2 (much of the information from which has been updated in this volume). Instead, the focus of this book is entirely upon factors that have had a direct or indirect influence upon the form and flow of aerial warfare over Ukraine from 24 February 2022 until around the mid-March of the same year. In similar fashion, in this volume, we have completely focused on major Russian offensives in northern-central, north-eastern, south-eastern and southern Ukraine in late February and early March 2022. Operations in eastern Ukraine, and the long-range missile campaign initiated in late February will be covered in a following volume.

1

THINK RUSSIAN

During the Cold War, Soviet military art was studied extensively and Western intelligence agencies accumulated immense volumes of expertise on this topic. Due to a mixture of other priorities and complacency, much of this knowledge has been lost since the early 1990s: indeed, through the late 2010s, Western experts tended to prattle on about the Russian military 'high-tech modernisation' and began massively overestimating its capacities and misinterpreting its capabilities. Nowhere was this as clear as when it came to the Russian Aerospace Forces (*Vozdushno-kosmicheskiye sily*, VKS), which is why the way it was equipped, trained, and then deployed in combat through the decades up to 2022 came as a rude shock for many in the West, and remains widely misunderstood even at the time this book is about to be published.

The Brain(s)

As described in Volume 2 of this mini-series, at least nominally, in the Russian Federation in 2022 the business of strategic planning was the task of the Security Council: an inter-ministerial body chaired by high-level officials, most of whom had an intelligence and/or security background, and all of whom were closely associated with Vladimir Putin. In practice, Putin had the final say in regards of everything that followed.

The task of bridging Putin's strategic planning with the military operational art was that of the General Staff of the Armed Forces of the Russian Federation (*GenStab*). As of 2022, the Chief of the Russian *GenStab* was Army General Valery Gerasimov. The body commanded by Gerasimov was staffed by a caste of professional analysts and planners, never rotated through joint assignments and thus never 'fixed' to a specific branch of arms. This is of particular significance because while the *GenStab* has far wider authorisation and function than comparable command nodes in the West (for example: its US equivalent, the Joint Chiefs of Staff), it had no operational control of the force. However, it was still responsible for developing doctrine and capabilities, for planning at strategic and operational levels, and was the sole procurement authority. In other words: the *GenStab* bore the full range of responsibilities, determining what future wars might look like, via obtaining the necessary equipment, organising and training all the branches of the Armed Forces of the Russian Federation, to planning major combat operations.

The crucial role of the *GenStab* was that of 'thinking' – and of being supposed to know – what future wars would look like, how they would be fought, and thus what kind of strategy, doctrine, weapons and other equipment the Russian armed forces would need. This is why whenever discussing Russian – and prior to that, Soviet – aircraft design and the way their air force operated – one always has to start with the *GenStab*.

The primary origin of the *GenStab*'s mindset ever since 1945 has been the Second World War. Experience from this conflict was insistently studied and restudied by generations of Soviet, and then Russian, military officers and also formed the core of their way of thinking about how to fight a war in 2022. While experience from so-called 'local conflicts' – primarily those in the Middle East and South East Asia in the 1960s, 1970s, and 1980s – have always played an important role for military thinking in the West, the Soviet and

Russian studies of such wars remained at least very limited: the known studies are renowned for containing a mass of factual errors and omitting the key data, usually for reasons related to ideology and politics. More recent Soviet and Russian combat experience – including Afghanistan in the 1980s, Chechnya in the 1990s, and Georgia in 2008 – have had rather temporary effects in regards of equipment and training of a relatively limited number of units. As a consequence, even when the *GenStab* considered local and regional conflicts as the most likely manifestations of war, as in the 2000s and 2010s, it was still equipping and training the entire Russian armed forces to fight the most dangerous form of warfare: a large-scale, conventional war under nuclear-threat conditions. This is what formed the fundamental requirements for most modern-day Russian military aircraft and shaped the organisation and training of the VKS.

Lowest Common Denominators

Because most combat aircraft operated by the VKS as of 2022, and since, were based on designs developed during the Cold War, for a better understanding of their actual purposes and the way they are deployed in combat, it is necessary to take an in-depth look back to those times: at least back to the 1970s and 1980s. Once the *GenStab* had issued a requirement for a new military aircraft, it would also pick the suitable design bureau. This in turn would then request the most advanced currently available aerodynamic configuration for the purpose from the Central Aerohydrodynamic Institute (*TsAGI*). *TsAGI* would issue its recommendations and then it would be up to the design bureau to design and research correspondingly. At some point during this process, the task of manufacturing prototypes and then the pre-series aircraft was given to selected factories, and the design would run state-acceptance trials. Obviously, the usual procedure was that if the design was successful, it would be ordered into full-scale production. However, at least as often it happened that the *GenStab* or the branch in question would select its favourite, and full-scale production would be launched before the state-acceptance trials.

As mentioned above, for most of the Cold War the *GenStab* saw an all-out nuclear war as the ultimate form of warfare. Unsurprisingly, it issued requirements for new weapons systems capable of fighting exactly this kind of conflict. With the ultimate opponent of the Union of Soviet Socialist Republics (USSR; colloquially 'Soviet Union') being intercontinental ballistic missiles operated by the powers of the North Atlantic Treaty Organization (NATO), the *GenStab* emphasised development of their own nuclear weapons and intercontinental ballistic missiles, and the means of defence against such weaponry. With the next tier of the ultimate threat being represented by strategic bombers and tactical fighter-bombers armed with nuclear weapons, logic dictated that the *GenStab* demand the development of manned interceptors capable of destroying these before they could unleash their nuclear weapons. Considering the sheer size of the Soviet territory, this was a gargantuan task requiring the continual development of new types of manned interceptors capable of scrambling on short notice, rapidly climbing to operational altitude, and then intercepting either high-flying bombers or low-flying fighter-bombers, and (preferably) destroying these with a single attack. The basic requirements for such aircraft were correspondingly to take-off, climb, destroy the target, and return to base.

For example, in the mid-1950s, Western bomber forces – foremost the Strategic Air Command of the USA and Bomber Command of the Royal Air Force in the UK – began receiving the predecessors of cruise missiles: they were armed with weapons they could release from 100 kilometres or more away from their targets, without having to actually overfly heavily-protected major urban centres or military facilities in the USSR. This resulted in the Soviets launching work on manned interceptors capable of destroying such bombers before they could release their stand-off weapons: aircraft like the Mikoyan i Gurevich MiG-21 and Sukhoi Su-15. A few years later, many of NATO's members began placing large orders for Lockheed F-104G Starfighter fighter-bombers, while the USAF acquired the Republic F-105 Thunderjet. Both types were meant to deliver 'tactical' nuclear bombs while flying very fast and very low. Correspondingly, the *GenStab* requested the development of a manned interceptor capable of destroying such targets. The resulting MiG-23 was manufactured in huge numbers. However, barely was it in service, when NATO began introducing a new generation of fighters, including types like the Grumman F-14 Tomcat, McDonnell-Douglas F-15 Eagle, General Dynamics F-16 Fighting Falcon and others. Correspondingly, the *GenStab* reacted with requirements that led to the development of the MiG-29. Moreover, because of the requirement to intercept US-made Rockwell B-1 bombers and the cruise missiles they could carry, and do so over the vast expanses of Siberia, it ordered the development of the MiG-31. Finally, as a complement for the MiG-31, and because there were limits in how many aircraft the Soviet Group of Forces in Germany could deploy at air bases in East Germany, the *GenStab* requested a bigger 'variant' of the MiG-29 design, capable of either operating over the northern USSR or of reaching the battlefields in Central Europe when based in Poland and Ukraine. Thus came into being the Sukhoi Su-27.

Through all of these times and processes, and irrespective of how much the technology developed, the fundaments of the *GenStab*'s requirements remained the same: they were still based on experience from the Second World War. Using the statistics from 1941–45, when issuing specifications for new combat aircraft, the 'brains' of the *GenStab* 'knew' that in an all-out nuclear war tactical combat aircraft were unlikely to survive more than 120–150, perhaps 200 hours of combat operations. This much-overlooked factor is what dictated the *GenStab*'s requirements for manufacturing quality, and also the maintenance schedules for the resulting equipment. Correspondingly, through the 1950s and 1960s, the Soviet combat aircraft were designed with an emphasis on simplicity and to be operated for 120-, 150-, 200- and then 400 hours without requiring any complex maintenance. This also made them cheap to acquire and operate in peacetime. In turn, once flown beyond such hours, they required a complete rebuild, requiring their return to the factory that manufactured them, or to works specialised in overhauling combat aircraft. This interval was only gradually increased in the case of types introduced to service in the 1970s and 1980s, to between 600 and 800 flight hours, though with the result of Soviet aircraft becoming much more expensive.

Another important factor for the development of Soviet military aircraft were the *GenStab*'s obsession with centralised command and control and the fact that in the 1960s the USSR began lagging behind the West in regards of the development of micro-technologies. In the first case, and essentially: the Soviet military 'brains' expected the all-out nuclear war to be commanded from selected main headquarters – the only place with the necessary situational awareness, even more so if supported by computers and data-links, and almost by remote control. In the second, the centralisation of command and control made the issue of equipment for future combat aircraft a lot cheaper: they needed less of the expensive advanced technologies, which in turn kept both their production price low, and lowered their maintenance requirements. Instead of 'dissipating the effort', the *GenStab* sought to 'focus the effort': instead of placing orders for ever more complex and ever more expensive aircraft packed with high technologies, as the West did, the Soviets sought to develop aircraft that kept the application of advanced computers 'limited' to their ground-based headquarters, to which they were connected either via radio or such datalink systems as Lazur. Certainly enough, the Soviet aircraft were also designed to 'outfly' their Western opponents – in terms of speed, operational altitude, or manoeuvring at high acceleration – but also carried far simpler avionics systems: the *GenStab*'s standpoint was that all the targeting intelligence necessary was to be supplied to the pilot by ground-based headquarters, the only node with the necessary situational awareness to make decisions.

The resulting interceptors and fighter-bombers were custom-tailored to their expected mission, but ill-suited for anything else. Most of them were interceptors designed to scramble, be vectored by ground control along a precise intercept course, destroy their target, and return to base. They carried little or no extra fuel, no extra avionics, and only enough weapons for their sole mission. Even their avionics were designed to the 'minimum requirement imaginable': the resulting aircraft were all equipped for operations (literally) 'by remote control' – with the help of so-called 'automated tactical management systems' (ATMS). The ATMS was the tool of remote control: a system supported by computers installed in ground-based headquarters, capable of integrating the input from all available intelligence sources and sensors (including intelligence information, early warning and surveillance radars, electronic support and warfare stations, and information provided by ground-based air defences), and then coordinating and controlling the work of – depending on the task – either manned interceptors, or fighter-bombers, and of their own ground-based air defences, or a combination of *all* these.

Within such a system, the Soviet – and later Russian – pilots or flight crews were never equipped, nor required – and thus never trained – to have more situational awareness than necessary for their immediate mission. Their job was to take-off, control the work of onboard systems (engine, avionics, hydraulics, and weapons), and – if necessary at all, because on specific types even this could be done by remote control – to release weapons upon orders from the ground. It was the job of their ground controllers to have the situational awareness, and commanders in ground-based headquarters to make decisions.

The severe economic crisis and massive political turbulence of the 1990s, followed by the gradual take over and imposition of the dictatorship by the small clique of strongmen around Vladimir Putin – all linked to the Federal Security Service (*Federalnaya Sluzhba Bezopasnosti*, FSB), combined with the insistence of the top minds within the *GenStab* upon traditional methods of military decision-making – prevented the Russian air force from developing beyond this point. This is why the VKS of the 2010s and early 2020s never trained its flight personnel to fly their aircraft to the maximum of their flight envelope, nor to operate independently from the control of their commanders, exercised with help of ATMS: just as during the times of the USSR, they did not need to do so – which in turn made not only the research and development of their aircraft, but also their training, and their peacetime and combat operations much cheaper, and ascertained improved flight safety during training operations, while offering the promise of fulfilling the task. Unsurprisingly, and despite lots of public announcements and even more wishful thinking by some of the air force's top commanders of the 1990s and even in the 2000s, the training of VKS flight crews remained dominated by the stolid conservativism of Soviet times. With flight safety being a paramount issue, both training and operational methods were curbed, while pilots and flight crews usually spent an entire working day solely upon preparing for their next training sortie. In other words: regardless of the availability of modern technologies, by 2022 all aspects of Russian air warfare were brought to their lowest common denominator.

Tolkachev Affair

As unlikely as it is to sound at first, much of the organisation, equipment, and tactics of the VKS in 2022 was a result of a chain of events that began back in the late 1970s. Adolf Georgievich Tolkachev – an electronics engineer who was working as one of the chief designers at the Scientific Research Institute of Radar (NIIR or NII Radar, better-known as the Phazotron Design Bureau); the Soviet Union's largest developer of military radars and avionics – became disillusioned by the persecution of his wife's parents and by communist rule in general. As a result, he established clandestine links to the Central Intelligence Agency (CIA) of the USA and began delivering immense volumes of highly classified and extremely sensitive data about the most important radars and weapons systems installed in Soviet-made military aircraft and air defence systems. The amount of materials Tolkachev provided was such that the CIA translators could not keep up with their task: indeed, US intelligence was still busy translating and studying the information supplied by him well into the 1990s, years after he had been revealed to the Soviets by one of their spies within the US intelligence community, and arrested, sometime in early 1985. While the CIA never released precise details, the available information emphasised that the intelligence provided by Tolkachev was crucial to the USAF completely redesigning the electronic package for its latest fighter jets as early as 1979. An internal evaluation by the CIA from March 1980 praised Tolkachev for providing details of unprecedented quality, including details of combat aircraft that were only just about to enter operational service. In April 1980, another internal CIA memorandum called his information on jam-proofing tests for Soviet fighter aircraft radar systems 'unique': obviously, he provided data that was not obtainable by any other means. Only a few months later, Tolkachev was credited with, 'providing unique information on a new Soviet fighter aircraft, and documents on several new models of airborne missile systems'. Similarly, a memorandum from the Department of Defense from September 1980 praised the impact of Tolkachev's reporting as, 'limitless in terms of enhancing US military systems' effectiveness, and 'in the potential to save lives and equipment…instrumental in shaping the course of billions of dollars of US research and development activities…'[1]

Black Hole of the 1990s and 2000s

While Moscow has remained zip-lipped about the Tolkachev affair to this day, deductions from the information available means it is possible to draw the conclusion that he caused irreparable damage to the Soviet – and thus Russian – defence sector, and to their aviation industry in particular. Indeed, keeping in mind that he betrayed an entire generation of the latest fighter jets – including the MiG-29,

MiG-31, and Su-27 – and their weapon systems, as well as several ground-based air defence systems (such as the S-300) before these entered operational service, and in combination with the Chernobyl catastrophe that bankrupted the empire (leading to the dissolution of the USSR), the conclusion is that the Russian aviation industry never fully recovered from this series of blows.

Almost the same can be concluded about the development of the military thinking of the *GenStab*: this has never fully comprehended the impact of advanced technologies, nor realised what exactly happened in several local wars of the 1980s that exercised such strong influence upon the Western way of thinking about future wars (like Lebanon in 1982 and Libya of 1986, and after). As a result, by the late 1980s the development of the Soviet military art not only began falling behind that of several of their allies, but well behind that of the West. There then followed the 1990s and early 2000s, when there was no funding for development in regards of strategy and tactics at all. Indeed, the situation reached a point where the Russian aviation industry began acting on its own initiative in order to survive – independently from the *GenStab*. Thus, making use of foreign high-technologies it developed a new aircraft type – the Sukhoi Su-30 – along with a few new weapons systems based on the requirements of (and with funding help from), an export customer: India. In turn, and primarily because of the lack of money, the rest of that industry degenerated to the point where it became unable to deliver what the *GenStab* demanded: hundreds, if not thousands, of engineers it used to employ were bought up by Western – especially US – industry: more often than not, they took with them all their technical documentation, too.

The situation was similar in the air force: massive losses of aircraft, units, facilities, and personnel caused by the dissolution of the USSR, followed by years of massive budget shortfalls, resulted in its near collapse in the mid-1990s. Indeed, the service was still vegetating for much of the following decade. Preoccupied with political and economic reforms, the Kremlin was too disinterested and 'busy with other affairs' to properly finance its armed forces, including air power. In an attempt to reduce operational expenses, on 1 January 1999 the Kremlin integrated the former Air Defence Force (*Protivovozdushnaya Oborona*, PVO) into the Air Force (until 2015 still named the *Voyenno-Vozdushnye Sily*, VVS). In the course of this integration, the air force moved most of its own headquarters to those of the PVO, because the latter were much better equipped with command, control, and communication systems – with ATMS – than its own facilities. Simultaneously, the number of regiments was reduced from 340 to 180 and the service vacated 32 air bases and 310 housing estates. To no avail: just as during most of the 1990s and through much of the 2000s, Russian military pilots were happy if they could get an operational aircraft and clock anything between 20 and 40 hours of continuation training annually. Serious tactical exercises and evaluations were conducted by only a handful of instruction and research units, and almost exclusively on behalf of foreign customers.

United Aircraft Corporation[2]

As a President of the Russian Federation, Vladimir Putin might never have had a clearly defined political programme, however, he never had doubts about how to impose his authority upon the state and all of its functions. He did so – with the help of the FSB – by ascertaining control over major sources of income, its oil and gas sectors, followed by banks and insurance, and organised crime. Immediately after, he reached out for other branches of the economy. In 2000, he established JSC Rosoboronexport as the sole (state-owned) agency for all arms exports and imports, and the control of dual-use products, technologies and services. In February 2006, Putin then went a step further and signed a decree ordering the creation of the United Aircraft Corporation (*Obyedinyonnaya Aviastoritelnaya Korporaciya*, OAK).

The purpose of the OAK was to centralise the control of the entire aviation industry of the Russian Federation. Although envisaged as a high-tech enterprise, the board of the OAK almost completely consisted of Putin's favourites: while they promptly secured his dominant position, next to none had any kind of experience, and even fewer had skills, in industrial management; nobody dared take decisions without securing authorisation from the president. Combined with the Russian tradition of governments never allocating the funds promised, and Putin's decision to prevent any kind of serious foreign influence, a corporation expected to generate an income of US$15 billion per year by 2025 found itself starved of nearly everything including the knowhow and the workforce, and was also cut off from possible sources of foreign investment. Unsurprisingly, over the following 15 years it proved unable to realise even one of the bombastically announced major projects for future aircraft and helicopters. The much-lauded Sukhoi Su-57 'stealth' fighter (ASCC/NATO reporting name 'Felon'), supposed to be equal to the US-made Lockheed Martin F-22 Raptor and re-establish Russia as one of the leaders in this field, was not only delayed for years but – despite all the announcements to the contrary – never completely developed, and was neither in series production nor in operational service as of 2022. Indeed, other than continuing production of existent designs with minor updates for export customers, the OAK failed even to fully develop subvariants entirely equipped with avionics made in the Russian Federation, let alone launch series production of guided weapons. Numerous other ambitious projects only experienced ever further delays: the research and development of the Beriev A-100 airborne early warning and control system (AWACS) was constantly delayed, while projects for a new strategic bomber and a fighter with vertical take-off and landing capabilities never ventured beyond initial announcements.

Part of the reason was that around the time he created the OAK, Putin realised that Russia could neither afford an overhaul and upgrade of its entire armed forces, nor was Russian industry capable of manufacturing the high technologies, both of which were necessary for one of his most ambitious projects: the complete reform of the Armed Forces of the Russian Federation.

New Look

Initiated on 1 January 2003 – when the former Army Aviation was subordinated to the Air Force – and eventually becoming known as the 'New Look' once it reached nationwide proportions in 2008, the reform of the Russian military and defence sector had the primary aim of streamlining the former Soviet system and its bloated command structure into a modern and combat-ready force, largely depending on professional soldiers. The New Look was managed by a new minister of defence, the economist Anatoly Serdyukov who – against fierce resistance from the *GenStab* – drastically downsized both the number of active units, and officers (who used to account for about one third of the total manpower), and other ranks, while creating a professional corps of non-commissioned officers. In 2010, Serdyukov also reformed the seven existent Military Districts into four Strategic Operational Commands (*Ob'edinyonnoye strategicheskoe komandovanie*, OSKs).

The Air Force had all of its divisions disbanded, the number of regiments reduced from 180 to 70, and the number of air bases from 70 to 52. Regiments were reorganised as air bases, which became the basic structural element of the VVS, each including a headquarters, between one and seven squadrons, an airfield service battalion, and communication units. In similar fashion, all the former air defence divisions of the PVO were disbanded and replaced by 13 airspace defence brigades, distributed into seven commands.

Before long, the VVS appeared to profit immensely from this reform: with the *GenStab* being granted the necessary funding, it began ordering an entirely new generation of combat aircraft with much-improved capabilities and performance, such as the Sukhoi Su-30, Su-34, and Su-35. Moreover, its reorganised units were granted enough funds, spares, and fuel for their pilots to fly up to 80–120 hours per year, including serious tactical training. After decades of degeneration and a life in shame following the dissolution of the USSR, officers and other ranks serving with the Air Force were proud of themselves, their service and their aircraft.

Victory of the Red Man[3]

Soon, Serdyukov's New Look placed him on a direct collision course with the *GenStab*. Not only did the top generals consider it an insult because he was a civilian; they were disgusted when he brought in a team of civilian accountants to control the defence budget (largely because ever-growing parts of the budget were disappearing without a trace); they were furious over the work of Serdyukov's accountants 'causing problems for young and promising officers' sacked for corruption; and the *GenStab* was aghast when Serdyukov launched his effort to liquidate 30 percent of the central administration and to halve the number of active officers, not to mention his efforts to transform the armed forces from a mass-mobilisation army to a professional force…. By 2012, tensions reached such proportions that Putin was left without choice but to replace him with one of his favourites and close aides, Sergey Shoygu. Although another civilian, Shoygu skilfully took care to appease the *GenStab* through revoking some of Serdyukov's reforms: he pardoned numerous officers, reinstated Soviet military traditions, and reestablished some of the army's divisions, thus reaffirming the position of what the Russian military officers termed as the 'Red Man' in the armed forces (also known as 'Homo Sovieticus' within academic circles).

When it came to the VVS, Shoygu not only reversed the reorganisation into air bases and reinstated regiments: he also allowed the *GenStab* – on the basis of experience from Chechnya and Georgia, though in faithful pursuance of Soviet traditions since the 1930s – to cement the position of the air force as that of an administrator: a service responsible for air bases, maintenance, aircraft and the training of their flight and ground crews *in peace*, but without any kind of influence upon combat operations. Indeed, for operational purposes, the Air Force's tactical arm (Frontal Aviation, equipped with interceptors and attack aircraft) and the Army Aviation (equipped with attack, assault, and transport helicopters) remained operationally subordinated to the respective Joint Strategic Commands, i.e. front commanders. With the headquarters of the OSKs always being dominated by army officers, there was not much left for the VKS to do but to support 'local' operational needs.

Moreover – and as it became clear at least during the Russian military intervention in Syria in 2015 and after – nothing changed in regards of development of doctrine and tactics of the Air Force, the quality of its equipment and tactics, the quality of its leadership, or operational plans: permitting its unit commanders to make autonomous decisions remained anathema, and regardless how many new and 'multi-role' Su-30, Su-34, and Su-35 'fighter-bombers' the service received, the air force remained a tool for supporting the ground forces – in the form of air defence, escort, and close air support (CAS) operations. Indeed, experience from the wars in Chechnya, Georgia, and Syria made the *GenStab* feel confirmed in its theories that CAS was, and remained, the primary purpose of air power, and also insistent that all the decision-making must remain reserved for higher levels: because its officers were convinced it belonged there. Regimental commanders thus remained tied to the practice of training norms and standards: to gradual, slow, repetitive build-up of skills of their flight and ground crews, well-known from Soviet times, in which pilots (or flight crews) took 8 to 12 years to fully qualify and spent most of their flight time flying circles within visual distance of their air bases. While the total number of flight hours per pilot/crew per annum remained at around 80–100 hours, tactical exercises were limited to a bare minimum and heavily prescribed, with crews rarely experiencing surprise from unexpected opponents or obstacles.[4]

Dissimilar air combat training (i.e. training between different aircraft types) remained limited, and if undertaken, it involved the top ranks of the regiment only. Finally, even the classification of specific aircraft types experienced a dogmatic approach. Correspondingly, and regardless of being advertised as 'multi-role' abroad, in the VKS the Su-30SM was declared an interceptor and its crews trained correspondingly; the Su-34 was considered a bomber (and a replacement for the Su-24) – and their crews trained as such. When, in 2013, a few Su-34 crews publicly complained about lacking training even in the deployment of R-73 short-range air-to-air missiles for self-defence purposes, somebody up the chain of command 'gave them a few to play with' and left it at that. Fundamental to their training remained the tactical manual for bombers (abbreviated as KBT).

The 'dot on the i' for the Russian aircraft industry and the VKS was the loss of contact with dozens of high-technology enterprises in Ukraine – which were responsible for the mass of research and development – caused by the invasions of the Crimea and Donbas in 2014, and the resulting international sanctions. Even as of 2018, the Russian defence sector was still experiencing major problems in replacing Ukrainian knowhow, capabilities, and production capacity: the resulting crisis reached such proportions that the Ministry of Defence experienced significant problems launching domestic production of any kind of guided weapons.[5]

VKS Organisation in 2022

As of 2022, the Armed Forces of the Russian Federation (*Vooruzhonnije Síly Rossíyskoj Federátsii*, VSRF) was organised into three military branches and two independent corps, the commanders of which were responsible to the National Defence Management Centre:

Ground Troops (branch)
Aerospace Forces (branch)
Navy (branch)
Strategic Rocket Troops (corps)
Airborne Assault Troops (VDV) (corps)

The VKS was commanded by the Main Command of the Aerospace Forces, headquartered at Znamyenika Street in Moscow, and its everyday operations managed by the Commander-in-Chief Executive and the Main Staff of the Aerospace Forces. At the next level, the VKS was organised into three corps:

Air Force (VVS) (operator of all fixed-wing aircraft and helicopters)
Air and Missile Defence Troops (operator of ground-based air defences)
Space Troops (operator of the ballistic missile warning system, space launches, and space surveillance)

As mentioned above, the purpose of the VKS was administrative by nature: for operational purposes, its elements were subjected to the control of four Joint Strategic Commands from 2010 (increased to five from 2014), which were organised on a territorial principle:

Western OSK (HQ St. Petersburg)
Northern OSK (also Northern Fleet) (HQ Severomorsk)
Southern OSK (HQ Rosov-na-Donu)
Central OSK (HQ Yekaterinenburg)
Eastern OSK (HQ Khabarovsk)

Correspondingly, the VKS was divided into several direct-reporting units, the Long-Range Aviation, Military Transport Aviation (VTA), and five Air Force and Air Defence Armies:

6th Leningrad Red Banner Army of Air Forces and Air Defence (Western OSK)
45th Army of Air Forces and Air Defence (Northern OSK)
4th Red Banner Army of Air Forces and Air Defence (Southern OSK)
14th Red Banner Army of Air Forces and Air Defence (Central OSK)
11th Red Banner Army of Air Forces and Air Defence (Eastern OSK)

At the tactical level the VKS was organised into aviation regiments. On average, a single regiment was commanded by a colonel (supported by a team of staff officers, the regimental command post, flight operations management team, and sub-unit commanders), and included two squadrons of 12 aircraft or three or more squadrons of 12 helicopters each. As of 2015, the VKS had 1.3 crews per aircraft or helicopter on average. Maintenance of all the equipment of a regiment was the task of its Engineering Service and the Technical Operation Unit; communications and navigation were managed by the Battalion of Communication and Radio Support; while the maintenance of the home-base and related equipment was the task of the Battalion of Airfield and Technical Maintenance. Overall, and depending on the type of aircraft or helicopter it operated, a regiment comprised around 1,000–1,200 military officers and other ranks, and up to 250 civilian employees.

Direct Reporting Units

Directly reporting to the High Command VKS were units for special purposes, aviation-evaluation and research purposes and the Group of Russian Federation's Forces in Syria, including Hmeimim Air Base (555th Air Base). The most prominent amongst special purpose units was the 8th Aviation Division, based at Chkalovsky, operating VIP transports for top military commanders and – in the time of war – for the top civilian authorities. Much more relevant to the combat operations in Ukraine since 2022 were the research institutions. Foremost amongst these was the Central Research Institute of the Air Force of the Ministry of Defence of the Russian Federation at Shcholkovo: this included six Research Centres, of which the three most relevant for operations in Ukraine were:

NITs AT V: responsible for defining the place and role of military aviation within the VSRF and requirements for its future aircraft and helicopters

NITs ERAT: responsible for development of flight and technical manuals

2 TsNII MO RF: responsible for studies related to air and missile defence

Another major research facility was the 929th State Flight Test Centre of the Ministry of Defence of the Russian Federation. Based at Akhtubinsk Test Centre, but maintaining proving grounds in the Astrakhan area (in Kazakhstan), in the Fedosia area (on the Black Sea Coast), and in Nalchik (in Kabardino-Balkaria), the 929th included six test centres for various purposes (including test-flying, engines, evaluation for Naval Aviation use, engineering and weapons, and static testing), while the seventh – the 1338th Test Centre at Chkalovsky – operated Ilyushin Il-80 airborne command posts and Il-82 airborne communications relay aircraft of the 4th Airborne Control Post of the VSRF: essentially, strategic command and control aircraft serving as survivable, mobile command posts for the president, the minister of defence, or their successors in the event of a strategic emergency.

Of similar importance, but slightly more specialised purpose, was the 4th State Air Personnel Preparation and Military Evaluation Centre of the Ministry of Defence of the Russian Federation, based at Lipetsk. This institution was primarily responsible for the evaluation of new aircraft types before their service entry with the VKS. For this purpose, it comprised the 968th Fighter Aviation Regiment (*istryebityel'niy aviatsionniy polk*, IAP) and the 968th Research Instructor Composite Aviation Regiment (usually the first VKS unit to receive any new types of combat aircraft when these were entering service), both based at Lipetsk Air Base (AB). Other elements of the 4th Centre included the 237th Aviation Technology Demonstration Centre at Kubinka AB (including two aerobatic teams), the 344th State Combat Training and Flight Crew Conversion Centre of Army Aviation at Torzhok AB (responsible for evaluation of new helicopter types), and the 924th State Unmanned Aviation Centre of the Ministry of Defence of the Russian Federation (responsible for evaluation of unmanned aerial vehicles, UAVs). Finally, also subordinated to the 4th Centre were the 'aggressor' assets of the VKS

– the 185th Combat Training and Combat Application Centre of the Aerospace Forces, based at Astrakhan AB, and the 116th Combat Application Training Centre of Fighter Aviation – of which the latter operated MiG-29s of several subvariants.

Reconnaissance-Strike Complex and Automated Tactical Management Systems[6]

For most of the last 50 years, the *GenStab*'s thinking about modern warfare was heavily influenced by Army General Makhmut Akhmetovic Gareev. The former military advisor to Egypt, commander of the Ural Military District, Head of the Military Scientific Directorate of the General Staff, Deputy Director of the Main Operational Directorate of the General Staff, Deputy Director of the *GenStab* (starting in 1984), and President of the Academy of Military Sciences, Gareev was widely considered the greatest Russian military theoretician of his times. Under his influence, the *GenStab* remained insistent on traditionalist ways of thinking, emphasising continuous studies of the Soviet experience from the Second World War. It was only with the demise of the traditionalist influence and then Putin's and Serdyukov's reforms that officers of the *GenStab* began demanding the modernisation of doctrine, tactics, and weapons. Thus, it has only been since the early 2000s that the Russian Ministry of Defence began investing into serious digitalisation of its command, control, and communication functions.

Once the *GenStab* initiated its own reforms, new terminology began appearing in the Russian military vocabulary, most of which can be summarised with the Reconnaissance-Strike Complex (*razveyvatelno-udarnnyy komplekx*, RUK). The concept of the RUK can be only roughly compared to the Western concept C4ISR (Command, Control, Communications, Computers, Intelligence, Surveillance and Reconnaissance): its actual essence was, once again, that of a lowest common denominator. Essentially, the concept emphasised the synergy of collected intelligence for the purpose of accelerating military decision-making, aiming to deliver quick, determined, and precise strikes where these were expected to matter.

Following several years of research and development, the idea of the RUK was first realised in 2010, when OSK headquarters came into being, followed – in 2014 – by the construction of the National Defence Management Centre (NTsUO) in Moscow. The NTsUO integrated command and control of all defence and security structures

Starting in 2016, Russia launched production of the Forpost UAV: a version of the Israeli Aircraft Industries Searcher Mk II manufactured under licence. The VKS acquired a total of 30 systems with three aircraft each, and in 2020 launched production of the Forpost-R armed with X-BPLA anti-tank guided missiles. In February–March 2022, the system was to cause much trouble to the Ukrainian armed forces in the Kyiv area in particular. (Photo by Daniele Faccioli)

in real time. The creation of the NTsUO in turn lead to the idea to network this node not only to OSK headquarters but also down to tactical-level units. Originally planned to be realised by 2027, as far as known, this effort failed years ago. Arguably, over the years the Russians have developed a number of automated tactical management systems for their air and ground forces, but only those coordinating the work of their air defence systems and navy's warships have actually entered regular service. Arguably, the Unified System for Command and Control at the Tactical Level (YeSU-TZ) was undergoing trials as of 2010–12, but due to problems with design, the lack of necessary technologies and suitable communication systems, and excessive cost overruns, it enabled inter-branch cooperation only at the level of the OSK headquarters and upwards. When it comes to the VKS, its use remained limited to the rapid download of information collected by intelligence-gathering aircraft and UAVs. Although the development of such and similar systems was continued through 2016–20 and the digitalisation was successful at the strategic- and operational levels, it regularly failed at the tactical level. Arguably, the VDV introduced to service the Andromeda-D ATMS, and the VSRF followed with the Akatsiya-M system at the level of the 12 combined arms armies and four army corps existing at that time. However, the Metronome system that was to enable automated coordination of tactical fighters with ground forces was cancelled following its testing in Syria in 2016–17, while – despite related announcements – both Andromeda-D and Akatsiya-M had not been integrated into the YeSU-TZ even as of 2022.

Instead, the *GenStab* appears to have decided to stop troubling itself with such issues: it began heavily prescribing all exercises and, later on, even all planning and operations. The unsurprising result was that the speed of the Russian military decision-making during the first stages of the all-out invasion of Ukraine was extremely slow: many ground units were out of touch with their commanders for days, and thus unable to call for air or artillery support. Moreover, although the VSRF and the VKS also began excelling in the execution of well-rehearsed operations during exercises, in combat their tactical commanders had no solutions to hand whenever things went wrong – which was exactly what was about to happen in dozens, if not in hundreds, of cases in Ukraine in February and March 2022, several of which were decisive for the flow of the resulting war.

The overall result was a system of self-deception: the combination of bombastic announcements in the Russian and international media, and the relatively good performance of the VSRF in Ukraine in 2014, created the impression of the Russian armed forces as a highly-modern, technologically advanced force, and the VKS – equipped with its powerful Su-30s, Su-34s, Su-35s, and hypersonic missiles – as a highly potent air force, capable of overrunning even countries like Ukraine in a matter of days. However, as subsequent developments were to show, the actual situation was dramatically different.

Force Multipliers

The most important of the combat-support assets of the VKS as of 2022 were units operating airborne early warning aircraft, airborne command posts, or for aircraft equipped for electronic warfare (EW) purposes. The most important amongst these was the Aviation Squadron of Long-Range Radar Surveillance Aircraft: subordinated to the (direct-reporting) 610th Combat Application and Flight Crew Conversion Centre, and based at Ivanovo Severnyi AB. In 2022 this unit operated all seven Beriev A-50U airborne early warning and control (AWACS) aircraft available.

Of similar importance were a range of subvariants of the VKS's fleet of Ilyushin Il-20M, Il-22PP, and Tupolev Tu-214R reconnaissance aircraft. Because their operations were tightly controlled by the Main Intelligence Directorate (*Glavnoye Razvedyatelnoye Upravleniye*, GRU), very little was known about their organisation, except that most of the Il-20Ms (ASCC/NATO reporting name 'Coot-A') were operated by relatively small squadrons based at Chkalovskiy AB, with regular detachments of one or two aircraft at Kubinka, Khabarovsk-Bolshoy, Rostov-na-Donu, Kacha (in Crimea), and Hmeimim ABs. Since February 2022, at least one Il-22M and at least one Il-22P were also regularly forward deployed at Seshcha AB.

Back in the 2010s, the Russian Ministry of Defence planned to replace the old and worn-out Il-20s with specially-modified Kazan Aircraft Production Association (KAPO) Tu-214Rs (ASCC/NATO reporting name 'Mullet'): however, and although this type was declared 'combat-ready' following its deployment to Syria in 2016, its research and development experienced significant delays. As of 2022, only four were available, of which two were still regularly based at the KAPO facility in Kazan, indicating they were still undergoing further development and testing. Slightly different was the situation with three Ilyushin Il-22PP EW aircraft: these were permanently assigned to the 117th Military Transport Aviation Regiment/18th Military Transport Aviation Division, home-based at Orenburg AB, and intensively deployed over southern Belarus in February and March 2022.

Army General Makhmut Akhmetovic Gareev, the most influential Russian military theoretician of the 1980s and 1990s. Always insistent on 'defending the historical truth about the Second World War', he continued publishing about military science and actively participating in numerous conferences despite his age, and thus essentially cocreated the VSRF and the VKS as they were in 2022. (Russian Ministry of Defence)

SRDLO: THE SAGA OF THE RUSSIAN AWACS, PART 1

Theoretically the centrepiece of VKS operations, the Beriev A-50 (ASCC/NATO reporting name 'Mainstay') was an airborne early warning and control aircraft (abbreviated to SRDLO in Russian) based on the Ilyushin Il-76 transport. As in the case of so many other projects, its existence – and performance – was revealed to the CIA by Adolf Tolkachev in 1978, while it was still undergoing research and development.

Between 1985 and 1993, a total of three prototypes and 24 operational A-50s were manufactured by State Aircraft Factory 84 in Tashkent. The original variant entered service in a great hurry and was never considered a definitive solution. Its deficiencies were obvious in the early 1980s and included a rather short detection range for low-flying fighter-sized targets (220km), onboard computers enabling the simultaneous tracking of just 50 targets (and simultaneous control of intercepts of 10 of these), and low-bypass-ratio turbofans with poor fuel efficiency.[7]

Therefore, multiple upgrade projects were initiated over the following years, including A-50U, A-50M, then another A-50U, and then the A-100. However, next to nothing of this was ever realised. Eventually, much of the fleet was put into 'open storage' or sold abroad, and only about a dozen kept operational for most of the 2000s and 2010s. Originally initiated in 1999, then cancelled, then relaunched in 2000, the research and development of the final A-50U variant progressed very slowly. The essence was an overhaul of selected airframes and the installation of modern processors and flat-screen displays, which enabled a single A-50 to simultaneously track up to 150 targets, and direct up to 12 interceptors. Usually operating at flight altitudes of 5–10,000m, the aircraft had an endurance of seven hours and 40 minutes. The first of the overhauled jets (Bort 37) was rolled out in 2005: it served as a prototype and was handed over to the VKS only in 2014. By 2022, it had been followed by just six additional aircraft, as listed in the Table 1.

Table 1: A-50Us of the VKS, 2022

Bort Number	Registration	Notes
33	RF-50602	service entry 2013; named *Vladimir Ivanov*
37	RF-93966	prototype, service entry 2014; named *Sergey Atayanc*
41	RF-94268	service entry 2017; named *Taganrog*
42	RF-50610	service entry 2019
43	RF-50608	service entry 2022, damaged on 26 February 2023
45	RF-93952	service entry 2018
47	RF-93957	service entry 2011
51	RF-50606	undergoing overhauls and upgrade; service entry Sep 2023

In 2006, the *GenStab* contracted the Vega Group for another upgrade: the A-100, code-named Premier. One non-upgraded A-50, Bort 52 (RF-93953), was converted into the first prototype, followed by two pre-series aircraft based on newly-manufactured Il-76MD airframes (78651 and 78652). However, the project then stalled before being reorganised as Premier-476 in 2013. The first flights by one of the prototypes were undertaken in 2017, and the A-100 was announced to be ready to enter service in 2020: in actuality it was still undergoing trials as of April 2021, when one was monitored while shadowing the flight of a US Northrop Grumman RQ-4 Global Hawk reconnaissance UAV over the Black Sea. According to unofficial sources in Russia, all further work on the A-100 was cancelled in February 2024, primarily because the project was over-reliant on imported electronics of Western origin.[8]

The A-50U Bort 43 (RF-50608) seen at Makulishchi AB in Belarus in February 2023. This was the last example of this variant confirmed as upgraded and handed over to the VKS in early 2022. (Russian Ministry of Defence)

Bomber Fleet

The spearhead of the VKS during the war in Ukraine – the primary tool for delivery of long-range air strikes – were the bombers of the Long-Range Aviation Command. Headquartered in Moscow, this was directly subordinated to the General Staff of the Russian Armed Forces and as such the only element of the VKS operating semi-independently. The centrepiece of the Long-Range Aviation was the 22nd Guards Heavy Bomber Aviation Division: a unit the traditions of which dated back to 1942, and which as of 2022 consisted of four major sub-units:

- 121st Guards Heavy Bomber Aviation Regiment, based at Engels-2 Air Base, operating 16 Tupolev Tu-160 heavy bombers
- 184th Guards Heavy Bomber Aviation Regiment, based at Engels-2 Air Base, operating Tupolev Tu-95MS heavy bombers
- 52nd Guards Heavy Bomber Aviation Regiment, based at Shaykovka Air Base, operating Tu-22M3 medium bombers
- 840th Heavy Bomber Aviation Regiment, based at Soltsy Air Base, operating Tu-22M3 medium bombers

The Tu-160 supersonic, variable-sweep-wing, heavy strategic bomber was the most-powerful available type. Manufactured in the late 1980s, the fleet of 15 aircraft was overhauled and upgraded in 2002–06, becoming capable of deploying Kh-555 cruise missiles in addition to Kh-101s and Kh-102s: each Tu-160 was capable of carrying up to 12 cruise missiles in its internal bomb bay. In 2014–18 an additional example was assembled from the available spare parts, and the fleet was in the process of being upgraded to the Tu-160M2 standard, in part because the type was suffering from chronic engine-related problems and lack of spares. Although time and again hinted at being involved in operations against Ukraine, and even sighted as close as 100 kilometres to the border, as of 2022–24 there has been no confirmation of the use of Tu-160s in the current conflict.

Escorted by a Su-30SM fighter-interceptor, this Tu-160 was photographed while releasing a Kh-555 cruise missile against a target in Syria on 20 November 2015. (Russian Ministry of Defence)

A Tu-95SM releasing a Kh-101 missile over Syria in 2017. (Russian Ministry of Defence)

With its series production ending in 1992, the Tu-95MS fleet was about as old as the Tu-160s. Despite overhauls and modernisations in the mid-1990s, these aircraft were in only reasonably good condition: around 55 were in service as of early 2022, of which about a dozen were fully mission capable on average. The primary armament of the Tu-95MS was the Kh-555 cruise missile, six of which could be installed on each aircraft, but the type was also adapted to deploy the Kh-101 long-range cruise missiles.

Table 2: Known Tu-95MS of the VKS, 2022

Registration	Bort	Notes
RF-94116	28	c/n 10002137187; named *Sevastopol*
RF-94117	27	c/n 10002137345; named *Izborsk*
RF-94119	25	c/n 10002134444
RF-94120	22	c/n 10002134278; named *Kozelsk*
RF-94121	21	c/n 10002134446; named *Samara*
RF-94122	20	c/n 10002134666; named *Dubna*
RF-94123	19	c/n 10002136177; named *Krasnoyarsk*
RF-94124	16	c/n 1000234135; named *Veliky Novgorod*
RF-94125	15	c/n 10002134108; named *Kaluga*
RF-94126	12	c/n 10002133299; named *Moskva*
RF-94127	11	c/n 10002134757; named *Vorkuta*
RF-94128	10	c/n 1000235199; named *Saratov*
RF-94129	23	c/n 10002134379
RF-94130	24	c/n 10002128382; named *Murmansk*
RF-94131	18	c/n 10002133622
RF-94132	14	c/n 10002133412; named *Voronezh*
RF-94170	28	c/n 10002128561
RF-94172	26	c/n 10002135249; unidentified badge below the cockpit
RF-94176	22	c/n 10002127615, wearing Long-Range Aviation badge
RF-94177	25	c/n 10002128373
RF-94178	29	c/n 10002137566; named *Smolensk*
RF-94179	07	c/n 10002136583
RF-94180	06	c/n 10002136785
RF-94182	04	c/n 10002135367; named *Kurgan*
RF-94183	03	c/n 10002137098
RF-94184	02	c/n 1000236487; named *Mozdok*
RF-94185	01	c/n 1000235793; named *Irkutsk*
RF-94186	41	c/n 10002123107
RF-94188	43	c/n 10002123103
RF-94189	45	c/n 10002115105
RF-94190	48	c/n 1000219743
RF-94191	49	c/n 1000219429
RF-94192	50	c/n 64034200822
RF-94193	51	c/n 10002124532
RF-94194	52	c/n 64034200003
RF-94195	53	c/n 10002119421
RF-94196	54	c/n 10002121906
RF-94197	55	c/n 10002121914
RF-94198	56	c/n 10002121802
RF-94199	57	c/n 10002123419
RF-94200	58	c/n 6403400201
RF-94201	47	c/n 10002116202
RF-94202	60	c/n 1000219215
RF-94205	23	c/n 64034200875; named *Ryazan* (removed in 2015)
RF-94206	59	c/n 10002133144; named *Blagoveshchensk*
RF-94207	21	c/n 10002128593; wearing Long-Range Aviation badge
RF-94255	20	c/n 64034200905; named *Ryazan*
RF-94257	22	c/n 64034200903; named *Chelyabinsk*
RF-94259	17	c/n 10002133412
-	23	c/n 64034200843; named *Tambov*; ground instructional airframe Voronezh-Baltimor

No fewer than 497 Tu-22Ms were manufactured in the 1970s and 1980s, primarily for the Soviet Naval Aviation. As of 2021, around 70 were still in service, but meanwhile all assigned to the 52nd and 840th Heavy Bomber Aviation Regiments of the VKS. They saw operational service as conventional bombers against Chechnya, Georgia and Syria prior to being subjected to a mid-life update that added compatibility with the new Kh-32 and a range of other projected weapons. Theoretically, each Tu-22M3 was capable of carrying up to three Kh-22s or Kh-32s: over Ukraine, two, or even only one, are usually installed. Moreover, as of March–April 2022, the VKS began deploying them as conventional bombers, armed with 500kg, 1,500kg, and even 3,000kg free-fall bombs.

A Tu-95MS returning from a training sortie during Exercise Amur in September 2022. (Russian Ministry of Defence)

Tu-22M3, Bort 43, registration RF-94140, of the 52nd Guards Heavy Bomber Aviation Regiment taking-off from Shaikovka AB during the AviaDarts exercise in 2021. (Photo by Daniele Faccioli)

Cruise Missiles

In place of the tactical bombers and fighter-bombers of the VKS, the primary long-range tool early during the Russian campaign in Ukraine of 2022 were ballistic and cruise missiles. The latter were also the longest-ranged weapons of this kind. The oldest of the cruise missiles was the Kh-55 (ASCC/NATO reporting name 'AS-15 Kent'). Originally developed in the 1970s, by 2022 they were available in multiple variants, two of which are known to have been in regular service. The original Kh-55 was nuclear-armed and had been upgraded to the Kh-55SM standard, carrying a conventional warhead and two conformal fuel tanks to stretch the range. The more recent Kh-555 was a mid-life upgrade applied to some Kh-55s; this saw the replacement of the nuclear warhead with a conventional one, the installation of conformal fuel tanks, and the installation of a new turbofan engine and a GPS/GLONASS receiver. Early during the war, these weapons became the primary armament of Tu-95MS bombers, though gradually replaced by the more recent weapons of the Kh-101 family.

The development of the advanced Kh-101 began in 1991, with the first test-releases following in 2004, by when two subvariants became available, both having facetted front sections and sides to decrease their radar cross section. In addition to terrain counter matching, they used an inertial navigation system and a GPS/GLONASS receiver, and an electro-optical digital scene matching correlation system for the terminal flight phase. At least as important was the fact that Kh-101s were equipped with a

small EW system, a chaff and flare dispenser, and – in some cases – even a towed decoy. As of 2022, two variants were available: the Kh-101 was conventionally-armed and saw combat deployment from Tu-160s in Syria, starting in November 2015, and then from Tu-95MS a year later; the Kh-102 was the nuclear-armed subvariant and was reserved for deployment from Tu-160 bombers.

Both the Kh-55/555 and the Kh-101 missiles travelled at high-subsonic speeds (950–1,000km/h), and – depending on local terrain and man-made obstacles – could be programmed to fly at altitudes of 30–60 metres.

The oldest, and shortest-ranged, Russian cruise missiles deployed from bombers of the VKS in Ukraine belonged to the Kh-22 family (ASCC/NATO reporting name 'AS-4 Kitchen'). Developed in the late 1950s and early 1960s, these were relatively crude weapons originally designed to outperform the multi-layered defences of aircraft carrier

A Kh-101 cruise missile installed on an underwing hardpoint of a Tu-95MS bomber in November 2022. (Russian Ministry of Defence)

groups of the US Navy through their hypersonic speed and very high altitude of operations. When fired over their maximum range (as usually in operations over Ukraine), Kh-22s accelerated to a speed of Mach 2 and climbed to an altitude of 22–23,000 metres, before diving on the target at 30–40 degrees and accelerating to about Mach 4. When fired over a shorter range, they dived at 80–90 degrees, and is why they are sometimes described as 'semi-' or 'quasi-ballistic' weapons. In 2008–12, about a dozen Kh-22s were upgraded to the Kh-32 standard, and the development of an upgraded Kh-32M was announced, but this project proceeded at a very slow pace over the years. As of 2022, both Kh-22s and Kh-32s were deployed solely from Tu-22M3 bombers.

Poor Reliability Record

The primary issue with the Russian cruise missiles of 2022 was their poor reliability record. During operations against Syria during 2015–16, the majority of Kh-555s and Kh-101s were released from Iranian airspace and had to travel to their targets via Iraqi airspace. Numerous crashed upon release or malfunctioned shortly after while still underway over Iran. The avionics of dozens of others failed to survive the torture of flying over 1,000 kilometres at low altitude and the resulting turbulence-induced vibrations. For example: out of six missiles that approached the area of Kansafra in western Aleppo on 19 November 2015, five failed shortly before reaching their presumed target. One disappeared without a trace; two crashed into an empty field without detonating; one 'went ballistic', and another overshot the target by about 100 metres (which was just as well because the 'terrorist headquarters' they appear to have targeted turned out to be an elementary school full of children).

Over the following years, the MOD in Moscow scrambled to explain all such failures as being 'corrected' and in 2017, demonstratively reported the much-improved performance of its Kh-555s and Kh-101s in Syria. However, this time, Moscow released far fewer details about such operations – in turn making a serious cross-examination much harder. Certainly enough, with nuclear-armed cruise missiles representing one of the major Russian deterrence factors vis-à-vis NATO, the top brass of the VSRF and the VKS was neither in position nor keen to inform the West that these were 'not really working as advertised'. As is clear from VKS cruise missile operations against targets in Ukraine since February 2022, any kind of improvements to the Kh-555s and Kh-101s remained limited. The principal issue was that the Russian Federation lagged so much in the development of microtechnology and software, that the microprocessors necessary for upgrades to the Kh-101s and Kh-555s were all imported from abroad, primarily the USA. Due to the international sanctions imposed in reaction to the Russian invasion of Crimea in 2014, sourcing such items became a problematic and costly issue, greatly reducing the total number of available rounds.

One consequence was that for the first two years of the all-out invasion of Ukraine the majority of Russian air-launched cruise missiles were released from as far away as the Caspian Sea, to assure that any missiles malfunctioning upon release would harmlessly crash into the water below, instead of exposing their poor technical reliability to the public if crashing over land. This resulted in the missiles having to travel over very long ranges – which not only further increased the likelihood of malfunction while reducing the number of weapons actually reaching the target zone, but also increasing the likelihood of their early detection, both by NATO and by Ukrainian air defences.

Routeing and Electronic Warfare Support

Early during the all-out invasion of Ukraine, most Kh-555s and Kh-101s were either routed via Belarus, or over the Crimean Peninsula and then via the airspace of the (neutral) Republic of Moldova to western Ukraine. In this fashion, the Russian planners sought to further lessen the chances of their successful detection and tracking by Ukrainian air defences, and to prevent their early interception by Ukrainian interceptors and surface-to-air missiles (SAMs). Moreover, most of the missiles were pre-programmed so that once inside Ukrainian airspace they would fly low along rivers, and around or between known major concentrations of Ukrainian air defences.

The body of a Kh-555 shot down by Ukrainian air defences seen in a field outside Odesa in November 2023. (Ukrainian Internet)

The workstation of an EW operator on a Tu-22M3 bomber of the VKS. (Russian Ministry of Defence)

For example: cruise missiles targeting the Lviv or Ivano-Frankivsk Oblasts were frequently programmed to overfly Moldova, then follow the Dniestr River (which offered plenty of geographic references for their navigation systems, thus making sure these were still on the right route), before turning towards their targets. In similar fashion, those targeting the Vinnitsa area were either routed via Moldova, or to pass roughly in between the Ukrainian air defences of Odesa and Mykolaiv, and then follow the Bug River.

Since 24 February 2022, every deployment of air-launched cruise missiles against Ukraine has been supported by the deployment of heavy and multi-layered electronic countermeasures (ECM). For example, attributed with an effective range of 1,000 kilometres, Murmansk BN systems of the 475th Independent Electronic Warfare Centre of the Russian Navy, set up in Crimea, were used to disturb Ukrainian long-range communications, including their High-Frequency Global Communications System. Similarly,

Although better than in 2015–16, the failure rates of Russian cruise missiles remained relatively high throughout 2022. While most of those that malfunctioned were released over the Caspian Sea and thus crashed into the water, leaving no evidence behind, one Kh-101 is known to have struck the ground, roughly halfway between Astrakhan and Rostov-na-Donu, on 10 October 2022. This photograph shows the wreckage of a Kh-101 that crashed in the Yelansky District, on 16 December 2022, after release from a Tu-95MS underway south-west of Engels AB. (Russian social media)

numerous 1L260 Krasukha-2 and 1RL257 Krasukha-4 EW systems were deployed to disturb not only the work of PSZSU long-range surveillance radars but also NATO's Boeing E-3 Sentry AWACS aircraft on stations over Poland and Romania through broadband active jamming.

A Murmansk BN electronic warfare system as installed on a KamAZ 530501 truck. By 2022, the VSRF operated a large number of EW systems, covering literally every band used by Ukrainian radars and telecommunications. (Russian Ministry of Defence)

Table 3: Principal Air-Launched Guided Missiles in service with VKS, 2022

Russian designation	ASCC/NATO reporting name	Notes
Air-to-Ground		
Kh-22/32	AS-4 Kitchen	tactical anti-ship missile (range: 600km/320nm) deployed for ground attack purposes; ARH; Kh-32 was an upgraded land-attack variant with INS guidance and lighter warhead to extend the range (range: 1,000km/540nm); deployed by Tu-22M3s only
Kh-25	AS-12 Kegler	tactical PGM (range 10–60km/6–32nm); PRH (Kh-25P); deployed by Su-24 & Su-34
Kh-29	AS-14 Kedge	tactical PGM (range: 10–30km/6–16nm); laser (Kh-29L) or EO (Kh-29T) guidance; deployed by Su-24 & Su-34
Kh-31	AS-17 Krypton	tactical PGM (range: 7–110km/4–60nm); PRH (Kh-31A), PRH or IR (Kh-31P); deployed by Su-30, Su-34, Su-35
Kh-35	AS-20 Kayak	tactical PGM and/or anti-ship missile (range:130km/70nm); INS, ARH and IR; deployed by Su-34
Kh-58	AS-11 Kilter	tactical PGM (range: 120–200km/65–130nm); PRH; deployed by Su-24 and Su-34
Kh-59	AS-13 Kingbolt	tactical PGM (range: 115km/62nm); EO (Kh-59T) or laser (Kh-59L); deployed by Su-24 and Su-34
Kh-59	AS-18 Kazoo	tactical PGM (range: 200–290km/110–160nm); EO; deployed by Su-24 and Su-34
Kh-101	AS-23 Kodiak	cruise missile (range: 3,000km/1,300nm); INS/GPS/GLONASS and EO-SMG; deployed by Tu-95MS and Tu-160
Kh-555	AS-15 Kent	cruise missile (range: 3,000km/1,300nm); INS/GPS/GLONASS and TCM; deployed by Tu-95MS and Tu-160
Air-to-Air		
R-33	AA-9 Amos	long-range (160km/65nm); SARH (R-33) or ARH (R-33S)
R-37	AA-13 Axehead	long-range (208km/112nm), ARH
R-40	AA-6 Acrid	medium-range (50–80km/31–50nm); SARH on R-40RD and IR on R-40TD
R-60	AA-8 Aphid	short-range (8km/5nm); IR
R-73/R-74	AA-11 Archer	short-range (20–30km/11–19nm); IR
R-77/R-77-1	AA-12 Adder	medium-range (80km/50nm); ARH

ARH = active radar homing, CM = contour matching, EO = electro-optical (or TV) guidance, GAI = ground aided inertial, GPS/GLONASS = global satellite positioning system, INS = inertial navigation system, IR = infrared, Laser = laser homing, PRH = passive radar homing, SMG = scene matching guidance, SAGG = seeker-aided ground guidance, SARH = semi-active radar homing, TCM = terrain contour matching/mapping, TVM = track-via-missile

Interceptor Fleet

Although not directly involved in early operations against Ukraine in 2022, at the forefront of the VKS fighter fleet at that time were Mikoyan i Gurevich (MiG) MiG-31 interceptors. Developed from the design of the Mach-3-capable MiG-25, this big and powerful, twin-engined, two-seat, long-range, high-speed interceptor was designed for autonomous operations over the northern regions of Russia. The centrepieces of its weapons system were the RP-31 Zaslon electronically scanned phased-array radar and the (retractable) 8TK infrared search and track system (IRST). Capable of detecting bomber-sized targets at high altitude over a range up to 280km (151nm), and fighter-sized targets flying at low altitude out to 65km (35nm), the Zaslon could simultaneously track up to 10 targets, and engage four of them, all provided they were approaching head-on: tail-on engagement ranges were around 50 percent shorter. Originally, the MiG-31 was usually armed with four R-33 SARH missiles, with a maximum launch range of 120km (65nm): these could be complemented with either two R-40 medium-range, or four R-60 short-range, air-to-air missiles, while a six-barrel 23mm GSh-6-23 autocannon was installed low in the starboard fuselage, together with 260 rounds. Overall, some 520 had been manufactured by 1994.

As soon as Tolkachev's treachery became known in 1985, the Soviets scrambled to introduce upgrades, resulting in the variant designated the MiG-31B. Entering production in 1990, this had an upgraded Zaslon-A radar, new software, and improved R-33S missiles with active radar homing and a maximum launch range of 160km (84nm). About a dozen MiG-31s upgraded to a similar standard received the designation MiG-31BS. However, the ultimate fighter variant became the MiG-31BM: this included a mid-life overhaul, installation of the Zaslon-AM radar – with a claimed detection range of 240km (130nm) for fighter-sized targets – and compatibility with R-37 long-range, and R-77-1 medium-range, air-to-air missiles. It entered service in 2008 and by 2022 all the 113 operational MiG-31s had been upgraded to the MiG-31BM standard, while another 150 airframes were kept in long-term storage: in 2021, the Ministry of Defence in Moscow reported that five additional examples had been overhauled and modified and delivered to the 712th Fighter Aviation Regiment.

Starting in 2017, 10 selected MiG-31BM airframes were modified to the MiG-31K standard, which enabled them to carry one Kinzhal hypersonic air-launched ballistic missile under the centreline. Announced in the Russian media with much fanfare, the Kinzhal was developed from the ground-launched 9K720 Iskander ballistic missile and praised as capable of reaching terminal speeds of Mach 10 over a range of 2,000km (1,100nm). Depending on altitude and speed of the aircraft at launch, it actually had a combat range of 460–480km (248–259nm) and its top speed during the terminal flight phase was approximately Mach 3.6.[9]

Because Putin's planers expected only minimal Ukrainian resistance, in late February 2022 it fell to two other types to serve as the primary interceptors of the VKS. The first of these was the Su-30SM: essentially a derivative of the Su-30MKI originally developed for India in the 1990s. Equipped with the massive N011M Bars pulse-Doppler radar (which necessitated the installation of canards and thrust-vectoring engines to retain the airframe's original manoeuvrability), this type was full of foreign electronics, including French-made holographic head-up displays, and Indian- and Israeli-made computers. Some 116 Su-30SMs were handed over to the VKS (and the Naval Aviation, V-MF) by 2020, by when production switched to the Su-30SM2 variant: this was equipped with the slightly lighter N035 Irbis radar and more powerful AL-41F1S engines. Additionally, the VKS also acquired 20 Su-30M2 two-seaters, which acted as lead-in trainers for its Su-30SMs.

The actual 'star of the show' was the Su-35S. Originally developed as a major upgrade of the Su-27, then nearly cancelled before being relaunched to 'bridge the gap pending availability of the Su-57', this type became something like the ultimate single-seat, multi-role subvariant of this family. Featuring thrust-vectoring AL-41F1S engines, Irbis-E radar, OLS-35 IRST, and L175M Khybni-M pods for electronic countermeasures, the Su-35S promptly proved technologically superior to anything in service with the Ukrainian air force and continued dominating the air-to-air discipline in this war for the next few years. As of late 2021, a total of 99 Su-35S were delivered to the VKS, and the Ministry of Defence placed an order for another batch of 24.

While praised by both the representatives of Rosoboronexport and many Western experts as 'multi-role' fighter-bombers, in the VKS in 2022 both the Su-30SM and Su-35S were considered interceptors – and their crews trained correspondingly, spending just 10 percent of their time exercising for air-to-ground operations. Therefore, early during the all-out invasion of Ukraine, they were primarily tasked with intercept operations, flying top cover for heliborne assaults or combat air patrols further to the rear. That the VKS figured out that one type was superior to the other was obvious from their armament: while the Su-35S was usually armed with four R-77-1s and four R-73s or R-74s, Su-30SMs were rarely sighted while armed with R-77-1s and then only with two. These were usually complemented by two to four older R-27s, and two or four R-73s or R-74s. It was only during operations in support of heliborne assaults that both types were also armed with a pair of Kh-31 anti-radiation missiles, to help suppress heavier Ukrainian SAM systems. Finally, both were equipped with the best ECM systems that Russian industry was capable of delivering: Su-30SMs usually carried SAP-518 pods, while the Su-35S was usually equipped with L175M Khybni-M electronic warfare pods on wingtips. Both systems proved rather heavy and had a negative influence upon their flight performance.

A MiG-31BM interceptor armed with R-37M (under the fuselage) and R-77-1 (underwing station) air-to-air missiles. The bort number and registration of this aircraft have been deleted by the Russian military censor. (Russian Ministry of Defence)

Su-30SM, Bort 52, registration RF-81871, of the 14th Guards Fighter Aviation Regiment, seen in 2021. (Photo by Daniele Faccioli)

Su-35S, Bort 17, registration RF-81861, armed with B-13M pods for 130mm unguided rockets, seen during the AviaDarts exercise in 2021. Notable on the inboard underwing pylon is an AKU-170 launch rail for R-77 air-to-air missiles. (Photo by Daniele Faccioli)

Tactical Bombers and Attack Aircraft

As of 2022, the VKS was still in the process of replacing its venerable Sukhoi Su-24M tactical bombers (ASCC/NATO reporting name 'Fencer'). Forty years earlier, when the first examples entered service, they were some of the most advanced tactical aircraft in Soviet service: their avionics included the PNS-24M Tigr weapons system with the Relyef terrain-following radar, DISS-7 Doppler navigation radar, advanced navigation devices and self-protection systems, and made them compatible with almost all the guided weapons in Soviet service of the period. While very fast at low altitude, this type was always a handful to maintain and fly, and thus the one with the worst flight safety record in service: although more than 1,300 Su-24s were manufactured in the 1970s and 1980s, only around 150 were still in service as of 2022. About 50 of these were modified through the installation of the SVP-24 targeting system, and another 30 overhauled and brought up to the Su-24M2 standard. Another 80 aircraft of the specialised Su-24MR variant served as the primary tactical reconnaissance fighters. Although compatible with precision-guided munitions like the Kh-25 and Kh-29, even with guided bombs with GPS/GLONASS-supported homing systems, in action over Georgia and Syria the fleet was rarely equipped with anything other than free-fall bombs of the FAB-250 and FAB-500 series, parachute-retarded bombs like the FAB-500ShN, and cluster bombs like the RBK-250 and RBK-500.

With ageing Su-24s being heavily utilised in Syria (where they flew more than 50 percent of all the combat sorties undertaken by the VKS), both the Main Command of the Aerospace Forces and the *GenStab* was relieved when, in 2008, the Kremlin granted funding for procurement of Sukhoi Su-34 bombers (ASCC/NATO reporting name 'Fullback'). Originally developed from a two-seat conversion trainer variant for the V-MF, the Su-34 was equipped with the Leninets V-004 passive electronically scanned radar (with terrain-following and terrain-avoidance working modes). Although heavy, the system had potent capabilities, including a maximum detection range of 200–250km (110–130nm) for large surface targets, and the capability to simultaneously track 10 and engage four targets whether in the air, on land, or on the water. The ventrally installed I255 B1/02 Platan laser and TV sight made it compatible with all tactical PGMs in service with the VKS at the time. Moreover, the Su-34 possessed the capability to haul up to 8,000kg (17,637lbs) of weaponry on 12 hardpoints over a combat radius of 1,100km (683 miles). Protected by two L265 Khibny-MV self-protection pods, the type also had significant capabilities in regards of EW. A total of 131 Su-34s were delivered by 2020 with another 20 of the upgraded variant Su-34M due for delivery by 2023: indeed, the total production run was planned to reach 153 by the end of 2024.[10]

That said, the Su-34 proved almost as much of a handful to maintain and prepare for missions as the Su-24: it was susceptible to foreign object damage and dust, and much too inflexible for high-tempo operations over a rapidly changing battlefield. This is why the *GenStab* retained in service the old Sukhoi Su-25 (ASCC/NATO reporting name 'Frogfoot') attack aircraft. Designed as a subsonic, armoured fighter for CAS to ground troops, the majority of about 140 aircraft still in service were manufactured in the late 1980s. Due to their low utilisation over the following 20 years, most still had plenty of service life in their airframes and from 2006 were subjected to extensive overhauls and upgrades to Su-25SM/SM-1 and SM-2 standards. However, while these upgrades were praised as adding compatibility with guided weapons, the fact was that the VKS had such low stocks of PGMs that these were reserved for more advanced types – mainly the Su-34s. Moreover, despite significant investment in research and testing, neither the air force nor the army ever managed to develop a fully-functional automatic tactical management system for their cooperation. Therefore, regardless of their avionics standard, Su-25s of the VKS in 2022 continued soldiering on with their primary armament consisting of either B-8M or B-13M pods for unguided rockets (80mm and 130mm respectively), and their internally-installed 30mm GSh-30-2 autocannon.

Helicopters

The branch of the VKS deployed most intensively against Ukraine, right from the start of the all-out invasion of February 2022, was the Army Aviation. Its star – and the type that was to cause the most problems to the Ukrainians – was the Kamov Ka-52 attack helicopter (ASCC/NATO reporting name 'Hokum'). Originally developed for reconnaissance, to command strike groups of helicopters, and destroying ground and aerial targets out to a range of up to 15km (8nm), it was unusual for two reasons: its coaxial rotor system

THE R-77 SAGA

For much of the 1990s and 2000s, ever more reports appeared in public, emphasising the excellent performance of the latest Russian medium-range air-to-air missile. Designated the R-77, this received the ASCC/NATO reporting name 'AA-12 Adder' and was widely considered to be in service with the Russian air force and matching nearly every comparable Western or Chinese weapon.[11]

Originally developed by what used to be the Vympel Design Bureau (now known as GosMKB Vympel), starting in 1982, this medium-range missile with active radar homing originally carried the designation K-77. It was cancelled five years later over issues related to the 9B-1348 seeker head and replaced by the Project K-77M (or Izdeliye-170). This featured the improved 9B-1348M1 seeker head, but its development was halted from 1989 to 1991 due to funding shortages amid the collapse of the USSR. Even then, most of the K-77M's components were made by the Ukrainian company KAKhK Artem in Kyiv, even if they were assembled in Russia by OAO Duks (formerly Kommunar). The latter put together some 200 test rounds by 1991, when Ukrainian independence made the weapon a property of that country. This left the Russians in possession of about a dozen examples, all still undergoing testing at Akhtubinsk: with the K-77 always being closely associated with the Su-27M – realised only in the form of the Su-35, 15 years later – it never entered operational service.

Financing by export customers brought the project back to life and thus in 1996 Vympel launched the production of a 'variant' designated the Izdeliye-190 (or RVV-AE) and equipped with the Agat 9B-1348E seeker head. Containing Ukrainian components but assembled in Russia with very poor quality-control, this was exported to Algeria, China, Ethiopia, India, Indonesia, Malaysia, Sudan, Syria, Uganda, and Venezuela. However, while Vympel began advertising further variants (including the infrared homing R-77T, the passive radar homing R-77P, and the ramjet-powered R-77-PD), none were acquired for the VKS. This remained the case even once an improved variant – designated R-77-1 and

equipped with a streamlined nose cap covering the new 9B-1248 seeker head, and a rocket motor enabling a flight time of 100 seconds compared to 60 seconds for the older R-27R – was test-fired from a Su-27SM at Akhtubinsk in September 2010. Certainly enough, over the following years the VKS showed several of its MiG-31s, Su-30SMs, and then Su-35s equipped with the associated AKU-170 launch rails. However, these rails were manufactured and delivered separately and their availability did not mean that any R-77s were in service with the VKS.

It was only in August 2015 that the Ministry of Defence in Moscow announced a tender for the production of the R-77-1. Even then, nothing happened for months: at least not before, on 24 November 2015, a Russian Su-24M fighter-bomber of the VVS was shot down by Lockheed Martin F-16C Fighting Falcon fighters of the Turkish air force, after violating Turkish airspace. While the VKS scrambled to borrow a batch of old R-77s from the Syrian Arab Air Force to arm its Su-30SMs deployed in the country, in Moscow, the Ministry of Defence rushed into opening an official tender. Then it took over a year to find a company capable of manufacturing the weapon – KTRV (Russian abbreviation for 'Tactical Missile Armament Corporation') – and initiate series production.

Eventually, the R-77-1 entered production with KTRV in late 2016. In March 2017, GosMKB Vympel announced to the Ministry of Defence that a total of 91 rounds had been manufactured by then, and that delivery of another 109 was planned by the end of the same year. Despite subsequent reporting indicating a production rate of up to 170 rounds per annum, the R-77-1 remained rather scarce even four years later – if for no other reason than because in 2019, 75 rounds were manufactured for export to Egypt, and in 2020 a similar-sized batch was sold to India. Correspondingly, early during the all-out invasion of Ukraine, R-77-1s were mainly reserved for Su-35 units and very few were sighted while carried by Su-30SMs or Su-27SMs. Indeed: for reasons explained elsewhere in this book, none were ever installed on Su-34s.

An R-77-1 from the first production batch seen installed on a Su-35 of the 23rd Fighter Aviation Regiment at Dzyomgi AB (Khabarovsk Krai, Russian Far East) in 2019. In February 2022, this regiment was deployed in Belarus and became involved in numerous air combats with interceptors of the Ukrainian air force. (Russian Ministry of Defence)

Su-34, Bort 21, registration RF-81857, of the Chelyabinsk-based 2nd Bomber Aviation Regiment, seen at AviaDarts in 2021. The type could haul up to 8,000kg of guided weapons, bombs, or unguided rockets and was the primary tactical bomber of the VKS in 2022. (Photo by Daniele Faccioli)

Thanks to its low utilisation in the 1990s and 2000s, and due to the lack of money for acquisition of advanced high-technology weaponry, the VKS's fleet of around 140 Su-25s continued playing a highly important role as the principal tool to provide close air support to ground troops. This example – Bort 14, registration RF-92260 – is a Su-25SM3 that was operated by the Budennovsk-based 368th Attack Aviation Regiment. (Photo by Daniele Facioli)

(making a tail-rotor redundant), and its cockpit for a crew of crew of two seated side-by-side on – uniquely for any helicopters – Zvezda/Tomilino K-37-800M ejection seats.

The Ka-52's BREO-2 avionics suite was probably the best manufactured in Russia during the 2010s: it integrated the work of targeting sensors, flight navigation and the communication system. The weapons system included the Myech-1U radar and the GOES-451.24 electro-optical turret and was compatible with a wide range of weaponry. Internally installed was the Shipunov 2A42 30mm autocannon with up to 460 rounds, mounted low on the starboard side of the fuselage: its barrel could be moved -37/+3.5° in elevation, but had to be aimed by positioning the helicopter. In 2022 its principal guided weaponry included 9K113U Shturm-VU laser beam-riding anti-tank guided missiles (ATGMs), four of which were usually strapped under each winglet. Alternatively, it could be armed with B-8M1 pods for 80mm S-8 unguided rockets, or B-13Ms for 130mm S-13 rockets, or carry up to four drop tanks, while in air-to-air configuration, two 9M39 Igla-V air-to-air missiles could be attached to each outer underwing pylon. This fast, well armoured and excellently equipped helicopter also had the powerful L370P52 Vitebsk self-protection suite: it comprised the L370-1 radar warning receiver, the L370-3 electronic countermeasures suite, the L140 Otklik laser- and L370-2 ultraviolet warning sensors, and an L370-5 infrared jammer: it had two rotating jamming modules installed on the sides of the lower fuselage, and also controlled the work of the

UV-26 chaff and flare dispensers installed into each wingtip. As of 2022, the VKS had received about 196 Ka-52s.

Originally intended to form the backbone of the future attack helicopter fleet of the VKS, the Mil Mi-28 proved something of a disappointment in service, primarily because of its relatively low reliability. Therefore, very few were seen in action early during the Russian invasion of 2022, although the VKS had acquired a total of 167 since 2005. Like the Ka-52, the Mi-28 was operated by a crew of two, but they were seated in tandem, inside a cockpit protected by 370kg of armour to withstand hits by bullets of up to 12.7mm calibre. The Mi-28N was equipped with the BREO-28 integrated avionics suite that combined the work of targeting sensors, navigation, communication, and self-defence systems. Targeting sensors included the OPS-28 turret with TV and FLIR (forward looking infrared) camera, a laser rangefinder, and a radio-command datalink. A mast-mounted turret (when installed) included the N025 single-range millimetre-wave radar for surface mapping, target detection, and their presentation in the sights or to the weapons. In addition to a 30mm 2A42-2 autocannon, with 250 rounds, mounted under the chin, the primary armament consisted of 9M120 Ataka-VN ATGMs, up to 16 of which could be installed under the winglets. Unlike the Ka-52, Mi-28s did not receive the Vitebsk self-protection suites, but were equipped with a radar warning receiver, a laser warning receiver, and UV-26 chaff and flare dispensers.

The principal utility and assault helicopter of the VKS was the venerable Mil Mi-8. In service since the early 1960s, as of 2022 it was available in a wide range of second and third generation variants, the most-widely used of which were the Mi-8MTV-5 and Mi-8AMTSh series, respectively. Weighing about 7,055kg (15,554lbs) when empty, and a maximum of 13,000kg (28,660lbs) on take-off, on average the Mi-8 could carry a payload of up to 2,000kg (4,400lbs) over a maximum of 580–590km. Depending on the variant, some had a Doppler navigation radar (installed in a housing under the boom), and the Kontur-10C weather radar was standard for both Mi-8MTV-5 and Mi-8AMTSh. While self-protection equipment usually included the L-166V1A infrared jammer and UV-26M chaff and flare dispensers, the Mi-8AMTSh were equipped with the L-370ES Vitebsk suite. The Russian Ministry of Defence actually stopped purchasing Mi-8s in the early 1990s, but in 2008–11 placed two large orders, comprising 140 Mi-8MTV-5s and 132 Mi-8AMTShs. As of 2022, more than 500 were still in service as utility and assault helicopters, with another 50 serving as specialised EW versions. The most advanced amongst the latter were 18 Mi-8MTPRIs, acquired in 2015–16: based on newly-built Mi-8MTV-5s, they carried the L187A Rychag-AV electronic warfare suite, capable of jamming enemy air defence radars.

Roughly similar was true for another type available in large numbers: the Mi-24 attack helicopter. Developed in the early 1970s, this was manufactured in large numbers and widely exported during the 1980s and 1990s. The Russian air force acquired a total of 49 Mi-35Ms in 2010, as a cheaper alternative and more reliable option than the Mi-28N. Never meant to be operated in the fashion of Western attack helicopter types – from a hover – regardless the variant, in combat the Mi-24 was always flown like a fighter aircraft conducting attack runs. Because of this, it had heavy armour protection for its cockpit, engines, and transmission. As well as the older variants like the Mi-24V and Mi-24P, by 2022 much more advanced versions like the Mi-24VM (upgraded Mi-24P) and Mi-35Ms became available. Both had GOES-342.10 electro-optical turrets and could deploy the same 9K113 Shturm ATGMs as the Ka-52 as an alternative to other weaponry: that said, in combat in Ukraine, they were rarely seen armed with anything other than B-8M rocket pods. Finally, both variants had L370E24 Vitebsk self-protection suites including L370-2 ultraviolet sensors, L370-5 infrared jammers, and UV-26 chaff and flare dispensers.

The Ka-52 was the most advanced attack helicopter in service with the VKS in 2022. A total of 146 had been manufactured by 2018, and by 2022, this figure had increased to more than 196. In combat over Ukraine, they led both the onslaughts on Kyiv in the north, and those on Kherson and Mykolaiv in the south. Bort 43 (registration RF-91335) was operated by the Ostrov-based 15th Army Aviation Brigade. (Photo by Daniele Faccioli)

Originally intended to replace the old Mi-24 series, the Mi-28N proved far more expensive and much more problematic to maintain and operate, which in turn resulted in much larger orders for the Ka-52 than originally intended. This example, photographed during AviaDarts 2021, was assigned to the Kubinka-based 237th Aviation Technology Demonstration Centre. Notably, it still lacked the mast-mounted radar. (Photo by Daniele Faccioli)

With more than 8,000 manufactured examples (in some 30 or more different variants), the Mi-8 family were some of the most-widely available helicopter types both in the world and for the VKS. In February 2028, they were primarily deployed for heliborne assaults, usually in conjunction with Ka-52s and Mi-24/35s. The Mi-8AMTSh variant shown here was the most advanced in service with the VKS: this example (Bort 20, registration RF-94994) served with the Rostov-na-Donu-based 30th Helicopter Aviation Regiment. (Photo by Daniele Faccioli)

The ultimate variant of the other major helicopter family in service with the VKS in 2022 – the Mi-24 family – was the Mi-35M. Originally acquired because it was expected to be cheaper than the more recent Mi-28 and Ka-52, following the installation of the Vitebsk self-protection suite and other advanced avionics, it proved almost as expensive as Mi-28N. This photo shows the Mi-35 with Bort 51 and registration RF-13027. (Photo by Daniele Faccioli)

The RUK Concept: Sea- and Land-Launched Missiles

No description of Russian air power as of 2022 is complete without providing at least a basic insight into the long-range strike capability of the VSRF in total. The most advanced Russian tactical ballistic missile system – and also the most dangerous of all such weapons – as of 2022 was the 9K720 Iskander. Based on the RUK concept – where a network of intelligence sources and sensors was expected to enable prompt strike against selected targets anywhere within the theatre of operations – the Iskander was envisioned as a missile that could be set up in a matter of minutes, and then deployed to strike not only fixed enemy installations (such as air bases, headquarters, industrial facilities, or storage sites), but also so-called 'time-sensitive' targets, such as objects that made a temporary stop. The Strategic Rocket Troops, as of 2022 operated a total of 13 missile brigades, two or more of which were assigned to the headquarters of each OSK.

These missile brigades were the epitome of the RUK concept and another example of the 'lowest common denominator' aspect of the *GenStab*'s thinking about future wars. Instead of depending on

air power to find the target, and then organising and conducting a complex and expensive operation to suppress or destroy enemy air defences in order to enable an effective strike – which might still result in only partial- or no success even in the event of successful release of weaponry – the availability of quick-reacting and (relatively) precise Iskander missiles would enable the commanders of the OSKs to act decisively and in a matter of minutes to new intelligence input.

The appropriate weapon for this task would need to require minimal prelaunch preparation and be particularly precise, something beyond the reach of the 9K720's immediate predecessor, the 9M723/OTR-23 Oka (ASCC/NATO reporting name 'SS-23 Spider'), when it entered service in the 1980s. Its inertial guidance and an early digitised scene-mapping area correlator provided relatively advanced means of guidance in the terminal phase, but required a very large target and well-mapped terrain to achieve a circular error probable (CEP) of around 50–100 metres.[12] Targets for the 9K720 Iskander could be located by satellite, aircraft, artillery observers, or other means of intelligence gathering (such as informants behind enemy lines), or by photographs scanned into a computer, and the missiles could be retargeted even once airborne. Moreover, the weapon had a guided warhead, controllable via encrypted radio transmission, in addition to self-homing capability.

The centrepiece of each Iskander system were the 9S552 and 9S920 processing stations: by 2022, both of these were capable of processing real-time full-motion video from UAVs such as the Forpost and Orlan-10, and could be connected to the Strelets ATMS operated by GRU reconnaissance formations. Strelets enabled the selection of the target on a map, transfer of the resulting coordinates to the missile, and its programming for the engagement. The missile was then elevated from the horizontal to the vertical position and launched, with two missiles carried by the same transporter-erector-launcher (TEL) being ready for action within less than a minute of each other. Moreover, the same TEL could carry two different missile variants and these were programmable to arrive at the target at the same time, thus complicating defence efforts. Finally, Iskanders could be combined with the fire of 300mm BM-30 Smerch multiple rocket launchers, with a maximum firing range 120km/65 nautical miles, to strike the same target.

Each Iskander-equipped brigade in 2022 comprised three battalions, each including four 9P78-1 TELs (each carrying two missiles), four 9T250E transporter-loader vehicles, the 9S552 command post vehicle, and the 9S920 information processing station. Thus, a single brigade included 12 TELs and 24 ready-to-use missiles.

The 9K270 system had two principal types of missiles:

Iskander-M: 9M723 or 9M723K1 quasi-ballistic missiles (capable of terminal phase manoeuvres), with electro-optical seeker reducing their CEP to 5–10 metres, warheads weighing between 480kg and 700kg (including cluster munition options), 9B999 decoys, and a range of around 500km (if carrying a 700kg warhead).

Iskander-K: 9M727, 9M728 (also known as R-500) and 9M729 cruise missiles (based on the 3M-14 family of sea-launched cruise missiles), with inertial navigation system supported by GPS/GLONASS, active radar homing and EO-guidance in the terminal flight phase, a warhead of 480kg, and range of 500km.

Another weapons system that played an important role was deployed from warships and submarines of the Russian Black Sea Fleet. These were armed with the 3M-54 and 3M-15 Kalibr, and 3M-14K Kalibr-PL land-attack cruise missiles (ASCC/NATO reporting name 'SS-N-30 Sagaris'). The conventionally-armed variant (450kg warhead) has been variously claimed as having a range of 1,400km to 'almost 1,500km'. Like most weapons in this class, Kalibr flies at a speed of Mach 0.8 to 0.9 and an altitude of 20 to 50 metres (66-164ft) for most of its route. During the terminal flight phase it could accelerate to between Mach 2.5 to 2.9 and fly high-angled manoeuvres, thus greatly complicating its timely detection and interception. The land-attack version has inertial guidance, the capability to update its route mid-course with via satellite communication, and a CEP of about 10 metres. As of 2022, the Russian warships that could deploy Kalibrs included:

Project 11356R Admiral Grigorovich-class frigates (*Admiral Grigorovich*, *Admiral Essen*, and *Admiral Makarov*, all assigned to the Black Sea Fleet)

Project 11661 Gepard-class frigates (*Tatarstan* and *Dagestan*, both assigned to the Caspian Sea Fleet)

Project 21631 Buyan-M-class corvettes (*Vyshniy Volochyok*, *Orekhovo-Zuyevo*, *Ingushetiya*, and *Grayvoron* in the Black Sea and *Grad Sviyazhsk*, *Uglich*, and *Velikiy Ustyug* in the Caspian Sea).[13]

In addition to surface warships, the 3M-14 Kalibr variant was regularly deployed from Project 636-3 conventionally-powered attack submarines (ASCC/NATO reporting name 'Improved Kilo') of which there were four in the Black Sea Fleet as of February 2022. Reportedly, up to 30 Kalibr cruise missiles were deployed during the opening wave of the Russian all-out invasion of Ukraine on 24 February 2022; as far as is known, from the Admiral Grigorovich-class frigates, Buyan-class corvettes, and Kilo-class submarines.

Both Iskanders and Kalibrs were to see extensive application in combat in Ukraine in 2022 and since.[14]

Conclusions

The practice of heavily prescribing the tactical exercises of the VKS was no exception: on the contrary, as demonstrated during the major exercise Zapad-2021, it was the norm at the operational and strategic levels of the entire VSRF. Moreover, while large, that exercise was 'defensive' in nature: it rehearsed a Russian military intervention in Belarus in reaction to a NATO attack on that country. Correspondingly, even though obtaining valuable conventional combat experience under similar circumstances in eastern Ukraine in 2014–15, and then some experience in expeditionary and counterinsurgency operations in Syria in 2015–21, overall, the Russian armed forces have never exercised nor had experience in running a large-scale offensive operation of the kind they were about to launch against Ukraine. This was even more the case with the VKS. Arguably, the air force flew over 100,000 combat sorties over Syria, but most of these consisted of air strikes against preselected geographic coordinates, flown at medium altitudes and low speeds, against an opponent with no serious air defences, and thus resulted in next to no useful combat experience at all, other than how to maintain aircraft under the conditions of expeditionary operations in the Middle East. Nevertheless, when sent to operate over Ukraine, the VKS changed

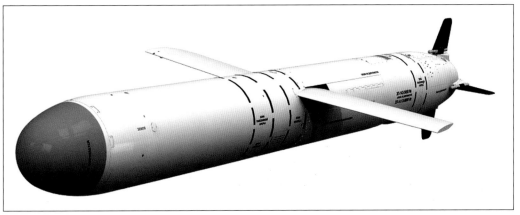

3M54 Kalibr cruise missile. (Federal Service for Military Technical Cooperation of the Russian Federation)

very little about its targeting practices: its crews were provided with a set of geographic coordinates during pre-mission briefings; they then programmed these into the navigation systems of their tactical bombers, launched and orbited well away from the battlefield until the selected coordinates were confirmed by A-50s or Il-20Ms. In the end, they were flying their attacks without any second thoughts about the nature of the target, and often without a clear picture about possible Ukrainian air defences in the area in question.

Combined with the delusional expectations of the political leadership, ad-hoc planning of the invasion of Ukraine, lack of information about the aims and tasks for reasons of secrecy, and widespread corruption and incompetence within the officer corps, this was to result in the massive logistical and tactical failures that doomed the invasion to failure right from the start. Under such circumstances, the role of the VKS was always to remain limited to that of a fire brigade: quick-reaction, extended-range artillery. This was something neither planned for nor rehearsed in any of the pre-war thinking of the *GenStab*: unsurprisingly, it took the Russian air force more than a year to adapt to the circumstances.

A 9P78-1 TEL with a 9M723 Iskander-M missile in fully erected position. (Russian Ministry of Defence)

A 9P78-1 TEL with a launch tube for 9M727/728/729 cruise missiles of the Iskander-K system. (Russian Ministry of Defence)

2

GUERRILLA AIR FORCE

The histories of Ukrainian military aviation commonly start with the declaration of Ukrainian independence on 24 August 1991 and the dissolution of the USSR on 26 December 1991. However, the history of military flying in the country can be traced back at least to the creation of the Ukrainian People's Republic Air Fleet – a flying branch of the armed forces of the Ukrainian People's Republic – in 1917–21 (recognised by the Provisional Russian Government of the time). Indeed, as of 1918–19 there were two such services; the separatists of the short-lived West Ukrainian People's Republic established their own aviation corps as a branch of the Ukrainian Galician Army. Of course, both air forces went down together with the states that maintained them, following the conclusion of the First World War and with the Peace of Riga, which resulted in Ukraine being partitioned between Poland and Bolshevik Russia. Indeed, in 1922, the Ukrainian Soviet Socialist Republic was one of the founding members of the USSR. Correspondingly, whatever was left of the Ukrainian pilots, ground personnel and aircraft was integrated into the Soviet Air Force. It was in this form that thousands of Ukrainian officers and other ranks came to serve in the VVS during the Second World War, and one of them, Ivan Kozhedub from the Chernihiv area, became the highest-scoring Soviet or Allied fighter pilot of that conflict.

Disarmament and Decay

Following the Ukrainian declaration of independence in 1991, the Air Force of Ukraine was officially established on 17 March 1992 on the basis of the command structure of the 24th Air Army VVS, headquartered in Vinnitsya. Nominally, the new service found itself in control of three Frontal Aviation Armies (5th, 14th and 17th), two Strategic Air Armies (26th and 46th), two Air Defence Armies (2nd and 8th PVO, including the 28th, 49th, and 60th Air Defence Corps), two Military Transport divisions, at least nine regiments of Army Aviation from three Military Districts, and a large part of the Naval Aviation of the Black Sea Fleet. This was a total of 49 regiments and 11 independent squadrons, with more than 2,800 aircraft and helicopters. Unsurprisingly, one of the first Ukrainian decisions was to combine all the flying assets into the air force – although the ground-based elements of the former PVO continued to exist in the form of the Air Defence Force of Ukraine until 2004. Next, the air force was gradually decreased: while the Treaty on Conventional Armed Forces in Europe (CFE) limited Ukraine to operating 1,090 aircraft and 330 attack helicopters, by 1998, it was down to 966 combat aircraft and 290 attack helicopters. Amongst the aircraft disposed of at that time were all of the 60 Tu-22M-2/3 bombers of the former 37th Air Army. With the exception of a few examples retained for local museums, and together with 423 Kh-22 cruise missiles, they were scrapped between 1994 and 2003. In 1999, Ukraine also lost its fleet of strategic bombers and associated nuclear weapons; most of the 19 Tu-160s based at Priluki and 23 Tu-95MS based at Uzin were scrapped under a contract issued by the US government: just eight Tu-160s and three Tu-95MSs from these (all manufactured in 1991), were handed over to Moscow, together with 575 Kh-55MS cruise missiles, to settle Ukrainian debts for natural gas imported from the Russian Federation.

Meanwhile, by 1995–96, old MiG-23, MiG-25, and Su-15 interceptors were withdrawn from service and the fighter-interceptor fleet was reduced to units operating MiG-29s and Su-27s. In the next phase of reorganisations, the PSZSU sought to improve efficiency and reduce costs through restructuring. The Air Defence Force was inaugurated in 2004, creating the service existent ever since as the Air Force of the Armed Forces of Ukraine (*Povitriyani syly Zbroiynyh syl Ukrayini*, PSZSU). This included a centralised automated command and control system integrating all flying operations and the operations of ground-based air defences.

The scrapping of one of the last Ukrainian Tu-22M3 bombers in 2002. (Defense Threat Reduction Agency)

However, while local industry offered several types of new radars and other surveillance equipment, comprehensive modifications for existing aircraft and SAMs, and there was talk about a purchase of advanced combat aircraft, a chronic lack of funding caused ever further postponements in their acquisition. Instead, the PSZSU was constantly downsized. By 2011, it was reduced to only one regiment and two squadrons equipped with Su-24 fighter-bombers and Su-24MR reconnaissance fighters, five regiments operating MiG-29s and Su-27s, one regiment with Su-25s, three transport regiments, several helicopter squadrons, and one training squadron flying the Aero L-39 Albatros, all operated by about 43,000 officers and other ranks.

The Russian invasion of Crimea, followed by that of Donbass, in 2014 caught the PSZSU as ill-prepared for combat operations as the rest of the Ukrainian armed forces. For example, the entire 7th Tactical Aviation Brigade had only 10 operational Sukhoi Su-24Ms and Su-24MRs in February that year. Despite its poor condition, the air force operated intensively during the war in Donbass and managed to inflict heavy losses on the 'army' of Russian mercenaries and local collaborators, even if suffering heavy losses to ground-based air defences: about 20 aircraft were shot down in combat or lost in accidents, while 126 were captured by the Russians at bases in Crimea; 51 servicemen of the PSZSU were killed, including 16 pilots. Nevertheless, the air force gave its best and operated intensively up to early September 2014 when, following a crushing defeat of the ZSU at Ilovaisk, Moscow demanded a total ban on the Ukrainian use of air power as a condition for the Minsk I peace agreement.

In reaction to the Russian invasion, the government in Kyiv attempted to negotiate licence production of Saab JAS.39 Gripen fighter-bombers and an acquisition of Embraer EMB.312 training aircraft (i.e. the A-29 variant of the latter, equipped with the US-made AGM-114 Hellfire guided missiles): eventually, negotiations were cancelled for reasons of cost in August 2014. Immediately after, Kyiv issued order No. 499, allocating financing to upgrade as many available helicopters, MiG-29s, Su-24s, Su-25s, Su-27s, and transports as possible: the works in question were possible thanks to the clandestine acquisition of spare parts for Russian-made aircraft abroad. Moreover, during Soviet times, Ukraine had been a main hub of aerospace engineering and manufacturing, and thus inherited hundreds of factories involved in production, maintenance, and upgrades of all types of military aircraft, and were even manufacturing guided missiles. Major enterprises still active as of 2010–22 were:

AVIAKON: based in Kontop, specialised in the overhaul, maintenance, and repair of helicopters

Artem: based in Kyiv, manufacturing R-27 air-to-air missiles

Lviv State Aircraft Repair Plant (LSARP or LDARZ): certified for overhauls of MiG-29s, Su-24s, Su-25s, and Su-27s

Nikolayev Aircraft Repair Plant (NARP): certified for overhauls of Su-24s

Zaporizhzhya State Aircraft Repair Plant (ZDARZ, also known as 'MiGremont'); specialised in overhauls and upgrades of Su-25s

Odessa Aircraft Repair Plant (ODARZ, also known as 'Odessaviaremservis')

Lutsk Repair Plant Motor: production, maintenance, and repair of engines for aircraft and helicopters (including AL-21F-3 engines for Su-24s; AL-31F engines for Su-27, RD-33 engines for MiG-29s, and GTDE-117 gas-turbines for MiG-29s and Su-27s)

Moreover, the PSZSU was provided with enough founding to reactivate the former air bases at Kanatovo (Kirovograd), Voznesensk (Mykolaiv Oblast), Velykyi Buialyk and Artsyz (both in Odesa Oblast).[1]

Bombers

In 2022, the most potent offensive aircraft type operated by the PSZSU was the fleet of Sukhoi Su-24 bombers. Ukraine inherited at least 283 aircraft of this type, of which 119 were Su-24M, 122 were older Su-24s, 35 Su-24MR reconnaissance fighters, and seven Su-24MP EW aircraft, operated by a total of 10 different units. As of early 2022, 142 were still intact and there was just one active unit still operating this type: the 7th Tactical Aviation Brigade. Home-based at Starokostiantyniv AB in Khmelnytskyi Oblast, this also maintained regular forward detachments at Kanatove AB (Kirovohrad) and Myrhorod AB (Poltava). The 7th Brigade was assigned a total of 68 aircraft, but actually operated just 18 fully mission capable Su-24Ms and nine Su-24MRs (in addition to three L-39M1s used for continuation training). Only seven of these (four Su-24Ms and three Su-24MRs) had been overhauled by NAPR by this time (they were recognisable by their digital camouflage pattern): the rest of the active fleet consisted of jets last overhauled before 2014. Another 17 'nearly airworthy' aircraft and 30 'in relatively good condition' were stored in the open at Bila Tserkva AB.[2]

With regards to their equipment and armament, as of February–March 2022, Ukrainian Su-24s were equipped with exactly the same avionics as their brethren flown by the VKS. The centrepieces of their PNS-24M Tigr weapons system were the Relyef terrain-following radar and the DISS-7 Doppler navigation radar. Their underwing and fuselage hardpoints were compatible with the full range of free-fall 250kg, 500kg, and 1,500kg bombs, parachute-retarded OFAB-500ShN and OFAB-500ShR bombs, B-8M pods for S-8 80mm unguided rockets, and with PGMs such as the Kh-25 and Kh-29. Significantly different were the Su-24MRs: instead of the usual armament, they had the BKR-1 reconnaissance complex, including the Shtyk synthetic aperture side-looking radar (installed in the nose), the stabilised Aist-M TV camera for reconnaissance, the Zima infrared linescanner, and radar detection, -location, and -tracking systems such as the SRS-13 Tangazh ELINT pods. Moreover, in reaction to the invasion of 24 February, the personnel of the 7th Brigade started mounting bombs on the underwing pylons of their Su-24MRs.

Table 4: Su-24s of the PSZSU, February–March 2022

Bort	Variant	Notes
02 White	Su-24M	overhauled at NARP since 2014; pixel camouflage pattern
04 White	Su-24M	dark grey camouflage pattern
06 White	Su-24M	
08 White	Su-24M	overhauled at NARP since 2014; pixel camouflage pattern
09 White	Su-24M	overhauled at NARP since 2014; pixel camouflage pattern
11 Yellow	Su-24MR	dark grey camouflage pattern
12 White	Su-24M	returned to service since February 2022
16 Yellow	Su-24MR	
17 Yellow	Su-24MR	
18 White	Su-24M	
20 White	Su-24M	overhauled at NARP since 2014; pixel camouflage pattern
21 White	Su-24M	
22 White	Su-24M	

A Su-24MR undergoing overhaul at the NARP. (UkrOboronProm)

Bort	Variant	Notes
26 White	Su-24M	
28 White	Su-24M	
35 Yellow	Su-24MR	
36 Yellow	Su-24MR	
41 White	Su-24M	returned to service since February 2022
44 White	Su-24M	returned to service since February 2022
45 White	Su-24M	
46 White	Su-24M	
49 White	Su-24M	shot down 22 March 2022
54 Yellow	Su-24MR	overhauled at NARP since 2014; pixel camouflage pattern
59 Yellow	Su-24MR	overhauled at NARP since 2014; pixel camouflage pattern
60 Yellow	Su-24MR	overhauled at NARP since 2014; pixel camouflage pattern
66 White	Su-24M	
69 White	Su-24M	returned to service since February 2022
77 White	Su-24M	shot down 27 February 2022
84 White	Su-24M	returned to service since February 2022; pixel camouflage pattern
93 Yellow	Su-24MR	

Attack Aircraft[3]

As a result of experience from 2014, when slower jets capable of providing close air support to ground troops proved more efficient than faster but less-flexible Su-24s, the condition of the PSZSU's Su-25 fleet was significantly different to that of other types. In 1992, Ukraine inherited 90 Su-25s, of which 75 were fully mission capable. Initially, 41 were operated by the 299th Naval Assault Aviation Regiment from Saki AB in Crimea, while 34 were assigned to the 452nd Independent Assault Aviation Regiment at Chortkiv AB in Ternopil Oblast. By 1996, the entire fleet was consolidated within the 299th Tactical Aviation Brigade, which transferred to Kulbaykine AB, while 15 were sold – to Chad, Democratic Republic of the Congo, Equatorial Guinea, Niger, and North Macedonia – before Chortkiv AB was closed in 2005. During the fighting of 2014, the

299th Brigade operated from Dnipro International Airport (IAP) and was the only unit of the PSZSU to have a full squadron of operational aircraft. Unsurprisingly, it also flew the most combat sorties of the force and also suffered highest losses: one Su-25 and four Su-25M1s were shot down in combat against the separatists and the Russian forces.

Over the following years, almost all the regularly operated aircraft – 26 out of 30 – underwent overhauls and upgrades to the Su-25M1 standard at ZDARZ. The upgrade included the installation of the SN-3307 satellite-supported navigation system, the ASP-17BTs8-M2 optical sight supported by a digital computer, the R-862M1 VHF/UHF radio and A-511 transponder: a few were even upgraded to the M1K standard, which added the MSD-2000V DME/TACAN receiver, the Kurs-93M-V VOR/ILS system, the BUR-4-1-10 flight data recorder, the SRVP-25 video recording system (replacing the Soviet-era gun camera) and KUV 26-50-1 chaff and flare dispensers (which were installed on all aircraft, regardless of whether overhauled and upgraded or not). Correspondingly, as of February 2022, the 299th had a total of 43 Su-25s available. Around 30 of these were fully mission capable (including 24 single- and six two-seaters), while one was undergoing overhaul at ZDARZ. Included in this total were 12 Su-25M1s, nine Su-25M1Ks, and two Su-25UBM1s. The other 12 were stored at Kulbaykine AB. The 299th also had six L-39s (two of which were stored), operated as continuation trainers.

Table 5: Su-25s of the PSZSU, February–March 2022

Bort	Variant	Notes
10 Blue	Su-25	
12 Blue	Su-25	stored at Kulbaykine AB, destroyed 24 February 2022
15 Blue	Su-25M1	dark pixel camouflage pattern
16 Blue	Su-25M1K	light pixel camouflage pattern
17 Blue	Su-25M1	dark pixel camouflage pattern
18 Blue	Su-25	
19 Blue	Su-25M1K	light pixel camouflage pattern, shot down 24 February 2022

Bort	Variant	Notes
20 Blue	Su-25M1K	light pixel camouflage pattern
21 Blue	Su-25M1	dark pixel camouflage pattern
22 Blue	Su-25	
25 Blue	Su-25	
27 Blue	Su-25	
29 Blue	Su-25M1	dark pixel camouflage pattern; shot down 2 March 2022
30 Blue	Su-25M1	dark pixel camouflage pattern; shot down 26 February 2022
31 Blue	Su-25M1	dark pixel camouflage pattern; shot down 26 February 2022
32 Blue	Su-25M1K	light pixel camouflage pattern
35 Blue	Su-25M1K	light pixel camouflage pattern
36 Blue	Su-25M1K	light pixel camouflage pattern
37 Blue	Su-25M1	dark pixel camouflage pattern
39 Blue	Su-25M1	dark pixel camouflage pattern; shot down 25 February 2022
40 Blue	Su-25M1	dark pixel camouflage pattern; shot down 3 March 2022
41 Blue	Su-25M1	
42 Blue	Su-25	stored; destroyed at Kulbaykine AB, 24 February 2022
44 Blue	Su-25	
45 Blue	Su-25M1	
46 Blue	Su-25M1K	
47 Blue	Su-25M1K	light pixel camouflage pattern
48 Blue	Su-25M1K	light pixel camouflage pattern
49 Blue	Su-25M1	dark pixel camouflage pattern; shot down 27 February 2022
60 Blue	Su-25UBM1K	light pixel camouflage pattern
61 Blue	Su-25UB	
62 Blue	Su-25UBM1	dark pixel camouflage pattern
63 Blue	Su-25UBM1K	dark pixel camouflage pattern
64 Blue	Su-25UBM1	dark pixel camouflage pattern
65 Blue	Su-25UB	
67 Blue	Su-25UBM1K	dark pixel camouflage pattern

Interceptor Fleet

The principal interceptor and air superiority fighter of the PSZSU was the Su-27, a total of 66–70 of which were inherited from the VVS in 1992. Included in this number was a mix of Su-27S single-seaters manufactured for the VVS, Su-27P single-seaters manufactured for the PVO, and Su-27UB and Su-27UP two-seat conversion trainers with full combat capability. The fire-control system of both variants included the N001 Myech pulse-Doppler radar with a search range of 85–100km (46–54 nautical miles) for a fighter-sized target in head-on engagement, or 30–40km (16–22nm) in a tail-on position. Another major sensor installed was the OLS-27 infrared search and track system coupled with a laser rangefinder with theoretical tracking range of up to 50km/27nm in a tail-on position.

For most of the following 20 years, their high maintenance requirements and a shortage of spares kept about half of the Ukrainian Su-27-fleet in storage, and – following the crash of one during an air show in 2002, and the sale of two examples to the USA in 2009 – only 19 were operational as of 2014. Following the Russian invasion, funding was granted to enable stored aircraft to be sent to ZDARZ to bring them up to 'NATO-similar standards', which included an overhaul of their radars, and minor upgrades of navigation and communication equipment that brought them to Su-27S1M/P1M and Su-27UB1M standards. Furthermore, in 2018, the same company overhauled and upgraded one of the two-seaters to an entirely new standard, designated Su-27UP2M, equipped with a new navigation system, digital weapons control system, and improved chaff and flare dispensers. However, during the same year, one of only a handful of Su-27UB two-seaters was lost in a fatal crash over the Khmelnytskyi Oblast during exercise Operation Clear Sky, leaving 37 examples in service as of 2022, as listed in Table 6. They were operated by the 39th Brigade, home-based at Ozerne AB in Zhytomyr Oblast, and the 831st Brigade, home-based at Myrhorod AB in Poltava Oblast.

As described in the first chapter, Ukrainian companies played a crucial role in the research and development of K-77 and R-77 active radar homing air-to-air missiles. However, none are known to have been manufactured in Ukraine, and they never entered service with the PSZSU. Thus, the principal armament of Ukrainian Su-27 were older Artem-manufactured R-27ER semi-active radar homing and R-27ET infrared homing, medium-range air-to-air missiles, of which a total of up to six could be carried underwing, on stations under intakes, and in the tunnel between the engine nacelles. The RLPK-27 Myech fire-control system enabled the N001 radar to simultaneously track 10 targets and engage two of these, but cockpit ergonomics were poor, and engagements with R-27ER missiles over their maximum range was sometimes described as too complex for a single-seat aircraft.

For short-range engagements, the type could carry up to six R-73E infrared homing air-to-air missiles, or use its 30mm GSh-30-1 internally-installed autocannon, for which it carried 150 rounds.[4] Like the Russian examples, Ukrainian Su-27Ss and Su-27UBs could also be armed with a full range of free-fall bombs of Soviet origin, including FAB-250 and FAB-500 general purpose bombs, KMGU sub-munitions dispensers, BETAB-500 runway piercing bombs, and RBK-250 and RBK-500 cluster bombs, as well as B-8M pods for S-8 80mm unguided rockets. However, ex-PVO Su-27Ps lacked the weapons control system for air-to-ground armament, and due to constant budget constraints, air-to-ground training was rarely undertaken by Ukrainian Su-27 units.

Table 6: Su-27s of the PSZSU, February–March 2022

Bort	Variant	Notes
04	Su-27S	831st Brigade
06	Su-27S	831st Brigade
08	Su-27S	831st Brigade
11	Su-27S1M	831st Brigade; overhauled and upgraded in 2020; shot down 28 February 2022
15	Su-27S	831st Brigade
21	Su-27S1M	39th Brigade
23	Su-27S	39th Brigade; overhauled and upgraded in 2017
24	Su-27S	39th Brigade; overhauled and upgraded in 2015
26	Su-27S	39th Brigade; overhauled and upgraded in 2011
27	Su-27S	831st Brigade
28	Su-27S	831st Brigade
30	Su-27S	831st Brigade
31	Su-27S1M	39th Brigade
33	Su-27S	831st Brigade; overhauled in 2015
36	Su-27S	39th Brigade; overhauled in 2016
37	Su-27P	39th Brigade; overhauled in 2015; destroyed at Ozerne AB, 24 February 2022
38	Su-27P	39th Brigade; shot down 5 June 2022
39	Su-27P	39th Brigade
41	Su-27S	831st Brigade
43	Su-27S	831st Brigade

A pair of Su-27s of the 39th Brigade, PSZSU, seen in the mid-2010s, both armed with R-27ER, R-27ET, and R-73 air-to-air missiles. The jet in the foreground, the Su-27UP2M, was still operational as of 2022. (Ukrainian government release)

Prototype of the Su-27UP2M seen during a take-off for flight-testing in November 2021. (PSZSU)

Bort	Variant	Notes	Bort	Variant	Notes
45	Su-27S	831st Brigade, overhauled in 2013	59	Su-27P1M	831st Brigade; overhauled and upgraded in 2020
46	Su-27S	831st Brigade; overhauled in 2013			
50	Su-27P1M	831st Brigade; overhauled and upgraded in 2015	67	Su-27UB1M	831st Brigade; overhauled and upgraded in 2012
52	Su-27S	831st Brigade; overhauled in 2012	69	Su-27UB	39th Brigade; overhauled in 2015
53	Su-27S	39th Brigade	71	Su-27UB1M	831st Brigade; overhauled and upgraded in 2017
54	Su-27P1M	831st Brigade; overhauled and upgraded in 2014			
56	Su-27P1M	831st Brigade; overhauled and upgraded in 2017	73	Su-27UP2M	39th Brigade; overhauled in 2013; upgraded in 2018–20
57	Su-27P1M	831st Brigade; overhauled and upgraded in 2016	74	Su-27P	831st Brigade; overhauled and upgraded in 2015
58	Su-57P1M	831st Brigade; overhauled and upgraded in 2015	100	Su-27P	831st Brigade; overhauled in 2012; shot down 25 February 2022
			101	Su-27P	831st Brigade; overhauled in 2012

The other interceptor type in service with the PSZSU was the MiG-29, up to 240 of which were inherited from the Soviet Union in 1991. For most of the following 20 years, four units of the air force (9th, 40th, 114th, and 204th Brigades) utilised some 70–80, although fewer than 20 were fully mission capable on average. Many were overhauled by local companies and then sold – including five to Algeria in 2000 and 14 to Azerbaijan in 2007 – while others were handed over to museums, before 63 of the oldest examples were withdrawn from service in 2008. Meanwhile, in 2005, and in cooperation with Rockwell Collins of the USA, LSARP developed an upgrade package designated the MiG-29MU1. This added the SN-3307 GPS/GLONASS-supported navigation system, a digital processor for the N019 radar (improving its detection range out to 100km/54nm), and the Omut radar homing and warning system with recording capability and an integrated countermeasures system. The first four MiG-29MU1s were handed over to the PSZSU in 2011. However, most of the fleet – the Ukrainians mostly kept MiG-29S (Izdeliye 9.13) and MiG-29UBs in service – was still in its original condition and in a poor state at the time of the Russian invasion of Crimea. Indeed, during their assault on Crimea, the Russians seized Balbek AB together with 52 MiG-29s and L-39M1s of the 204th Tactical Aviation Brigade. Following an agreement with Moscow to return 43 of its MiG-29s and one L-39M1, the unit had to redeploy to Kulbakino AB outside Mykolaiv, before, in 2018, being re-formed at Lutsk AB in north-western Ukraine.

By 2019, LSARP had upgraded one jet to the MiG-29MU2 standard – which added a new radio and the 20PM weapons-management system (including compatibility with R-27ER air-to-air missiles and with guided air-to-ground weapons, such as the Kh-29T and KAB-500KR guided bombs) – and was developing the MiG-29MU3. The latter project was never realised due to the Russian invasion. Finally, three MiG-29s of the Azerbaijan Air Force were undergoing overhauls at LSARP in February 2022 and seem to have been transferred to the Ukrainian air force following the Russian invasion. With this the MiG-29 fleet operated by the 40th and 204th Tactical Aviation Brigades would have been bolstered from around 55 to 58 aircraft.

Table 7: Known MiG-29s of the PSZSU, February–March 2022

Bort	Variant	Notes
01 White	MiG-29MU1	modified in 2016; pixel camouflage pattern
02 White	MiG-29MU1	second MiG-29MU1 with this bort number (first was shot down in 2014); modified in 2016; pixel camouflage pattern
03 Blue	MiG-29MU1	40th Brigade; Ukrainian Falcons pattern
04 White	MiG-29MU1	40th Brigade; pixel camouflage pattern
05 White	MiG-29S	40th Brigade; pixel camouflage pattern; shot down 24 February 2022
06	MiG-29S	restored in 2014–2018; 204th Brigade; pixel camouflage pattern
07 White	MiG-29MU1	204th Brigade; pixel camouflage pattern
08 White	MiG-29MU1	204th Brigade; pixel camouflage pattern
09 White	MiG-29S	restored in 2018; 40th Brigade; pixel camouflage pattern
10 White	MiG-29MU1	restored in 2016; 204th Brigade; pixel camouflage pattern; shot down 9 March 22
11 Blue	MiG-29MU1	40th Brigade
12 Blue	MiG-29MU2	modified in 2019; 40th Brigade; pixel camouflage pattern
15 White	MiG-29S	restored by 2022; 40th Brigade; pixel camouflage pattern; shot down 15 March 2022
16	MiG-29MU1	restored in 2014–2018; modified in 2020; 204th Brigade; pixel camouflage pattern
17	MiG-29MU1	restored in 2014–2018; modified in 2020; 204th Brigade; pixel camouflage pattern
19 White	MiG-29S	restored; 40th Brigade; pixel camouflage pattern
20 White	MiG-29S	restored
21 White	MiG-29S	restored
28	MiG-29S	restored in 2014–2018; 204th Brigade
29 Blue	MiG-29MU1	40th Brigade; pixel camouflage pattern
30	MiG-29UB	restored in 2015; 40th Brigade; pixel camouflage pattern
31 Blue	MiG-29S	restored; Ukrainian Falcons pattern
33 White	MiG-29MU1	restored in 2016; modified in 2020; 40th Brigade; pixel camouflage pattern
35 Blue	MiG-29MU1	restored in 2020; modified in 2020; 204th Brigade; pixel camouflage pattern; shot down 25 February 2022
36 White	MiG-29MU1	modified in 2021; 204th Brigade
40 White	MiG-29UB	restored in 2014–2018; pixel camouflage pattern
41 Blue	MiG-29S	restored in 2021; 204th Brigade; pixel camouflage pattern
43 Blue	MiG-29S	204th Brigade; pixel camouflage pattern
45	MiG-29S	restored in 2015; 204th Brigade; pixel camouflage pattern
46	MiG-29S	restored in 2019; 204th Brigade
47	MiG-29MU1	modified in 2020; 204th Brigade
48 Blue	MiG-29MU1	modified in 2019; 204th Brigade; pixel camouflage pattern
49	MiG-29S	restored in 2019; 204th Brigade; pixel camouflage pattern
57 White	MiG-29MU1	modified in 2014; 40th Brigade; pixel camouflage pattern
71 White	MiG-29S	restored in 2015; 40th Brigade; pixel camouflage pattern
72	MiG-29S	restored in 2017; 40th Brigade; pixel camouflage pattern
73	MiG-29S	restored in 2016; 40th Brigade; pixel camouflage pattern
74	MiG-29S	restored in 2018; 40th Brigade; pixel camouflage pattern

Bort	Variant	Notes
75	MiG-29S	restored in 2016; 40th Brigade, pixel camouflage pattern
76 Blue	MiG-29S	40th Brigade; pixel camouflage pattern
77 White	MiG-29S	restored in 2017; 40th Brigade; pixel camouflage pattern
81	MiG-29UB	restored in 2019; 204th Brigade; pixel camouflage pattern
82	MiG-29UB	restored in 2014–18; 204th Brigade
83	MiG-29UB	modified in 2018; 204th Brigade
85	MiG-29UB	modified in 2012; 40th Brigade
86	MiG-29UB	restored in 2014; 204th Brigade; pixel camouflage pattern
90 White	MiG-29UB	pixel camouflage pattern
91 Blue	MiG-29UB	restored in 2017; 40th Brigade; Ukrainian Falcons pattern
94 White	MiG-29S	restored
99 White	MiG-29UB	pixel camouflage pattern

Prototype of the MiG-29MU2 project while in the final stage of work at LSARP in 2020. (PSZSU)

The same jet during flight-testing, armed with a single Kh-29 air-to-ground guided missile. (PSZSU)

Transports, Helicopters, and Army Aviation

The balance of the PSZSU operated a mix of about 25 Antonov An-24, An-26, and An-30B transport aircraft (with three An-178s on order), and four Il-76MDs. The helicopter fleet of the air force was greatly downsized since the 1990s, and as of 2022 operated only about a dozen Mil Mi-2 training helicopters and some 20 Mi-8TB/MSB-V transport and utility helicopters.

The majority of combat-capable helicopters belonging to Ukraine in 2022 were assigned to the ground forces, which had its own flying branch organised into four Separate Army Aviation Brigades (OBrAA): 11th in Kherson, 12th in Novi Kalinov, 16th in Brody, and 18th in Poltava. Each Army Aviation brigade operated a mix of Mi-8MT/MTV/MSB-V and Mi-24P/PU1 helicopters, but the entire fleet comprised only some 30–35 of the former and 25–30 of the latter models. As clear from their designations, most had been not only overhauled, but also upgraded by Aviakon. For example, the Mi-24PU1 had received new engines, an omni-directional infrared jammer and flare dispensers, a GPS receiver, and cockpits compatible with night vision goggles. By 2018, a total of 23 Mi-8s had received similar improvements that brought them to the Mi-8MSB-V standard. Finally, about a dozen heavily modified Mi-8MSB-Vs served with the 18th Brigade for training purposes but could be armed with B-8M pods for 80mm unguided rockets.

That said, the Army Aviation suffered from exactly the same set of problems as the PSZSU: most of its fleet was old, the pay for its personnel was poor, and on average its crews flew fewer than 44 hours per annum in 2019, and only 50 in 2020. Certainly enough, all had extensive combat experience from operations in Donbas in 2014–15, but what actually kept the service in better condition were its operations in Africa as part of the United Nations peacekeeping efforts. For example, from 2004 until 2018, eight Ukrainian Mi-8s and six Mi-24s were deployed in Liberia, where their crews flew a staggering 55,000 sorties, logging over 60,000 flight hours. The other detachment was deployed in Democratic Republic of the Congo from 2012 to 2018, where its crews flew more than 3,000 combat sorties. Finally, numerous Ukrainian pilots and ground personnel served as private military contractors in Chad, Cote d'Ivoire, and Equatorial Guinea. Thus, this relatively small, and often overlooked, sub-branch of the armed forces was one of the most battle-hardened elements of the ZSU.

Unmanned Aerial Vehicles

As of 2014, Ukraine had very few unmanned aerial vehicles (UAVs) in service: indeed, the air force operated none at all. In August 2014, the PSZSU was granted the funding necessary to recommission, overhaul and partially upgrade 68 antiquated Tupolev Tu-141 and Tu-143 drones left over from the Soviet era. Their availability enabled the establishment of the first dedicated UAV unit of the air force, the 383rd Regiment, in 2016. The army acquired 64 of various other types by 2019, and another 46 through the next year, and initiated the production of indigenous models like the PD-2, and its advanced Shark version. Thus, it was a major breakthrough when in 2019 Kyiv acquired the first batch of six Bayraktar TB.2s from Turkey and then placed a follow-up order. By 2022, a total of 36 Turkish-made UAVs were in operational service with the air force and the navy.

Integrated Air Defence System

As of 2022, the PSZSU operated the third largest integrated air defence systems (IADS) in Europe (after those of NATO and Russia). Evolved from the former PVO system, Ukrainian IADS comprised a network of multi-layered, interconnected sensors, command and control nodes, and weapons systems, organised on a regional basis – which also formed the backbone of the organisation of the entire air force. In terms of equipment, the ground-based air defences of the PSZSU included a total of five radio technical brigades (operating radars), six communication regiments, three EW battalions, one rifle brigade, and two airfield engineer battalions. Its core comprised at least five brigades and three regiments operating a total of about 100 batteries equipped with S-300PS/PT/PMU and S-300V1 SAM systems.

An Mi-8MSB-V of the Army Aviation. Upgraded with improved navigation systems and night-vision-compatible cockpits, and operated by extremely courageous crews, the small fleet of venerable helicopters was to provide sterling service on the battlefields of Ukraine in 2022. (Ukrainian Ministry of Defence)

The launch of a Tu-143 UAV out of its transport container, assisted by a jettisonable booster. By 2022, the 383rd Regiment had a number of these ancient, jet-powered UAVs modified to carry 250kg warheads instead of their photo-reconnaissance equipment. (PSZSU)

The S-300PT was an early subvariant of the first generation of this powerful weapons system. Its centrepiece was the 30N6 surveillance radar, while launchers were semi-trailer trucks designated 5P85. As such, the system was semi-mobile: it took about one hour to set up for firing and used semi-active radar homing for guiding its 5V55 missiles over their maximum engagement range of 75km (40nm). The S-300PS represented the second generation of this family of SAM systems, in which all the heavy equipment and launchers were installed either on MAZ-7910 8x8 trucks (designated 5P85S and 5P85D), or on towed TELs designated 5P85T. Centred on the 30N6 mobile surveillance radar and the 76N6 mast-mounted radar for detection of low-flying targets, it also featured new 5V55R missiles with a maximum engagement range of 90km (49nm). Generally similar to the S-300PS, the S-300PMU system was originally developed as an export variant and equipped with 5V55K and 5V555R missiles with a maximum range of 45km/24nm and 90km/49nm, respectively. While the S-300 SAM system was widely advertised as having both anti-ballistic missile and anti-cruise missile capability, and the Ukrainians also operated the necessary 64N6 radars (theoretically capable of detecting ballistic missiles from as far away as 1,000km/540nm, and engaging targets travelling at 10,000km/h or 6,200mph), in combat its capability of engaging such objects proved very limited.

Little-known in 2022 was the fact that since 2014 the PSZSU had recovered dozens of additional systems from storage: amongst these were enough S-300V anti-ballistic missile systems on tracked vehicles to equip one full brigade and one regiment. Their maximum engagement range was 75km/40nm or 100km/54nm, depending on the type of missile deployed. Centred on 9S15 and 9S19 surveillance radars, and 9S32 fire-control radars, a typical S-300V battery included four TELs with four launchers for shorter-ranged 9M83 missiles, and two TELs with two launchers each for longer-ranged 9M82 missiles.

Complementing S-300-equipped units were three regiments operating a total of at least 72 9K37M1 tracked transporter erector launchers and radar vehicles (TELARs) for Buk M1s. Operated in units with a much smaller footprint than that of the S-300 – a typical battery included one command post vehicle, four or five technical service vehicles, one transloader, two TELARs with four missiles each, and one TEL with four missiles – this system was to prove more flexible and manoeuvrable (a well-trained crew could open fire within five minutes of stopping), while particularly dangerous for aircraft and helicopters – including those operating at very low altitudes – out to a range of 25km (13.5nm). Additionally, the PSZSU operated one or two reconditioned 2K12 Kub M2 mobile SAM systems, and several fixed S-125 Pechora 2D batteries. Lighter systems – like the 2K22 Tunguska, 9K33M3 Osa-AKM, and 9K330 Tor – as well as most of the man portable air defence systems (MANPADS) were operated by the Ukrainian army, as was most of the anti-aircraft artillery.

Although the majority of PSZSU heavy SAMs were mobile, its IADS was largely static, arrayed around major urban centres and capable of countering unidirectional and well-defined threats from manned aircraft and helicopters. The core of the system was a large number of early warning or surveillance radars: radars with long range, used to detect the approach of enemy aircraft, helicopters and missiles. The resulting radar picture was then forwarded to the dispersed network of additional radars, responsible for covering selected areas: by tracking the enemy aircraft, helicopters or missiles, these then distributed targets between the suitable SAM sites: these SAM sites then used their own radars to track and guide their weapons to the target.

That said, this IADS had several shortcomings: while potentially highly effective against the threat of combat aircraft and helicopters, it was woefully unprepared for the large-scale long-range missile campaign of the kind the Russians were about to unleash upon Ukraine. Indeed, the PSZSU had never planned for nor trained its operators to intercept targets like ballistic and cruise missiles, and – regardless of how much advertised as some sort of 'Gods of war' over the previous 30 or more years – the majority of SAM systems in service had no capability to intercept such ballistic missiles as the Russian-made Iskander. As the subsequent combat experience was to show, and although partially re-equipped with upgraded SAM systems, the PSZSU had no capability to intercept such air-launched supersonic missiles as the Kh-22, let alone the hypersonic missiles that the Russians were to deploy later during the war. Finally, due to the sheer size of Ukraine, and despite significant investment in research, development, and production of an entire generation of new, mobile surveillance radars (primarily Malachite, the local development of the old P-18MU) it proved technically and economically impossible to provide effective, nationwide air defence against all types of threats. Combined with that, Ukraine possessed no means to strike back at the sources of Russian missiles: their launchers – whether those based on the ground, in the air, or at sea. Correspondingly, the PSZSU was soon to find itself embroiled in a war of attrition, in which it was forced to target individual missiles, one at a time, instead of destroying launch sites, launchers, and associated equipment. Unsurprisingly, simply having a good IADS proved to be anything but good enough for Ukraine.

Table 8: Principal SAM Systems in Ukrainian Service, 2022

Russian designation	ASCC/NATO reporting name	Notes
S-125 Pechora 2D	SA-3 Goa	SARH/Command; operated by ZSU
2K22 Tunguska	SA-19 Grison	SARH/Command; operated by ZSU
9K33M3 Osa-AKM	SA-8B Gecko	SARH, operated by ZSU
9K35 Strela-10	SA-13 Gopher	IR homing; operated by ZSU
9K330 Tor	SA-15 Gauntlet	SARH; operated by ZSU
9K37M1 Buk M1	SA-11 Gadfly	SARH, operated by PSZSU
S-300PT/PS/PMU	SA-10B Grumble B	Command (PT), SAGG (PMU); operated by PSZSU
S-300V1	SA-12A/B Gladiator	GAI/SARH; operated by PSZSU

A pre-war photograph of the components of an S-300V1 SAM system. In the foreground are four 9A83-1 TELARs. This system was operated by the Pervomaisk-based 201st Anti-Aircraft Missile Brigade and the Uman-based 210th Anti-Aircraft Missile Regiment. (Ukrainian MOD)

A Buk M1 TELAR of the PSZSU participating in an exercise before the war. (Ukrainian MOD)

The Crisis of 2021

By 2017, the PSZSU had received over 60 completely overhauled combat aircraft and helicopters, and by 2019 was operating a total of 155 fighter-bombers, as well as over 150 SAM batteries. Combined with joint exercises with foreign air forces – like Clear Sky 2018, when Boeing F-15C Eagle interceptors of the California Air National Guard's 144th Fighter Wing visited Ukraine – this helped create the impression of the service undergoing not only a rapid modernisation, but also introducing new tactical methods to its operations, greatly improving its operational effectiveness.

The actual situation was anything but that. The cold fact was that most of the PSZSU's aircraft were old: even the newest MiG-29s and Su-27s were 30 years old, while the repairs and upgrade work remained limited in extent and quality. As if this or their low salaries and poor living conditions were not enough, the flight operations of Ukrainian units were marred by inefficient, obsolete, sometimes even absurd flight regulations engrained in the service since Soviet times and imposed by the Regulation Activities of the State Aviation of Ukraine. These included such measures as pilots having to spend a day with flight preparations before every single training mission, to regulations preventing them from introducing new tactics learned from their Western colleagues during joint exercises. As a result, most units flew only on two or three days every week. Finally, although the PSZSU was receiving enough spare parts and fuel,

the number of flight hours per annum per pilot decreased to as low as 35 hours: barely enough to keep them current on the type they were flying, and far too little for serious tactical training. Atop of this, senseless bureaucracy swamped pilots with paperwork, forcing them to maintain up to 50 different logs, registers, folders and forms. Rather unsurprisingly, through 2020–21, the service experienced its deepest crisis, with nearly 140 pilots leaving: the figure increased by another 40 by the end of 2021. With just 10–15 cadets graduating from the Ivan Kozhedub National Air Force University in Kharkiv every year, there were never enough replacements.[5]

Overall, the PSZSU thus found itself facing the Russian onslaught of February 2022 flying old, only partially upgraded aircraft and helicopters, equipped with shorter-ranged air-to-air weaponry, and crewed by pilots and weapons systems operators that had received even less tactical training than the Russians. Moreover, while its IADS was operational, most of its air defence units were still in their bases on the morning of 24 February 2022. In a matter of minutes, the service expected by the General Staff in Kyiv and Ukrainian intelligence services to deal with a similar scenario to that of 2014–15 was to find itself facing a poorly trained, even confused, but determined opponent in possession of vast qualitative and quantitative superiority. Under such circumstances, the PSZSU was left with few options but to learn quickly, disperse, and operate as a kind of aerial guerrilla.

Table 9: Order of Battle, PSZSU, Army Air Force, Naval Aviation, and National Guard, February–March 2022

Unit	Location	Notes
PSZSU		
101st Communications Regiment	Vinnytsia	directly subordinated to the Air Force General Command
182nd Communications Regiment	Vinnytsia	directly subordinated to the Air Force General Command
1st Air Force Rifle Brigade		directly subordinated to the Air Force General Command
Air Command West		
352nd Airfield Engineer Battalion	Khmelnytskyi	
76th Communications Regiment	Lypniki	
17th Electronic Warfare Battalion	Kolomyia	
1st Radio Technical Brigade	Lypniki	
11th Anti-Aircraft Missile Regiment	Shepetivka	Buk M1
39th Anti-Aircraft Missile Regiment	Volodymyr-Volynskyi	Army unit; Osa-AKM
223rd Anti-Aircraft Missile Regiment	Stryi	Buk M1
540th Anti-Aircraft Missile Regiment	Kamianka Buzka	S-300PS
7th Tactical Aviation Brigade	Starokostyantyniv AB	18 Su-24M (1st and 2nd Squadrons), 9 Su-24MR (3rd Squadron)
114th Tactical Aviation Brigade	Ivano-Frankivsk AB	18 MiG-29S/MU1, 3 MiG-29UB, L-39M1
204th Tactical Aviation Brigade	Lutsk AB	18 MiG-29S/MU1, 2–3 MiG-29UB, L-39M1
383rd Unmanned Aviation Regiment		Tu-141, Tu-143
Air Command Centre		
31st Communications Regiment	Kyiv	
19th Special Purpose Radio Intercept Brigade	Halytsynov	
2204th Electronic Warfare Battalion	Vasylkiv	
138th Radio Technical Brigade	Vasilkiv	
96th Anti-Aircraft Missile Brigade	Danylivka/Kyiv	S-300PS
210st Anti-Aircraft Missile Regiment	Uman	S-300V1
156th Anti-Aircraft Missile Regiment	Zolotonosha	Buk M1
1129th Anti-Aircraft Missile Regiment	Bila Tserkva	Army unit; Osa-AKM (5 batteries)
39th Tactical Aviation Brigade	Ozerne AB	23 Su-27S/P/P1M/UB, L-39M1
40th Tactical Aviation Brigade	Vasylkiv AB	9 MiG-29S, 11 MiG-29MU1, 4 MiG-29UB, L-39M1
831st Tactical Aviation Brigade	Myrhorod AB	22 Su-27P/M1/UB/UM (2 squadrons), L-39M1
15th Transport Aviation Brigade	Boryspil IAP	5 An-26, 3 An-30, 4 Mi-8, 1 Tu-134
456th Transport Aviation Brigade	Vinnytsia/ Havryshivka AB	9 An-26, 7 Mi-8
Air Command East		
57th Communications Regiment	Dnipro	

Unit	Location	Notes
164th Radio Technical Brigade	Kharkiv	
301st Anti-Aircraft Missile Brigade	Kharkiv	S-300PT
11th Anti-Aircraft Missile Regiment	Shepetivka	Buk M1
138th Anti-Aircraft Missile Brigade	Dnipro	S-300PS
301st Anti-Aircraft Missile Regiment	Nikopol	S-300PS
1039th Anti-Aircraft Missile Regiment	Hvardiske	Army unit; Osa-AKM
203rd Training Aviation Brigade	Chuihiv AB	16 L-39C, 1 L-39M1, 8 An-26, 2 Mi-8, 2 Mi-2
Air Command South		
28th Airfield Engineer Battalion	Mykolaiv	
43rd Communications Regiment	Odesa	
1194th Electronic Warfare Battalion	Pervomaisk	
14th Radio Technical Brigade	Odesa	
160th Anti-Aircraft Missile Brigade	Odesa	S-300PM
201st Anti-Aircraft Missile Brigade		
208th Anti-Aircraft Missile Brigade	Kherson	S-300PS, Buk M1
28th Anti-Aircraft Missile Regiment	Chornomorske	Army unit, Osa-AKM (5 batteries)
25th Transport Aviation Brigade	Melitopol IAP	22 Il-76M/MD & Il-78 (all stored, 1 undergoing overhauls), 1 An-26, 4 Mi-8
299th Tactical Aviation Brigade	Kulbakyne AB	24 Su-25/25M1/M1K, 7 Su-25UB/UBM1/UBM1K
Army Aviation		
11th OBrAA	Chornobaivka AB	Mi-24P/PU1, Mi-8MT/MTV/MSB-V
12th OBrAA	Novi Kalinov	Mi-24P/PU1, Mi-8MT/MTV/MSB-V
16th OBrAA	Brody	Mi-24P/PU1, Mi-8MT/MTV/MSB-V
18th OBrAA	Poltava AB	Mi-24P/PU1, Mi-8MT/MTV/MSB-V, Mi-2MSB-V
Naval Aviation		
10th Naval Aviation Brigade	Kulbakyne AB	10 Mi-8MSB-V, Ka-27, Ka-226 and Mi-14 helicopters, 2 An-2, 6 TB.2
National Guard		
Air Squadron	N/A	15 Mi-8MT/MSB-V, Mi-2MSB and Airbus H225

A map of air bases and forward operating air bases of the PSZSU, international airports and disused air bases in Ukraine in February 2022. (Map by Anderson Subtil)

3
COUP ATTEMPT

With hindsight, it can be deducted that, just as most political leaders in the West base their decisions on assessments by their respective intelligence agencies, Vladimir Putin's decision-making for Ukraine was based on assessments prepared by the FSB – as well as that he had begun developing a plot to destroy the country at least as far back as 2016–17, if not earlier. Like all other professional military intelligence services, in the event of a Russian invasion of Ukraine, the FSB prepared three sorts of assessments: 'worst case', 'best case', and 'in between'. Strongly influenced by the information from several Western intelligence services – most of which were excellently informed about Putin's intentions from at least November 2021 – the FSB provided the 'best case' assessment, because this was precisely what the President of the Russian Federation wanted to hear: the invasion would quickly remove the government of President Volodymyr Zelensky, and the majority of Ukrainians would greet Putin as a 'liberator'. Ironically enough, Putin then launched his invasion without ever informing the FSB about his intention: as far as is known, he kept only Shoygu, Gerasimov, and Viktor Vasilyevich Zolotov, commander of the Rosgvardiya (the Russian National Guard: a force designed to protect Putin's rule in the event of major internal unrest or mutiny) informed about his intentions. The reason was that he needed their services: Shoygu and Gerasimov were to plan the coup and deploy selected units of the Airborne Assault Troops (VDV) and the Spetsnaz (Russian special forces). Selected units of the (lightly armed) Rosgvardiya were to follow next.

On the contrary, although deployed en masse all-around Ukraine by February 2022, the Armed Forces of the Russian Federation (VSRF) were kept in darkness. Theoretically, its commanders did not need to know any details: their troops were assessed as equipped and trained well-enough to complete the task of following up the heliborne spearheads and the Rosgvardiya, and then to merely help secure the major urban centres, starting with Kyiv and Kharkiv, and followed by Czerhihiv, Sumy, Mariupol, Zaporizhzhya, Kherson, Mykolaiv, and Odesa, before linking-up with the Russian separatists in the so-called Transnistria, in eastern Moldova.

The immediate objectives of the coup plot might have been limited to a 'decapitation' of the Ukrainian government and subversion and disarmament of its armed forces, followed by rapid deployment of ground forces. However, its grand aim was not to take over specific parts of the country, but the complete destruction of Ukraine and any of its people opposing Putin's rule: like Czechoslovakia in 1968, or Afghanistan in 1979, the country was to be secured through a 'special military operation' within 3 to 14 days, and then systematically and completely eradicated as an independent entity.

In the light of such a plan, Russian air power was delegated a supporting task, limited in scope: a bigger campaign would be detrimental for the moment of surprise. Correspondingly, basing its targeting upon carefully obtained information from human intelligence (HUMINT) sources over the years, the VKS – in cooperation with the ground forces and the navy – was to deploy its cruise missiles to knock out the Ukrainian IADS, major air bases and fuel depots, and then to support assaults by the VDV and Spetsnaz with the aim of quickly securing a number of strategic points around the country. Correspondingly, the *GenStab* tasked the VKS with opening the war by blinding PSZSU communications, knocking out its early warning radar systems, shooting down any manned interceptors that might dare to take-off, disabling their air bases, and then blunting its ground-based air defences. To no small degree, this was exactly what the Western intelligence services had assessed that the Russians would do: with the VKS possessing something like tenfold quantitative, and an even bigger qualitative advantage vis-à-vis the Ukrainian air force, it was expected to rapidly establish itself in control of the skies and then protect friendly ground troops. Ironically, the *GenStab* planned, and the VKS attempted doing exactly that, though in their own fashion and not precisely the way expected in the West. Nevertheless, the initial Western reaction was that the 'Russian air force is nowhere to be seen'….

Special Military Operation
Starting at around 18.00hrs on 23 February 2022, a massive Russian cyberattack conducted by attackers with insider knowledge took down the ViaSat SAT-KA satellite broadband communication system in Ukraine and parts of the European Union. The hack – which relied on malware that wiped the contents of thousands of targeted modems via servers in northern Italy – not only disrupted internet services in most of the country, but completely crashed the communications between the top headquarters in Kyiv and all the brigades of the PSZSU and ZSU. Indeed, the Russian hackers rendered 40,000 out of 45,000 modems of the SAT-KA system inoperable, and then overwhelmed the network with fake requests that targeted selected terminals. Finally, once they had disrupted the network, the Russians used sophisticated methods to prevent it from being restored, thus keeping the system out of service for days, and then weeks.[1]

Next, between 03.00 and 04.00hrs in the morning of 24 February 2022, Tu-95 bombers underway over the northern Caspian Sea began releasing dozens of Kh-101 and Kh-555 cruise missiles. As these approached Ukraine, their numbers were bolstered by 3M54 Kalibr cruise missiles launched from warships of the Russian Black Sea Fleet. As the cruise missiles entered Ukrainian airspace, the Russian ground forces began firing a large number of 9K720 Iskander ballistic missiles, while A-50 AEW aircraft guided numerous Su-30 and Su-35 fighter-bombers into attacks with Kh-31 and Kh-58 anti-radiation missiles. However, fighter-bombers of the VKS flew next to no so-called 'deep strikes': attacks on targets deep inside Ukraine. As far as is known, all such attacks were undertaken by ballistic and cruise missiles only.

The reasons for this approach were manifold. Paramount amongst these were the way the VKS was equipped and trained, combined with the sheer size of the battlefield. As described in the previous chapter, the Russian Aerospace Forces was never meant, equipped or trained to fight something like 'its own air war', 'independently' of the other branches, but was subjected to the operational control of strategic commands dominated by the ground forces. As such, it was never meant to operate deeper than around 100–150 kilometres beyond the frontline. Irrespectively of the all-out invasion actually being planed as a 'big coup', the sheer size of Ukraine meant it also lacked the means of command, control and communications to fight over such distances. Another problem related to the size of Ukraine was the weather: on 22 February 2022, much of the north-east and east was covered by thick and low clouds, and snow was falling in several areas, making operations by VKS fighter-bombers and attack helicopters nearly impossible. Unsurprisingly, for the first week of the war, the Russian Aerospace Forces did exactly what it was designed, equipped, and trained for: conduct heliborne assaults and, even more so, provided close air support for advancing columns of mechanised troops – as requested, and wherever possible to do so – but nothing else.

A still from a video released by the Russian Ministry of Defence, showing the launch of a 3M54 Kalibr cruise missile from a warship of the Black Sea Fleet. (Russian Ministry of Defence)

First Blow

According to the Ministry of Defence in Moscow, a total of 75 VKS aircraft were involved in the first wave of strikes on Ukraine that hit its targets starting at 05.00hrs on 24 February 2022. Together with ballistic missiles fired by the VSRF and cruise missiles launched by warships of the Black Sea Fleet, they struck a total of 70 military targets, including 11 air bases. In a matter of a few hours, this number was increased to a total of 83 'land-based Ukrainian targets'. According to official Ukrainian sources, nearly all early warning/surveillance radars of the PSZSU came under attack during the opening Russian strike: the only detail in some dispute is whether

the opening Russian missile strike included a total of 160, or more ballistic and cruise missiles.[2]

The situation during this opening strike played into the hands of the planners in Moscow. Not only were the opening strikes to support what was expected to be a coup, but very few Ukrainian air defence units were on alert. The majority of ground-based air defence units were still in their bases: a handful had their minor elements involved in exercises. Thus, the Russians needed no dynamic targeting nor expected to be forced to search for mobile Ukrainian ground-based air defences. Moreover, they expected the conventional warheads of their ballistic and cruise missiles to be much more effective than they actually turned out to be.

The list of the bases attacked rapidly grew through the following day, and, according to Moscow, during the first 48 hours of the 'special military operation', the VKS alone targeted more than 100 installations related to Ukrainian air defences, including 19 air defence radar systems and 39 'other' radar stations. Notably, most of the facilities targeted were along the routes selected for the advance of VSRF ground formations.

The result of such a massive onslaught was that the PSZSU found itself under a near-simultaneous attack from multiple sides, and had all of its major air bases, air defence bases, communication sites, and radio technical units under pressure at the same time. Unsurprisingly considering the lack of effective protection for its bases, and especially its air defence assets, the air force suffered significant losses: up to 22 S-300 launchers and 17 launchers for other SAM systems were knocked out within the first 24 to 48 hours of the war. This in turn left the majority of Ukrainian command and control nodes, air bases, nearly all military bases, transportation hubs and logistic centres, ammunition depots, and power and water facilities entirely exposed to the Russian missile campaign. Finally, with its communication system down, the HQ in Vinnytsia was left with little option but to let local commanders act on their own – usually following pre-invasion planning.

Wreckage of a Russian Kh-31 anti-radiation missile that crashed in downtown Kyiv early on 24 February 2022. (Ukrainian social media)

Missiles Pawing the Way

Home-based in Lviv, the 1st Radar Brigade found itself on the receiving end of several Iskander ballistic missiles: there was only minimal advance warning and the unit suffered losses in equipment and personnel.[3] At Ivano-Frankivsk Air Base, MiG-29 pilots of the 40th Brigade were ordered to man their aircraft at 03.10hrs. Although freezing in their cockpits for more than an hour and a half, this measure proved a good idea when, shortly before 05.00hrs, the two jets standing quick-reaction alert were ordered to take-off. Just seconds after getting airborne, their pilots saw massive flashes in their rear-view mirrors, marking the impacts of several Russian missiles.[4] The same base was hit by another volley of 3M54 Kalibr sea-launched cruise missiles around 07.00hrs that morning.

At Starokostiantyniv AB, the 7th Fighter-Bomber Brigade, equipped with Su-24s, was put on alert at 02.00hrs and thus had enough time to prepare its pilots, ground crews and aircraft for evacuation. With most of the operational aircraft already dispersed, the few Su-24s still around were all flown out by the time of the Russian attack which targeted the local command post, fuel and ammunition depots, navigational systems, maintenance facilities, and aircraft dispersal areas with at least eight missiles. Indeed, Starokostiantyniv AB was hit heavily and took days to repair and return to operational condition.[5]

The situation at Ozerne AB, outside Zhytomyr, was different. The base was attacked by at least two Iskander-M missiles. One of these blew up a fuel truck, destroying a parked Su-27 and killing six ground personnel of the 39th Brigade. Another interceptor of the same unit crashed while taking-off from a damaged runway killing its pilot, Lieutenant Colonel Eduard Vahorovskyy. Ozerne was to receive hits from several additional Iskander-M missiles over the following days, even though most of these missed anything of value according to the Ukrainians.

In Vinnytsia, the base of the Radio Technical Brigade directly subordinated to the HQ of the PSZSU was hit by several ballistic missiles at 05.20hrs and suffered heavy losses in personnel and equipment. After recovering from this blow, surviving troops began the tedious work on repairing as much of the remaining equipment as possible: this process went on for days longer, and was disturbed by several additional Russian missile strikes.[6]

At 06.00 or 07.00hrs, Antonov IAP was hit by two 3M54 Kalibr cruise missiles: one hit the ground near an apartment building, while the other cratered a parade field at the airport. Meanwhile,

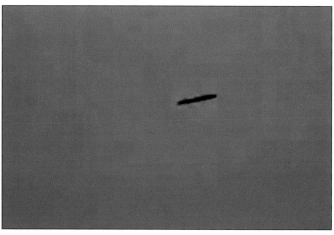

A 3M54 Kalibr cruise missile, captured on video while approaching the Ivano-Frankivsk area, underway at around 30 metres altitude. (Ukrainian social media)

Another Kalibr cruise missile, shortly before hitting one of the buildings at Ivano-Frankivsk airport early on 24 February 2022. (Ukrainian social media)

As of 24 February 2022, up to 17 'nearly airworthy' and 30 'non-airworthy' Su-24Ms were stored at Bila Tserkva AB. Although this was a well-known fact, the Russians targeted them anyway, causing severe damage to a number of airframes. While appearing an entirely pointless effort at that moment in time, in the long term, this proved a good decision. (Ukrainian social media)

The smouldering wreckage of the Su-27 Bort 37, destroyed by a Russian missile at Ozerne AB, early on 24 February 2022. (*GenStab-U*)

in Uman, the 210th Anti-Aircraft Missile Regiment (equipped with S-300V1s) was hit heavily, losing much equipment to the opening strike. Fortunately, most of its personnel survived and – reinforced by recalled reservists – rushed to salvage and repair whatever it could. By the next morning, it had several firing units ready for operations and was in the process of redeploying one of these to the Svyatopetrivske area, in south-western Kyiv.[7]

In Danylivka, a south-western suburb of Kyiv, the 96th Anti-Aircraft Missile Brigade was put on alert and ordered out of its barracks five minutes before 05.00hrs, just in time to evacuate because shortly afterwards the base received several very precise hits – which could have caused many casualties. The brigade not only survived, but rapidly dispersed its firing units into multiple firing positions.[8] The 138th Radio Technical Brigade was not evacuated in time but was still lucky: although one of its barracks received a direct hit from a cruise missile, 50 troops inside survived. Both units subsequently fanned out of their bases and, after bringing their equipment into working order, went into action on the morning of 25 February, greatly bolstering the air defences of the Ukrainian capital. A battalion of the S-300PS-equipped 160th Anti-Aircraft Brigade – home-based in the Odesa area – was on an exercise outside Kyiv when the Russians invaded. They suffered an unknown degree of damage in the opening strike but managed to recover and repair enough vehicles and other equipment to form a combined firing unit and deploy into the field. Commanded by Major Andriy, it became the first PSZSU unit to shoot down a Kalibr cruise missile in this war.[9]

The success of the 160th Anti-Aircraft Brigade was repeated by a Buk battalion commanded by Lieutenant Colonel Volodymyr Vesnin. Although taken by surprise by the Russian attack, the unit was quick to assemble and drove out of its barracks before experiencing some problems with finding a suitable firing position in the suburbs of Kyiv. Its first target were two cruise missiles. Vesnin's battalion continued fighting without respite for the next five days.[10]

Potential Bridgeheads

The missile strikes were still in full swing when the Russians set in motion their main coup: a heliborne assault on at least one airport in the vicinity of Kyiv, with the aim of establishing a bridgehead that would enable the bringing in of the airborne assault units necessary to stage a coup against the Ukrainian government.

As of 2022, there were three major airports and one minor airport in and around the Ukrainian capital. Constructed in the late 1950s, 29km outside Kyiv, Boryspil IAP was the biggest in the country, serving up to 65 percent of all passenger traffic, but also the most distant from the Russian bases in Belarus. The slightly smaller Sikorsky IAP (colloquially known as Zhuliany) came into being in the 1920s and was some seven kilometres southwest of the city centre. It was developed into a major civilian facility after the Second World War, before its further development was slowed down by proximity to major railway lines and rapid urban expansion. Antonov IAP was constructed outside Hostomel – about 10 kilometres outside Kyiv, and some 30km from the city centre – in the early 1960s at a former military flight-testing facility. Lying near the R02 highway, which the Russians intended to use as their primary approach avenue for Kyiv, it was also the closest to Belarus, while also relatively isolated, which was expected to play into the Russian hands. Finally, Sviatoshyn Airport had been constructed as part of the Antonov Works, just 11 kilometres north-west of the city centre. Its sole runway of 1,800 metres was long enough for aircraft like the Il-76, but it seems that the fact this facility was now surrounded by tall buildings rendered it unsuitable for an airborne assault.

As of February 2022, the 121st Guards Heavy Bomber Aviation Regiment had 12 Tupolev Tu-160 supersonic bombers in operation, and four undergoing overhaul and upgrade to the Tu-160M2 standard. Suffering from chronic engine-related problems and lack of spares, and because they may have been held in reserve for strategic deterrent purposes (for example, in the event of a NATO intervention), the type is not known to have been involved in launching cruise missiles against Ukraine. That said, it could carry up to 12 Kh-101s or Kh-555s on internal rotary launchers in its bomb bay. The main artwork shows Bort 06, named *Ilya Muromets*, in 2022. The inset shows the front section of Bort 17 (formerly 10), registration RF-94110, named *Valeriy Chkalov*. By the time of the all-out invasion of Ukraine, it had probably received the full service title – 'VKS Rossii' (in Russian, and in black Cyrillic characters) – applied low on the fin. (Artwork by Goran Sudar)

As of 2022, Tupolev Tu-95 bombers were operated by the 182nd Heavy Bomber Aviation Regiment (based at Ukrainka AB in the Far East), and one squadron of the 121st Heavy Bomber Aviation Regiment (based at Engels-2 AB). Most were painted in so-called silver-grey overall – essentially consisting of two layers of clear lacquer mixed with up to 10–15 percent aluminium powder. Some had their undersides painted in mid-grey-blue, which was also applied along the leading edges of their fins. About a third of the fleet wore the names and crests of major Russian cities – like *Moskva* or *Vorkuta* (as shown in the upper insets), while one – Bort 28, registration RF-94116 – wore the name *Sevastopol*. Principal armament consisted of Kh-101 and Kh-555 cruise missiles (shown in the lower insets, together with their silhouettes as seen from the ground). The service title had probably been changed to 'VKS Rossii' by 2022. (Artwork by Tom Cooper)

In the face of unexpectedly effective and bitter resistance from the Mariupol garrison of the ZSU, the *GenStab* in Moscow did not shy away from deploying Tupolev Tu-22M3 bombers of the 52nd and 840th Heavy Bomber Aviation Regiments to carpet-bomb the city. Indeed, once the garrison withdrew into the Azovstal compound, the VKS began deploying Tu-22M3s armed with old 3,000kg FAB-3000M-54 bombs to target the area. As of 2022, all the Tu-22M-3s were painted in the same medium grey on upper surfaces and sides, and dielectric white on lower surfaces as at the time of their service entry. A few examples – including the one shown here, Bort 55 (registration RF-34583) – were former Naval Aviation aircraft still showing their shark mouth, eye and gills insignia applied to the intakes. (Artwork by Tom Cooper)

With the project for an overhaul and upgrade of existing Beriev A-50s to the A-50U standard developing extremely slowly, the seven operational strategic airborne early warning and control aircraft of the 144th Aviation Regiment for Long-Range Radar Detection, of the 610th Combat Application and Flight Crew Conversion Centre, were in much demand through February and March 2022. Two were forward deployed to Machulischchy AB in Belarus at the time, one of which was regularly kept on station. The example illustrated here – Bort 42, registration RF-50610 – was the sixth A-50 upgraded to A-50U standard and handed over to the VKS on 28 March 2019. While the prototype for this variant, Bort 33, was painted in dark grey overall, the fleet-wide standard became the old livery in white on the upper half of the fuselage and grey on the lower half and on wings and horizonal stabilators. Unlike a few other examples, Bort 42 had no markings other than the usual national insignia, bort and registration. (Artwork by Tom Cooper)

At least four different subvariants of the venerable Ilyushin Il-20 COMINT/ELINT/SIGINT-gathering aircraft were in service with the VKS as of February–March 2022. While upgrades to the Anagramma and Monitor standards remained limited to a single aircraft each, and that to the Il-20MS Retsenzent progressing relatively slowly, the Il-20M was still the most numerous version around. This anonymised example – marked only with a white Z on the rear fuselage – was photographed while underway over Belarus in March 2022. Its equipment included two Vishnaya antennas atop the forward fuselage; a housing with A-87P cameras and the Romb-4 radio-locator on the sides of the forward fuselage; a huge ventral container for the Igla-1 SLAR; and a pair of domes of the Kvadrat-2 radio-locator under the rear fuselage. (Artwork by Tom Cooper)

Completing the airborne early warning and control triad of the VKS, the venerable Ilyushin Il-22 is an airborne command post version, usually deployed in support of operations at corps- or combined arms army level. A total of nine Il-22s and 22 Il-22Ms were manufactured between 1976 and 1985, and all wore civilian livery throughout their service (some including Aeroflot markings). As of 2022, some six Il-22s, 11 Il-22Ms, one Il-22K, and three Il-22PP escort jammers were operational. Mostly home-based at Chkalovsky AB outside Moscow, one or two were assigned to the command headquarters of the West and South OSKs, and co-stationed there. Illustrated here is an example still in the Il-22 Bison configuration as of 2022: registration RF-75899. (Artwork by Tom Cooper)

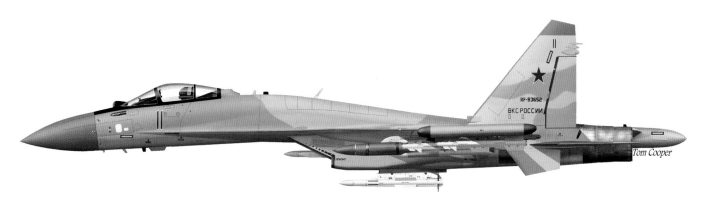

The majority of Su-35S models delivered through 2012–18 were painted in a disruptive camouflage pattern consisting of BS381C/172 pale roundel blue (or MRP-297 light blue), BS381C/625 camouflage grey (MRP-296 light grey), and BS381C/692 smoke grey (MRP-298 blue) on top surfaces and sides, and pale roundel blue overall on undersurfaces. Their radomes, the leading edges of wing and fins, and dielectric panels were painted in a colour similar to BS381C/637 medium sea grey, while much of both stabilators was left in unpainted titanium colour. Generally, borts were applied in red, but in 2016–17, a few had them reapplied in blue instead. Originally assigned to the 790th Fighter Aviation Regiment at Khotilovo AB (Tver Oblast), in early 2022, Bort 11 (registration RF-93652) was deployed with the 23rd Fighter Aviation Regiment at Baranovichi AB in Belarus. (Artwork by Tom Cooper)

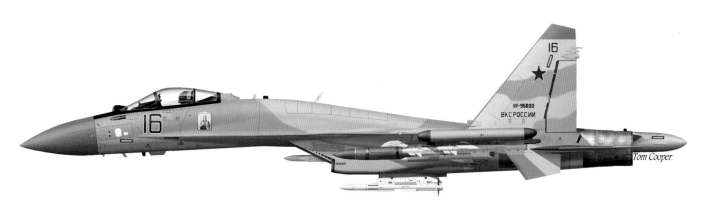

The 22nd Fighter Aviation Regiment is known to have deployed a squadron-worth of its Su-35S models for initial operations against Ukraine as well. The aircraft of this unit were relatively easy to recognise because of the application of *Ikona* (icon) religious images on the left side of their fuselages, behind the cockpit – in this case that of the Archangel Saint Michael. The aircraft shown here – Bort 16, registration RF-95800 – was confirmed as one having such an icon applied, but it remains unknown if it actually flew combat sorties against Ukraine in February–March 2022. Nevertheless, and like the aircraft in the preceding artwork, it is shown in a typical weapons configuration for the early days of the all-out invasion, including a total of four R-77-1s (two between the intakes and two under the intakes), two Kh-31P anti-radiation missiles, two or four R-74s on outboard underwing pylons, and L005 Sorbtsiya ECM pods on the wingtips. (Artwork by Tom Cooper)

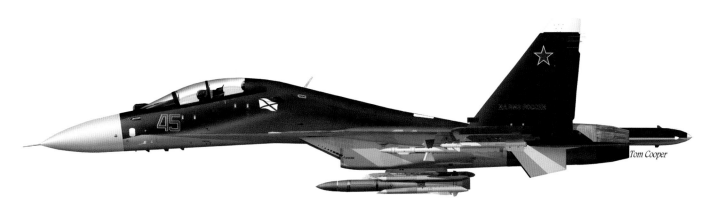

Starting in 2015, a squadron of the 43rd Composite Naval Aviation Regiment at Saki AB, in occupied Crimea, was re-equipped with Su-30SMs (the other two squadrons continued flying Su-24Ms and Su-24MRs). As far as is known, all of these were painted in the camouflage pattern known as 'Serdyukov' (though, amongst their crews also as 'Negro', because of its dark colour), consisting of a colour similar to RAF blue-grey (BS381C/633) on top surfaces and sides, and the same set of pale roundel blue, camouflage grey and smoke grey on undersurfaces as used on Su-35s. On 5 March 2022, two Su-30SMs of this unit were shot down over the Mykolaiv area, including the jet illustrated here: Bort 45 (registration RF-33787), crewed by Major Alexey Golovensky and Captain Andrey Kozlov, both of whom were captured. Whether it still wore the tile *Irkutsk*, applied behind the Russian Navy standard, and on intakes, as had been the case a few years earlier, remains unknown. (Artwork by Tom Cooper)

On 27 February 2022 the VKS suffered its first ever combat loss of a Su-34. The jet illustrated here, Bort 31, registration RF-81251, from the 277th Bomber Aviation Regiment, was involved in air strikes on Ukrainian positions on the western side of Borodyanka. When hit, the crew, comprising Captain Artur R. Gubaiduin and Major Maxim M Borona, ejected safely and was recovered. Wreckage of this Su-34 was found only following the Russian withdrawal from the region, in mid-April 2022. While precise details of its armament during the final mission remain unknown, it is shown here in one of the frequently seen configurations of that period, carrying a total of eight 250kg FAB-250M-62 bombs on underwing hardpoints, under the intakes, and in the tunnel between engines, and either R-73 or R-74 air-to-air missiles on outboard underwing pylons. (Artwork by Tom Cooper)

On 5 March the Ukrainian defenders of Chernihiv shot down two Su-34s. The first was the Su-34 Bort 24 (registration RF-81879) of the 47th Bomber Aviation Regiment, a reconstruction of which was shown in Volume 2 of this mini-series. The second was the jet illustrated here: Bort 26 (registration RF-81864) of the 2nd Composite Aviation Regiment, felled over the Hrabivka area. The crew, consisting of majors Ravil Romanovich Gattarov and Dmitry S Runov, was killed. Like the majority of Su-34s, both jets wore the standardised camouflage pattern in pale blue (BS381C/111 or light blue MRP-202), light green-blue (MRP-203), and dark green-blue (MPR-204) on upper surfaces and sides, and light blue overall on the undersides. Apparently, it was one of the last few still having its radome and other dielectric panels painted in fog grey, like early production batches: by 2022, most of these had been repainted in dielectric white. (Artwork by Tom Cooper)

Another 'significant first' related to the Russian Su-34 took place on 6 March 2022, when Bort 06, registration RF-95070 was felled by an Osa-AKM SAM of the 92nd Mechanised Brigade after descending under the cloud cover to bomb Kharkiv. It was the first aircraft of this type shot down over this part of Ukraine. The crew ejected: Lieutenant Colonel Maxim Sergyevich Krishtop (deputy commander of the 47th Bomber Aviation Regimen) was captured alive. His weapons system officer, Captain Arten Norin, was found only hours later, dead, under his parachute. The aircraft is illustrated as it appeared when photographed for the last time before the war – already showing significant signs of wear to its camouflage pattern – and armed with four ZAB-500 napalm tanks, and R-73 or R-74 air-to-air missiles. (Artwork by Tom Cooper)

Unlike operations over Syria in 2015–18, where Sukhoi Su-24s flew more than 50 percent of all the combat sorties by the VKS, over Ukraine in 2022, this type was overshadowed by the likes of Su-35s, Su-34s and Su-30s. Still, subvariants like the Su-24MR played an important role in regards of gathering intelligence on the work of the Ukrainian integrated air defence system in particular. Indeed, Su-24MRs are known to have flown dozens of related sorties before the all-out invasion of 24 February 2022, and they continued supporting all the strikes into north-western Ukraine through March, including operating from bases in Belarus. This example – Bort 40, registration RF-95040 – was shown on Russian TV while rolling for take-off, equipped with two drop tanks and the SRS-13 Tangazh pod under the centreline. (Artwork by Tom Cooper)

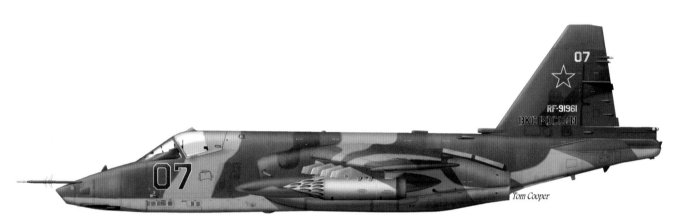

Right from the start of the all-out invasion, it was the venerable Sukhoi Su-25 attack fighters that flew the majority of close air support operations by the VKS: they supported most of the heliborne assaults, and then took part in every battle that developed on the ground. The most advanced subvariant as of 2022 was the Su-25SM3: although nominally compatible with precision-guided munitions, they were almost exclusively armed with pods for unguided rockets, the deployment of which required overflying Ukrainian positions. In consequence there were heavy losses: nine Russian Su-25s are confirmed to have been shot down within the first three weeks of the war. Amongst them was the example illustrated here: Bort 07, registration RF-91961, shot down on 2 March 2022 while attacking Ukrainian positions in the Irpin area. The pilot, Major Igor Redkokashin, was injured, but ejected safely and was recovered. (Artwork by Tom Cooper)

Although by 2022 over 100 Russian Su-25s had been upgraded to the Su-25SM/SM2/SM3 standards, the VKS still pressed its old Su-25s into combat as well. Amongst them was this relatively well-known example (photographed often in the 2010s and 2020s): Bort 28, registration RF-90969, assigned to the 266th Assault Aviation Regiment. The jet was shot down while attacking Ukrainian positions in the Myrotske area, outside Bucha, on 7 March 2022, and its pilot, Lieutenant Colonel Oleg Chervov, killed. Unlike the overhauled and upgraded Su-25SMs – most of which had received a standardised camouflage pattern as illustrated in the previous artwork – Bort 28 still wore one of the five camouflage patterns developed back in the mid-1980s: this consisted of two shades of green and one of dark brown on upper surfaces and sides (with some 're-touching' in light stone) and light admiralty grey (BS381C/697) on undersurfaces. (Artwork by Tom Cooper)

Conducted at a very unusual time of day – in broad daylight, late on the morning of 24 February – the Russian heliborne assault on Antonov IAP resulted in heavy losses for the VKS. At least eight helicopters are confirmed to have been shot down, or so heavily damaged that they were abandoned even if safely landed within the perimeter established by the VDV. One of the downed examples was Ka-52 Bort 17 (registration RF-90680) crewed by Captain Roman Stanisavlovich Kobets and Major Ivan Nikolayevich Boldyrev, which made an emergency landing on the tarmac of Antonov IAP. When it could not be repaired, it was blown up during the Russian withdrawal, sometime between 26 and 31 March. Like most of the VKS helicopters involved in this operation, the helicopter had all of its insignia crudely overpainted and a white 'V' applied on engine gondolas. (Artwork by Luca Canossa)

With this type regularly leading all the major Russian operations – including the heliborne assault on the Kakhovka Dam on the Dnipro, north of Kherson, early on 24 February 2022 – losses of Ka-52s remained high through March 2022. This example – Bort 74 (registration RF-13409) – was shot down by the Ukrainians while involved in mopping operations in the Skadovsk area, on or around 12 March 2022. One of its two crewmembers was killed, while Captain Andrey Lyulkin was seriously injured. Unlike the usual practice, this example seems to have been flown into combat with all of its markings still in place, as illustrated here. (Artwork by Luca Canossa)

Another of the helicopters written off in the course of the assault on Antonov IAP was this Mi-8AMTSh. Belonging to the latest assault and attack variant of this family acquired by the VKS, it was hit while approaching the target: the crew managed an emergency landing within the defence perimeter established by the VDV and was successfully evacuated. However, the helicopter (Bort 52; registration RF-91285; usually assigned to the 110th Helicopter Aviation Regiment) could not be recovered nor repaired before the Russian withdrawal and was blown up sometime between 26 and 31 March. As far as is known, Bort 52 was fully equipped with the Vitebsk self-protection suite and had exhaust diffusers painted in darker olive green than used in its camouflage pattern. (Artwork by Tom Cooper)

As of 2022, the Mi-8MTPR-1 was the newest electronic warfare variant of the Mi-8-family. Converted from Kazan-built Mi-8MTV-5 helicopters, it was equipped with the L187A Rychag-AV jammer (recognisable by its rectangular antenna installed in the position of the rearmost window on either side of the cabin) to counter enemy air defence radars, thus creating safe corridors for heliborne assaults, or to protect strikes by fighter-bombers. Although only 18 are known to have been acquired (under a contract issued in 2013), they were intensively deployed against Ukraine, right from the start of the all-out invasion. This example – Bort 77 (registration RF-19013) – is shown as it appeared in 2020. (Artwork by Tom Cooper)

As well as modern Ka-52s, Mi-35Ms and Mi-28Ns, early during the all-out invasion of Ukraine the VKS also deployed a large number of venerable Mi-24 helicopter gunships. This Mi-24P – Bort 24 (registration RF-94966) – was one of five helicopters shot down in quick succession between Rakove and Nova Odesa, while participating in the second assault on Voznesensk and escorting a number of Mi-8AMTSh assault transports. This reconstruction is based on pre-war photographs, which show it without the Vitebsk or other advanced self-protection systems and it seems that it was rushed into operation without even diffusers over its engine exhausts. Its camouflage pattern was rather unusual and consisted of light stone and dark camouflage desert sand (BS381C/420) on upper surfaces and sides and light admiralty grey on the undersides. (Artwork by Tom Cooper)

Mi-28s are not known to have been involved in the heliborne assault on Antonov IAP but they were deployed in combat in the Hostomel area over the following days. Indeed, on 25 February 2022, under as of yet unknown circumstances, a Mi-28UB conversion trainer was shot down almost directly over the airport and crashed next to its runways. Gauging by photographs taken before the war and those showing its wreckage, it wore a standardised disruptive camouflage pattern for this type, consisting of light stone (BS381C/361) and olive green (BS381C/220) on upper surfaces and sides, and light admiralty grey (BS381C/697) on the undersides, while the bort was applied in dark blue, and outlined in white. (Artwork by Tom Cooper)

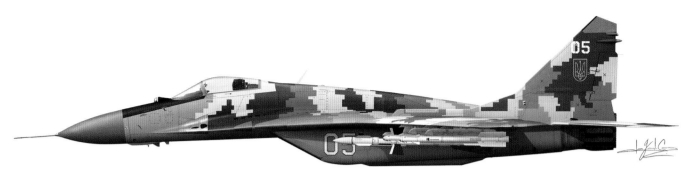

Lacking money for the acquisitions of modern aircraft and armament, the PSZSU was left with little choice but to fly its MiG-29s into combat still armed with R-27R and R-73 missiles that entered service back in the 1980s. Unsurprisingly, the losses during clashes with vastly superior Russian interceptors – regularly supported by powerful EW systems – were heavy. This is a reconstruction of one of five MiG-29s known to have been shot down on 24 February. On that morning, MiG-29S Bort 05 White was piloted by Lieutenant Colonel Vyacheslav Yerko, and according to Kyiv he was in a formation of five Ukrainian jets that engaged 12 Russian fighters and eight helicopters underway towards Kyiv. Yerko was credited with downing a Su-25 and two Mi-24s before his jet was hit by a Russian Su-35. The pilot managed to eject but was reportedly shot by Russian jets while descending under a parachute. (Artwork by Luca Canossa)

All Ukrainian MiG-29S and MiG-29MU1s overhauled and upgraded at LDARZ between 2008 and 2022 received the so-called 'digital' or 'pixel' camouflage pattern on upper surfaces and sides. This differed from aircraft to aircraft and sometimes included up to five different colours. One example (Bort 33) was repainted by the maintenance services of its unit. The undersides were always painted in grey-blue. Since the Russian all-out invasion, a number of jets have also received the so-called 'Ghost of Kyiv' insignia on the forward fuselage. Additionally, this example has three kill markings in the form of the Ukrainian Trident, applied in red and black. (Artwork by Luca Canossa)

Ukrainian Su-27s that underwent local upgrades and/or overhauls at the Zaporizhzhya State Aircraft Repair Plant between 2009 and 2020 received a new 'digital' or 'pixel' camouflage pattern, including grey (FS36375), blue (FS35250), and dark blue (FS15102) on upper surfaces, and light blue (FS35468) on undersurfaces. In addition to national insignia and their two- or three-digit borts (applied in blue and outlined in white), most aircraft had the insignia of the Sukhoi OKB on their fins – and the crest of the 831st Brigade with the inscription 'Galatskiy Aviapolk/PS ZS Ukraini' in red, on the fuselage behind the cockpit. As of 2022, the primary armament of this type was similar to – but longer-ranged than – that of Ukrainian MiG-29s: it included R-27ER SARH medium-range missiles (shown under intakes), R-27ET IRH medium-range missiles (shown on the inboard underwing pylon), and R-73 missiles. (Artwork by Luca Canossa)

Early on 25 February 2022, the VKS took the PSZSU by surprise by deploying one of its S-400 SAM systems almost directly on the border north of the Chernobyl area and then opening fire at Ukrainian interceptors underway over Kyiv. After travelling over 120 kilometres (64.79 nautical miles), one of these missiles hit Su-27P Bort 100 of the 831st Brigade, flown by Colonel Alexander Oksachenko. The pilot ejected but was found dead, while his jet crashed on private homes in south-eastern Kyiv, killing three civilians on the ground. (Artwork by Luca Canossa)

As of 2022, Ukrainian Su-25s wore two versions of the digital/pixel camouflage. One included pearl grey (FS26493), aircraft exterior grey (FS36300), dark gull grey (FS36231), and night camouflage black on upper surfaces; the other replaced night camouflage black dusty grey, as illustrated here. Undersurfaces were painted in signal grey. As of 2022, Su-25M1 Bort 19 of the 299th Brigade, PSZSU, wore the latter version. In the early afternoon of 24 February 2022, it was flown by Lieutenant Colonel Oleksandr Zhybrov in an attack on a column of Russian military vehicles in the Chorna Donlyna area. Although shot down by a Russian missile, Zhybrov's strike proved highly important because it targeted and destroyed the better part of an enemy PMP pontoon bridge, urgently needed to enable the 49th CAA cross the Buh River. (Artwork by Luca Canossa)

Lieutenant Colonel Gennady Matulyak is known to have flown a combat sortie late on the afternoon of 24 February 2022, when he was tasked with striking a Russian military column approaching Kherson from the south-east. Early the following morning, he flew an attack on another enemy column, this time in the Hostomel area, but around 07.00hrs local time was intercepted by a Russian fighter and shot down. Matulyak's body was found and buried by local villagers. As far as is known, the jet he flew on his final mission – Bort 39 – wore the darker version of the camouflage pattern, including night camouflage black, and would have been armed with four 240mm S-24 unguided rockets during that mission. (Artwork by Luca Canossa)

The PSZSU continued striking Russian columns underway from Armiyansk towards Nova Kakhovka and Kherson through 25 and 26 February 2022, too. On the latter date, a pair of Su-25M1s piloted by Major Rostislav Lazarenko and Captain Alexander Shcherbakov from the Melitopol Detachment of the 299th Brigade hit an enemy unit in the Chaplynka area with S-8 unguided rockets fired from B-8M1 rocket pods. During their second attack run, both Ukrainian jets were hit by Russian air defences: Bort 30 was shot down and Captain Shcherbakov was killed. Lazarenkov's Su-25M1 was badly damaged, but the pilot managed to nurse it back to a forward operating base in the Kherson area, where it was written off after landing. (Artwork by Luca Canossa)

The rate at which Ukrainian Su-24s were overhauled was significantly lower than that of other types operated, and thus the majority of machines of the 7th Brigade went into the war still painted in medium grey (FS73092) on upper surfaces and sides, and dielectric white (FS73125) on the radome, underside, and various dielectric panels. As shown in the example illustrated below, the latter was usually very worn out, because many of the jets in question had been stored for years. The majority of such examples had received the black dragon insignia of the 7th Brigade on the fuselage sides. Su-24M Bort 20 was one of a few that were overhauled at NARP and received a completely new, digital/pixel camouflage pattern consisting of three shades of grey. Bort 20 is shown as armed with four OFAB-500ShN parachute-retarded bombs, as regularly deployed for low-altitude strikes. (Artwork by Luca Canossa)

This is a reconstruction of Su-24M Bort 77 of the 7th Brigade, PSZSU. One of the examples operational as of February 2022, but not yet upgraded nor overhauled, this still wore its original camouflage pattern but had already received the black dragon insignia of its unit applied on the fuselage sides. The jet was flown on several ground attack missions during the first few days of the war. Late on 27 February 2022, while striking a column of Russian military vehicles in the Berzivka area (north-west of Kyiv), it was hit by enemy air defences and shot down, killing the crew consisting of Major Ruslan Bilous and Captain Roman Dovhalyuk. (Artwork by Luca Canossa)

This Mi-8MSB-V served with the 16th Brigade, ZSU. As in most other cases, its bort number, usually applied on the sides of the intakes, was removed once the Russians invaded. Instead, it had two wide white bands around the boom as 'quick identification aids', frequently applied on Ukrainian helicopters since 2014. This Mi-8 was shot down on 28 February 2022 while attacking Russian ground units advancing along the E40 highway south of Makariv. Videos of its final moments show it armed with B-8M-1 pods for 80mm S-8 unguided rockets. (Artwork by Luca Canossa)

A reconstruction of Mi-8MSB Bort 64 Blue, named *Za Babu Veru*. Operated by 16th Brigade ZSU, the helicopter was involved in resupply and MEDEVAC operations for the garrison in Mariupol. On 31 March 2022, while returning from such an operation, it was shot down by Russian-operated MANPADs in the Rybatskoye area. Out of the crew of three, and 15 passengers, only two of the latter survived and were captured. Due to the lack of visual evidence, it remains unclear if Bort 64 Blue received such markings, although these were worn by several other helicopters of the 16th Brigade around the same time. (Artwork by Luca Canossa)

All of the Ukrainian Mi-24s operated as of 2022 were assigned to the Army Aviation, and most of these were flown by the 11th Army Aviation Brigade, home-based at Chornobaivka AB/Kherson IAP. The predominant subvariant was the Mi-24P. Since undergoing overhauls, all had received a standardised camouflage pattern in dark stone and olive green on upper surfaces and sides, and light admiralty grey on undersurfaces. To be easily distinguishable as friendly by their own troops, all wore two wide white bands around the boom: in 2022, these means of visual identification were expanded through extensive use of additional Ukrainian national colours low on the front fuselage, along almost the full length of the cabin, and along the engine intakes. As well as their 23mm twin-barrel gun installed low on the right forward fuselage, early during the war, their principal armament consisted of B-8 pods for 80mm unguided rockets. (Artwork by Luca Canossa)

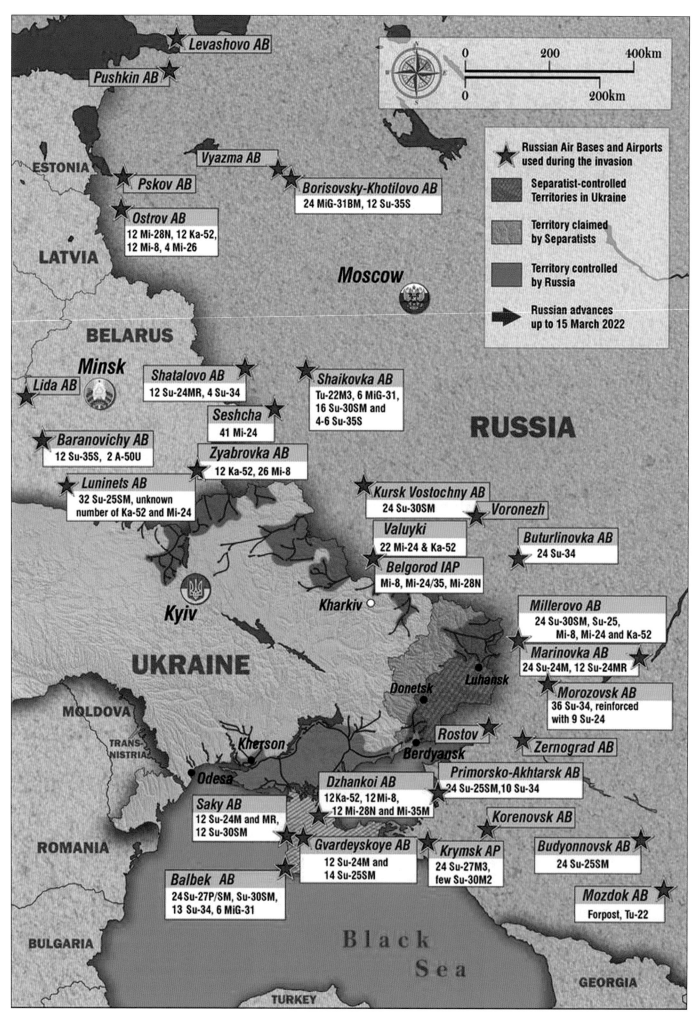

(Map by Anderson Subtil)

Table 10: VKS and VM-FA Units arrayed around northern and north-eastern Ukraine, 20–24 February 2022

6th Air Force and Air Defence Army (attached to OSK West, HQ St Petersburg)
Roughly 170 combat jet aircraft, Naval Aviation included. Reinforced with at least 50 combat jet aircraft, including those deployed in Belarus.

15th Army Aviation Brigade	Ostrov	one squadron each of Mi-28N, Ka-52 and Mi-8; Mi-26 detachment
33rd Transport Aviation Regiment	Levashovo	An-26, An-72, An-148, Tu-134, Mi-8
440th Helicopter Aviation Regiment	Vyazma	20 Mi-24 and Mi-28N, at least 10 Ka-52, around 20 Mi-8
549th Helicopter Aviation Regiment	Pushkin AB	one squadron each of Mi-8 and one of Mi-28N and Mi-35
2nd Air Defence Division	St Petersburg	5 regiments with a total of 1 S-300PM, four S-300PS, 12 S-400 batteries (S-300 probably replaced by 12 S-400 batteries) Each S-400 SAM site also included six Pantsyr S1 SAM close-in weapons systems for self-protection purposes.
32nd Air Defence Division	Tver	3 air defence regiments (2 S-400 batteries and 4 S-300 PS/PM batteries)
105th Composite Aviation Division	Voronezh	
14th Fighter Aviation Regiment	Khalino	2 squadrons Su-30SM
47th Composite Aviation Regiment	Buturlinovka	2 squadrons of Su-34
159th Fighter Aviation Regiment	Besovets	2 squadrons Su-35S
277th Bomber Aviation Regiment	-	2 squadrons Su-34, 1 squadron Su-24M2 & Su-34
790th Fighter Aviation Regiment	Khotilovo	2 squadrons MiG-31BM, 1 squadron Su-35S
4th Reconnaissance Aviation Regiment	Shatalovo	1 squadron Su-24MR (few operation), reinforced with 4 Su-34s on 20 February 2022
52nd Guards Heavy Bomber Aviation Regiment	Shaikovka	subordinated to Strategic Aviation; 20 Tu-22M3; reinforced with 6 MiG-31, 16 Su-30SM and several Su-35 by 20 February 2022
566th Transport Aviation Regiment	Seshcha	subordinated to Transport Aviation; An-124; reinforced with 41 Mi-24s by 20 February 2022
	Belgorod IAP	reinforced with a mix of Mi-8, Mi-24/35 and Mi-28N by 20 February 2022
	Valuyki	no runway; reinforced with 22 Mi-24 and Ka-52 by 20 February 2022

Naval Aviation of the Baltic Sea Fleet (attached to the OSK West, HQ Kaliningrad)
132nd SAD

4th Composite Aviation Regiment	Chkalovsk	1 squadron Su-24M, 1 squadron Su-30SM; flight of Forpost UAVs
689th Fighter Aviation Regiment	Chkalovsk	2 squadrons Su-27P

Table 11: VKS Units deployed in Belarus as of 20 February 2022

23rd Fighter Aviation Regiment	Baranovitchi	12 Su-35s, 2 A-50U at Ivanovo Svernyi
18th Attack Aviation Regiment	Luninets	32 Su-25SM, unknown number of Ka-52 and Mi-24
	Lida	16 Mi-8
	Zyabrovka	12 Ka-52, 6 Mi-8, unknown unit
	southern Belarus	unknown number of S-400 and Pantsir-S SAM sites

Air Battles for Kyiv

The first wave of the Russian assault on Kyiv included a battalion tactical group (BTG) made up from the 31st Guards VDV Brigade and the 45th Spetsnaz Brigade. For unknown reasons, the Russians did not launch their attack with similar ploys to those used in Prague in 1968 or Kabul in 1979, but went straight in.[11] Early on 24 February 2022, after ballistic- and cruise missile strikes knocked out a number of Ukrainian early warning radars in the Kyiv area, the Russian ground forces began deploying heavy electronic countermeasures. Next, an A-50U directed several pairs of high-flying Su-30 and Su-35 interceptors into the skies north of the Ukrainian capital and ordered at least a pair of Mi-8MTPRI electronic warfare helicopters

The Mi-8AMTSh assault helicopters seen lined up on a road outside Bragin, in southern Belarus, on 23 February 2022. (Russian social media)

An A-50U seen high above Belarus in March 2022. During the first month of the war, one of the Russian airborne early warning aircraft was on station over southern Belarus by day and by night. (Belarussian social media)

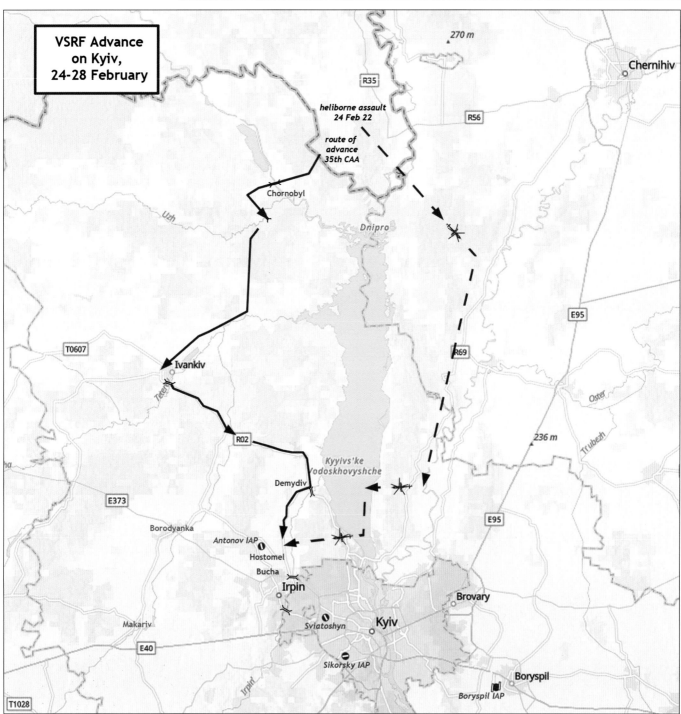

A map reconstructing the approximate course taken by the Russian helicopter formation carrying a BTG of the 31st Guards VDV and the 45th Spetsnaz brigades from Bragin to Antonov IAP. (Map by Tom Cooper)

into positions closer to the border. In this fashion, the Russians created a 'safe corridor' down the Dnipro River, along which they intended to conduct their heliborne assault. Meanwhile, the troops were loaded into some 15–16 Mi-8 helicopters lined up along a stretch of a road in the Bragin area in southern Belarus. Upon take-off at 10.00hrs, these grouped into a formation and entered Ukrainian airspace moving down the eastern side of the Dnipro River, escorted by about a dozen Ka-52, Mi-24, and Mi-35 attack helicopters. The entire operation was controlled from an Il-20M airborne command post that accompanied the A-50U. Additional Su-35s – mostly from the 23rd Fighter Aviation Regiment deployed at Baranovichi AB – were airborne at high altitude on two combat air patrol stations above southern Belarus. Although expecting only minimal Ukrainian opposition, each was armed with four R-77-1 active radar homing, medium-range air-to-air missiles, and two to four R-74 infrared homing, short-range air-to-air missiles.

While supported by missile strikes and electronic countermeasures, and although taking the Ukrainians completely by surprise, such massive activity did not escape attention of the PSZSU and the approaching helicopters were detected early enough for the 40th Brigade to scramble several MiG-29s in that direction. Due to the sheer size of Ukraine, the breakdown in Ukrainian military communications, and ongoing Russian missile strikes, these took some time to approach the Kyiv area: the helicopter formation thus remained undisturbed upon reaching a point on the eastern bank of the Dnipro reservoir, some 30km north of Kyiv. Whether this was part of the original plan, or if the formation was actually underway to Boryspil IAP remains unclear. What is certain is that around 10.30hrs it turned west to cross the Dnipro close to the point where a MANPAD team of the Ukrainian Territorial Defence, led by Junior Sergeant Anton K and armed with 9K38 Igla (ASCC/NATO reporting name 'SA-24') was deployed. One of the leading helicopters in the Russian formation – apparently misidentified by the Ukrainians as an Mi-8 – was an Mi-35M crewed by Major Nikolai V Bugay, Major Roman V Grovich, and Captain Aleksey D Belkov. It

was manoeuvring skilfully, constantly changing altitude and making minor adjustments in direction. Eventually, the Ukrainian Sergeant picked the right moment to open fire, just as the helicopter began another shallow climb. The missile guided and hit the target, causing a brilliant flash, and the helicopter crashed into the water, killing all three crewmembers. Fearing a possible counterattack on its position, the Ukrainian MANPAD team then quickly took cover, leaving the other helicopters to thunder by.[12]

However, another MANPAD team was deployed on the south-western side of the Dnipro reservoir and went into action shortly after. One of its Iglas hit the Mi-24P crewed by lieutenants Mankishev and Nasedkin: this was also shot down and the crew killed. Indeed, by the time this part of the action was over, at least one Mi-8AMTSh assault helicopter and one Ka-52 attack helicopter had also been damaged. The Ka-52 is known to have landed in a field outside Babintsy, a few kilometres from Borodyanka airport (about 20km north-west of Antonov IAP): the crew were recovered by the Russians, but the helicopter was captured intact by the Ukrainians. The damaged Mi-8 barely managed to reach the Hostomel area before making an emergency landing in a field outside Antonov airport, where it was abandoned.

As far as can be reconstructed from the currently available information, it was around the same time that the first pair of low-flying MiG-29s was about to approach Kyiv. Whether they were detected by the Russian A-50 airborne over southern Belarus – and if so, from what range – remains unknown, but very likely. If so, the Russian airborne early warning aircraft directed several Su-35s to the scene. According to all available Ukrainian sources, the leader of the PSZSU pair, Lieutenant Colonel Vyacheslav Yerko, then claimed a Su-25 and two Mi-24 helicopters as shot down – before his jet was hit by an R-77 air-to-air missile launched by a Russian Su-35. However, unless Yerko's jet was hit while returning to base, it is unlikely that this pair of MiG-29s reached the Russian helicopter formation because Yerko was killed when his MiG-29MU1 crashed into a forest in the Sosnivka area, well to the south-west of Kyiv.[13]

The wreckage of VKS Mi-35M Bort 29, crewed by Major Bugay, Major Grovich, and Captain Belkov seen after being raised from the bottom of the Dnipro reservoir in early June 2022. (Ukrainian Police)

The wreckage of VKS Mi-24P 04/RF-95290, crewed by lieutenants Mankishev and Nasedkin, and shot down over Dnipro reservoir early on 24 February 2022. (1+1 TV Channel, Ukraine)

A Ukrainian MiG-29 seen at high speed and low altitude in the Kyiv area early on 24 February 2024. (Ukrainian social media)

A still from a video showing a Ukrainian MiG-29 firing S-8 80mm unguided rockets while underway extremely low over the Kyiv area on 24 February 2022. The probable target was several Russian helicopters underway behind the person that recorded this action on video. (Ukrainian social media)

The wreckage of Yerkov's MiG-29MU1 '05 White', found in a forest in the Sosnivka area. (*GenStab-U*)

As the Su-35s directed by the A-50 moved deeper over Ukraine, another pair of MiG-29s was scrambled from Vasilkyiv AB and the one piloted by Lieutenant Vyacheslav Radionov was shot down by R-77s north of the town of the same name. Most likely, it was only the third Ukrainian pair that managed to reach the airspace over the capital, and while approaching the city from the south, probably by flying extremely low along the Dnipro. Although at least one of these MiGs was eventually caught on video firing S-8 unguided rockets from its B-8M pods from very low altitude, it remains unclear if they actually hit any of the Russian helicopters. What is certain is that a MiG-29 of the 40th Brigade, piloted by Lieutenant Roman Pasulko, was shot down over the Vyshgorodsky District, in northern Kyiv, and its pilot killed despite ejecting. Finally, the same unit then lost its fourth jet. Although the variant in question is presently still unclear, the aircraft was probably the MiG-29UB two-seater that crashed into the Dnipro River in the Kozyn area, south of Kyiv, from which at least one crewmember ejected safely.

As far as can be deducted from the available Russian publications and unofficial contacts, most of the Ukrainian losses were caused by Su-35S interceptors of the Baranovichi-based 23rd Fighter Aviation Regiment. According to the Russian Ministry of Defence, in late March 2022, Minister Shoygu decorated the Navigation Officer of that regiment, Major Viktor Dudin, for 'hitting an aerial target for the first time on the first day of the special military "Operation Z"'. However, Dudin's target may have been a Ukrainian Su-27 – and the PSZSU is not known to have lost any jets of this type on 24 February 2022. On the same occasion, Shoygu also decorated another pilot of the 23rd Fighter Aviation Regiment – Dudin's wingman Lieutenant Ivan Perepelkin – who was said to have shot down two Ukrainian aircraft. Months later, in July 2022, the deputy commander of the same regiment, Lieutenant Colonel Ilya Sizov was credited with two aerial victories against Ukrainian MiG-29s. In Sizov's case, it remains unknown if these were claimed on 24 February.[14]

What is also unknown is whether the Russians suffered any kind of confirmed losses to PSZSU interceptors during the heliborne assault on Antonov IAP. What can be deducted from published accounts by Ukrainian MiG-29 pilots is that the radars of their jets were regularly and severely disrupted by the Russian ECM. They did try to engage with their R-27Rs but high-flying Su-35s equipped with R-77-1s found it easy to target them with multiple missiles while remaining outside the reach of return fire. The Russians enjoyed the advantage of their missiles having active radar homing in the terminal flight phase: this meant that they did not have to wait and guide the missile until it hit – or missed – the target, unlike the Ukrainians when deploying their R-27s. Moreover, the high-flying Russians could launch their missiles from high altitudes and at high speeds, thus extending their range. Although the R-27ER's advertised range outmatched that of the R-77, it was significantly shorter when the missile was fired from an aircraft underway at low altitude – as was regularly the case with the PSZSU MiG-29s. Finally, because of Russian ECM and the damage to the Ukrainian radar network, the MiG pilots experienced significant problems with finding VKS helicopters that were flying low amongst the forests of northern Ukraine.

A still from a video showing a fighter involved in air combat in the Kyiv area going down in flames early on 24 February 2022. With the VKS not known to have suffered any losses in air combat this was most likely one of four Ukrainian MiG-29s shot down on that morning. (Ukrainian social media)

Viktor Dudin providing an interview in front of a Su-35S of the 23rd Fighter Aviation Regiment, armed with R-77-1 and R-74 air-to-air missiles. (Russian Ministry of Defence).

The Russian Minister of Defence Sergey Shoygu pinning the Golden Star of Hero of the Russian Federation to the uniform of Lieutenant Colonel Ilya Andreyevich Sizov, Su-35S pilot and Deputy Commander of the 23rd Fighter Aviation Regiment, in July 2022. Moscow styled Sizov as the top ace of the special military operation, with a total of 11 aerial victories. (Russian Ministry of Defence)

A still from a video documenting a Russian Su-25 heading towards Antonov IAP late on the morning of 24 February 2022. (Ukrainian social media)

Rather unsurprisingly, the only known Russian loss possibly related to operations by Ukrainian MiG-29s was the Su-25 piloted by Colonel Ruslan Igorevich Rudnev of the 266th Assault Aviation Regiment, which crashed outside the village of Orekhovo in southern Belarus, some 20km north of the border, while attempting to return to its base in Belarus. Furthermore, Lieutenant Colonel Denis Litvinov was highly decorated for saving his wingman as the latter was nursing his damaged aircraft back towards Belarus. By manoeuvring his jet behind his number two and then deploying countermeasures, he saved it from being hit by a Ukrainian missile.[15]

Heliborne Assault on Antonov IAP

This would not mean that the heliborne assault on Antonov IAP went without further problems. Thanks to the acquisition of precise intelligence about the Ukrainian defences of this vital facility, the Ka-52 attack helicopter crews of the 18th Attack Regiment were well-informed about enemy air defences, and they were successful in knocking out several Ukrainian vehicles with unguided rockets and gun fire before the arrival of the first wave of Mi-8s loaded with troops at around 11.00hrs. However, this proved to be an exceptionally dangerous business: the Russian pilots not only found the that the runway of the airport had been blocked by numerous heavy vehicles, but a team from the 4th Rapid Intervention Brigade equipped with 9K38 Igla (SA-18) MANPADs was deployed near the

local radar station and began firing its missiles in rapid succession. One of these hit the Ka-52 crewed by Major Ilya Rybakov and Lieutenant Aleksander Podshivalov, causing it to crash with both crewmembers killed. Another badly damaged the Ka-52 crewed by Captain Roman Stanislavovich Kobets and Major Ivan Nikolayevich Boldyrev – which claimed the destruction of six Ukrainian air defence vehicles – and it was forced to perform emergency landing at Antonov IAP. The crew were later recovered by Russian troops.[16] Finally, a third Ka-52 was damaged by an Igla and forced to make an emergency landing at Antonov IAP: it was subsequently destroyed by the withdrawing Russians and its wreckage discovered only in April.

Eventually, the first wave of the Russian BTG landed safely at Antonov IAP: the troops quickly fanned out to secure the facility and block all the approaches to it. They were constantly supported by pairs of Ka-52s and Su-25s, directed into action by the A-50 airborne over southern Belarus. The involved Mi-8s then returned to the stretch of road in the Bragin area to pick up the second wave. On the other hand, hampered by the loss of strategic telecommunications, and because most of the Hostomel-based 4th Rapid Reaction Brigade of the National Guard was deployed in Donbas (only around 200 officers and other ranks of this unit were tasked with the defence of Antonov IAP) – the Ukrainians proved rather slow to react – and when they did, it was their air force that did so.

At least five Mi-8s and one Mi-24 of the Russian formation can be seen on this video still taken in Hostomel, early on 24 February 2022, while converging on Antonov IAP. (Ukrainian social media)

A still from a video released by the Russian Ministry of Defence showing the head-up display of a Ka-52 helicopter (foreground) during an attack run with unguided rockets on an armoured fighting vehicle of the ZSU outside Antonov IAP. (Russian Ministry of Defence)

Another still from the same video, showing an Mi-24P passing from left to right in front of the Ka-52 from which this capture was taken. Note also the construction vehicle used to block the runway of Antonov IAP. (Russian Ministry of Defence)

A still from a video showing two Mi-8AMTSh and one Mi-24P that, reportedly, were involved in the heliborne assault on Antonov IAP. Notably, their bort numbers have been crudely overpainted and all have 'invasion stripes' around the boom, and large white chevrons on the rear fuselage. (Russian Ministry of Defence)

Battle of Hostomel

After recovering from the initial shock of the Russian onslaught, the 7th, 39th, and 40th Brigades of the PSZSU began launching additional fighter-bombers into action. The 7th dispatched a pair of Su-24Ms to bomb the Russian columns moving along the P56 highway in the Chernobyl area. It is very likely that it was in the course of this action that the L-39 piloted by Major Dmitro Kolomiets from the 39th Brigade was shot down by Russian interceptors while providing top cover for the low-flying fighter-bombers. In turn, the PSZSU pilots claimed two Su-30SMs as shot down in air combat.[18]

Around noon, the troops of the 4th Rapid Reaction Brigade began running out of ammunition and thus retreated from Antonov IAP. While most of them withdrew, about 20 defending the radar station were captured by the Russian airborne assault troops, who completed securing the facility by 13.00hrs. That said, their efforts were in vain: because they had no means to remove the heavy

vehicles blocking the runway, the third wave of the Russian assault – up to 2,000 airborne assault troops of the 76th VDV Division carried by 18 Il-76 transport aircraft from Pskov – never arrived. Instead, all the support they continued receiving was provided by pairs of Su-25 attack aircraft, that repeatedly roamed the area around the airport.

Meanwhile, the first elements of the 72nd Mechanised Brigade (commanded by Colonel Oleksandr Vdyovychenko), the 95th Airborne Assault Brigade, the 3rd Special Purpose Regiment of the Special Operations Forces (3rd SSO), and the Alfa Group of the Ukrainian Security Service (*Sluzhba Bezpeky Ukrayiny*, SBU) converged on Antonov IAP, where they were reinforced by 48 paratroopers of the 80th Airborne Brigade, deployed by three Mi-8 helicopters on the south-western side of the airport. Even then, it took the Ukrainians four hours to coordinate a counterattack. Initiated around 17.30hrs, this failed amid heavy Russian defensive fire. Immediately after, a pair of Ukrainian Su-24Ms bombed the

SRDLO: THE SAGA OF THE RUSSIAN AWACS, PART 2[17]

The A-50 was equipped with the Liana surveillance radar: in theory, this was a powerful system that promised excellent performance. In reality, it massively underperformed, which resulted in plans for improved variants emerging from the time it entered service, as described in Chapter 2. This was not the only problem: the USSR lagged behind the West in regards of micro-technologies so much that the installation of the mission equipment took up all the available space inside the Il-76 airframe: there was no room left for the additional communications and EW facilities considered necessary for the type to become effective. Because very little changed in this regard even through the A-50U upgrade, in operations over Ukraine the type was always accompanied by Ilyushin Il-20M electronic warfare aircraft and Il-22M airborne command posts.

Based on the airframe of the Ilyushin Il-18 turboprop-powered airliner, the Il-20Ms, of which about 15 were operational as of early 2022, were manufactured in the early 1970s. They had begun showing their age in the 1990s and were planned to be replaced by jet-powered Tupolev Tu-214Rs equipped with a mission suite of an entirely new generation. However, the development of that type experienced repeated delays and cost overruns. Moreover, the Tu-214Rs in Syria in 2016–18 revealed many shortcomings: amongst others, in one instance their side-looking airborne radars (SLARs) failed to detect multiple columns of the notorious 'Islamic State' underway in the open semi-desert from less than 50 kilometres away. Eventually, instead of completing more than three Tu-214Rs, the VKS and the GRU were left with no choice but to extend the service life of the old Il-20Ms. These had begun receiving a number of upgrades in the 2000s, the most numerous of which became known as Monitor and Anagramma, and were related to the installation of SLARs and digital COMINT, SIGINT, and ELINT equipment. Another subvariant, the Il-20PP, was claimed to be capable of jamming modern AWACS aircraft and even US-made MIM-104 Patriot SAMs. By 2022, the mission equipment of the surviving Il-20Ms had been modified so often – and included systems capable of tracking down smartphones – that rumour had it that no two aircraft of this type had exactly the same configuration.

The other military variant of the Il-18 is the Il-22M: an airborne command post with secondary ELINT capabilities. The variant is equipped with an extensive communication suite and also has a secondary ELINT capability – which is why the VKS frequently combined it with its A-50s, which lacked similar facilities. As of 2022, a total of 12 Il-22Ms were in service. Three of these were

Myasichev Il-22PPs, nicknamed *Porubshchik* (chopper). Equipped with the KNIRTI l-145 electronic warfare suite, they all entered service with the inauspicious 117th Transport Aviation Regiment at Orenburg AB in 2016–17. These Il-22PPs were the aircraft that were to cause some of the biggest problems to the PSZSU – not only during the first days of the war – because they had proven capable of jamming not only the onboard radars of Ukrainian MiG-29s and Su-27s, but also of all the SAM systems in Ukrainian service.[19]

Ironically, much of the equipment installed in the A-50s, Il-20M/PPs, and Il-22M/PPs was based on electronics made in the West. In peacetime, this was not a major issue because the Russians found it easy to continue purchasing the necessary electronics, despite sanctions imposed following their occupation of the Crimean Peninsula and then Donbas in 2014. However, severe sanctions imposed in the aftermath of the all-out invasion, and highly intensive deployment of this 'triad' during the following months soon began showing their effects: one after the other, the aircraft began suffering major malfunctions and were grounded. As a result, during the summer of 2022 the VKS was forced to curb their operations: by the end of the same year, only three or four A-50s and less than 50 percent of Il-20M/PPs and Il-22M/PPs were operational on average.

A rare photograph of one of only three An Il-22Ps known to have been operated by the VKS in 2022, underway over southern Belarus in March 2022. (Belarussian social media)

runway of Antonov: combined with continuous shelling by artillery of the 72nd Mechanised Brigade, this rendered the airport useless to the Russians. That said, Kyiv's boasting about the defeat of the enemy assailants and recovery of Antonov IAP by 21.00hrs local time was a massive exaggeration. Although a part of the Russian BTG suffered significant losses, other of its elements encountered not a single Ukrainian soldier. The Russians thus remained in control of the facility. Rather unsurprisingly, the final known PSZSU loss of 24 February 2022 occurred in the same area: around 20.20hrs, while attacking one of the Russian convoys underway down the R02 highway from Ivankyiv in the direction of Kyiv, the Su-24M crew consisting of majors Dmytro Kulykov and Mykola Savchuk reported

that its aircraft was hit. Twenty minutes later, contact with the crew was lost: the wreckage of their jet was subsequently found outside Borispil.[20]

Second Attempt

The morning of 25 February 2022 found both the Russians and Ukrainians in a state of scrambling: after figuring out that they could not count on using Antonov IAP nor any other of the airports in the Kyiv area for a quick coup inside the city, the assailants rushed most of the 35th Combined Arms Army (35th CAA) along the R02 highway towards the capital. Indeed, several of their columns managed to enter Kyiv before running into ambushes in which one after the other was

A view from the receiving end: a famous (and dramatic) photograph taken by one of the Russian VDV troops at Antonov IAP, late in the afternoon of 24 February, showing a pair of Ukrainian Su-24Ms in the process of releasing 500kg parachute-retarded bombs and decoy flares over the runway. (Russian social media)

smashed and the survivors scattered before Ukrainian sappers blew up a bridge carrying the R02 across the Irpin River near Kozarovichi, south of Demydiv. Combined with the first mining of a dam near the village of Kozarovychi (which caused only slight damage to the facility), this resulted in the flooding of the area between the Dnipro in the north and Irpin in the south, thus blocking the direct approach to the Ukrainian capital. The Russians now had to find an alternative route, and quickly. Inside the city, throughout the day the Ukrainians began improving their positions, and bolstered the defences of both Sikorsky and Boryspil IAPs and blocked their runways with obstacles. Combined with the Russian failure to reach at least Sviatoshyn Airport in western Kyiv, this pre-empted any possible attempts to establish a bridgehead inside the Ukrainian capital.

Meanwhile, ground-based air defence units of both sides went into action. During the night of 24 to 25 February, the Russians deployed one of their S-400 SAM systems right on the border with Ukraine. Shortly before dawn, this opened fire at a Su-27 of the 831st Brigade, piloted by Colonel Alexander Oksachenko, as it was underway over eastern Kyiv. One of the missiles scored a direct hit at a range of about 120 kilometres: the pilot ejected but was found dead, while the falling debris of his aircraft killed three civilians on the ground. About half an hour later, when a pair of Ukrainian Su-25s attacked one of several Russian military columns moving down the R02 highway towards Demydiv and Hostomel, the jet piloted

by Lieutenant Colonel Gennady Matulyak of the 299th Brigade was intercepted and shot down by a Russian Su-30SM. His wingman went on to hit the target and returned safely. Unable to return the favour in similar fashion, the Ukrainians attacked Millerovo AB in western Russia using at least one OTR-21 Tochka-U ballistic missile, destroying at least one Su-30SM and killing two pilots of the 31st Fighter Aviation Regiment and a helicopter pilot. Surprisingly enough – even more so considering Kyiv was in possession of satellite intelligence provided by NATO, and the fact that most of the Russian air bases around Ukraine were crammed full of aircraft and helicopters – this remained the only known and successful attack of this kind for a few days longer.

Airborne Assault on Vasylkiv Air Base

According to numerous Ukrainian accounts, the Russians launched their final attempt to capture one of the airports in the Kyiv area on the evening of 25 February. This time, the target was Vasylkiv AB, the home-base of the 40th Brigade PSZSU, but also a point where the E94 highway and the railway line connecting Kyiv with Bila Tserkva ran next to each other. Despite numerous official statements, exactly what went on in this area still remains unclear at the time of writing and there is an impression that the available Ukrainian version being a similar myth to the story about the complete liberation of Antonov IAP on the evening of 24 February.

A fiercely burning Su-30SM of the 31st Fighter Aviation Regiment at Millerovo AB, in the aftermath of the Ukrainian ballistic missile strike, early on 25 February 2022. (Russian social media)

A Ukrainian Su-27 in the sky low over Kyiv on 25 February 2022. The aircraft was armed with six R-27s and four R-73s. (Ukrainian social media)

What is certain is that the Russian assault began with infiltrated Spetsnaz operators wearing the uniforms of Ukrainian police and attacking different spots around Vasylkiv before using a police car to approach a checkpoint outside the air base and gun down the soldiers there. A few hours later, several Il-76 transports then attempted to approach and shortly after midnight on 25/26 February, a Su-27 piloted by Colonel Oleksander V Mostovoy (Deputy Commander of the 831st Brigade) was scrambled to intercept. Around 00.30hrs of 26 February, Mostovoy claimed to have shot down an Il-76 as it was about to disgorge VDV troops. No evidence for this claim was ever published, although the crash of such a big aircraft must have left significant amounts of wreckage. According to other Ukrainian reports, at least 20 Russian paratroopers managed to jump out and they were quickly eliminated by the ZSU on the ground. Around 03.20hrs, another Il-76 was then claimed as shot down over the Bila Tserkva area, apparently by a Ukrainian S-300 SAM. Immediately after, a formation of Russian helicopters was reported approaching Vasylikv AB and two of them were claimed as shot down by Colonel Mostovoy in his Su-27 again. Nevertheless, according to official Ukrainian sources, the Russians still managed to land enough troops to press home their attack that, at dawn, received support in the form of at least two Su-25s, one of which was also claimed as shot down. Ultimately, the assault was repelled by the security element of the 40th Brigade PSZSU and the National Guard, at a cost of about 30 Ukrainian casualties, including 10 killed, and the destruction of a POL depot nearby. By around 07.30hrs of 26 February, surviving Russian airborne troops withdrew into the forests of the Plesetske area.[21]

Unofficial Ukrainian sources recalled a significantly different course of events. Accordingly, on the afternoon of 25 February, as the infiltrated Spetsnaz teams were spreading confusion by attacking multiple points around Vasylkiv, the Russians launched a three-wave heliborne assault on the air base: at least some of the involved helicopters were shot down while approaching and quickly reacting ZSU troops then surrounded and completely destroyed the Russian airborne troops and Spetsnaz operators. However, once again, no evidence in the form of wreckage was ever provided.[22]

Something similar was true for another reported Russian heliborne attack – with the difference being that the following story is supported by at least one video that surfaced on Ukrainian social media. Accordingly, early on 26 February the Russians assaulted an unknown facility outside Lviv, prompting the deployment of Ukrainian Army Aviation Mi-24s and ground troops in return. Rather amazingly, except for that single video showing one of the attack helicopters unleashing its unguided rockets at an unknown target, no details about this action were ever released.

Through 25 February, fighter-bombers and helicopters of the PSZSU and the Ukrainian Army Aviation continued flying strikes against Russian columns rolling down the R02 highway. This Mi-24 was captured on video while approaching the Hostomel area early that morning. (Ukrainian social media)

The fin of the Su-25M1K '39', piloted by Gennady Matulyak, found near Hlibivka, on the western side of the Dnipro reservoir. The pilot was buried by local villagers. (*GenStab-U*)

4

FROM A COUP TO A WAR

Early on 27 February, another long column of Russian troops rolled down the R02 highway and then turned right in Demydiv, from where it drove for Antonov IAP. This included the heavy equipment – mainly BMD armoured fighting vehicles – of the 31st VDV Brigade. After a long march from Belarus, the vehicles were short on fuel and a refuelling point was set up in between the hangar of the Antonov An-225 Mriya and the Antonov building of the airport. Unknown to the Russians, this action was monitored both by a group of four Ukrainian special forces operators cut off at the airport since the 24th, and at least one reconnaissance UAV, and was promptly reported to Kyiv. The result was a massive artillery barrage by 2S9 Pion 203mm howitzers. In a matter of minutes, the entire BTG of the 31st Brigade was destroyed, together with a previously-damaged Russian helicopter and the sole operational Antonov An-225 Mriya: the biggest transport aircraft in the world.

That said, by that time the commander of the 35th CAA, Lieutenant General Aleksandr Semyonovich Sanchik, had enough troops in the Hostomel area to render the issue of possession of Antonov IAP irrelevant. Indeed, by the end of 27 February, his spearheads had managed to drive through Borodyanka, Nova Hrebyla, Lypivka and bypass Makariv in order to reach the vital E40/M06 highway and thus cut off the direct connection between Kyiv and Zhytomyr: for a while it appeared as if the Russians might manage to complete the isolation of Kyiv from western Ukraine.

Paradoxically, while appearing favourable for the Russians the situation was rapidly becoming critical for both sides. Amid continuous problems with their communications, and resulting lack of coordination and shortages of ammunition, the ZSU did manage to establish a coherent frontline along the Irpin River. Indeed, it spoiled the Russian coup attempt, destroyed multiple BTGs and thus bought the time necessary for the *GenStab-U* to mobilise the armed forces. However, even as ever additional brigades of the ZSU began converging on Kyiv, their overall numbers and firepower at best matched those of the 35th CAA, which was in the process of being bolstered by reinforcements from the 20th and the 36th CAAs. What helped the Ukrainians was the fact that the surviving units of the 35th Army were strewn all the way from Demydiv in the north-east, via Bucha to Makariv in the south, and entangled in a labyrinth of villages which they could not effectively control. Moreover, although the Russians had widened their invasion of northern-central Ukraine through an advance on Poliske and Rahivka, and thus were now able to use the northern section of the R02 highway for their advance in addition to the road from the Chernobyl area, south of Ivankyiv, snowy weather and soft terrain limited them to the use of only the southern sector of the R02 highway: any attempts to move heavy mechanised vehicles other than on the roads ended in these becoming bogged down in the mud. The result was a massive, 130-kilometres-long traffic jam consisting of additional BTGs and supply columns for the units already deployed in the Kyiv area. This was an issue that not only troubled the command of the 35th CAA for days, but ultimately sealed the fate of Putin's entire adventure: for all practical purposes, with the failure of his troops to establish even one bridgehead within Kyiv, the 'special military operation' converted from what was essentially a coup attempt into an all-out war, which Russia could not win.

Final Pushes West and South

Until the strategic-level communications of the ZSU were reestablished with help of StarLink satellite terminals, starting from 28 February, the PSZSU continued experiencing significant problems with command and control of its surviving assets. Certainly enough, most of the combat aircraft and helicopters were dispersed at different forward operating bases, and transports were flown out of the country, but relatively few of the dispersal facilities had all the necessary support infrastructure. Helicopter units frequently experienced shortages of S-5 and S-8 unguided rockets for their UV-16-57, UV-32-57, and B-8M pods, and most were limited to flying a single sortie a day. Similarly, while both MiG-29s and Su-25s were designed for operations from 'primitive' facilities, and their undercarriage enabled them to even make use of grass strips for take-off and landing, the Ukrainians often

Although failing to dislodge the VDV from Antonov IAP on 24 February, the Ukrainians did their utmost to disrupt the operations of the 35th CAA through air strikes with their Su-25s and helicopters against this area. This Mi-8 armed with two B-8M rocket photos was captured on a video while approaching the Hostomel area on 27 February 2022. (Ukrainian social media)

felt forced to park them 1,000–4,000 metres away from the runways in order to keep them well-concealed. While this made it extremely hard for the Russians to find and actually 'catch' any of the PSZSU's aircraft with their ballistic and cruise missiles, the command and control of a force scattered over many different FOBs caused a big problem for the HQ in Vinnytsia: the officers there frequently lacked a clear picture about which aircraft were deployed where, and which were available for immediate action. Unsurprisingly, intelligence provided to the pilots was often poor or belated. Moreover, once airborne, they continued facing severe ECM deployed both by Il-22PPs and Mi-8MTPRIs of the VKS, and by the Russian ground-based electronic warfare stations: these are known to have regularly caused such problems that even the intercept of cruise missiles with use of the onboard radars of MiG-29s and Su-27s were impossible.

On the other hand, and because the VKS was never equipped nor trained for tasks of this kind, the Russians found it extremely hard to actually find and catch any PSZSU aircraft on the ground. That said, faithful to their doctrine, the *GenStab* and the headquarters of the OSK West never arrived at the decision to deploy their air power for such purposes. Instead, supported by much intelligence provided by informants in Ukraine, they followed the RUK concept and continued targeting Ukrainian air bases with ballistic missiles. For example, on 27 February, the Ministry of Defence in Moscow claimed the destruction of no fewer than six MiG-29s at Ivano-Fankivsk AB. Only occasionally – apparently whenever no ballistic or cruise missiles were on hand for the task – were small formations (single or pairs of aircraft) sent to attack targets deeper behind the Line of Control. Instead, and starting from 29 February 2022, the *GenStab* and the OSK West ordered the VKS into close air support operations for ground troops of the 35th CAA in northern-central Ukraine, and other armies assaulting north-eastern Ukraine.[1] This is why the air warfare through March 2022 was dictated by, and tightly related to, developments on the ground.

Push to the E40

As the VKS increased its activity in the Kyiv area, and because from 28 February the Ukrainians began restoring their strategic military communications with the use of StarLink terminals, the PSZSU began coordinating the operations of its ground-based air defences. Correspondingly, dispersed Buk and S-300 firing units were deployed into favourable positions along the frontline and began engaging low-flying Russian Su-25s and Su-34s. Despite continuous and heavy deployment of Russian ECM, the S-300's maximum range of 75–90 kilometres usually kept the VKS at bay: primarily, it prevented the deployment of precious Il-20M and Tu-214R reconnaissance aircraft close enough to the combat zone to make a difference. Indeed, the dispersed deployment of Ukrainian Buks and S-300s, combined with massive deployment of MANPADs, took the Russians by surprise: on 27 February, while supporting ground troops assaulting Borodyanka, the VKS suffered its first loss of a Su-34 bomber in this war, when a jet with Bort 31 (registration RF-81251) from the 277th Bomber Aviation Regiment was shot down west of this town.[2] The crew, consisting of Captain Artur R. Gubaiduin and Major Maxim M Borona, ejected safely and was recovered.

Nevertheless, a BTG of the 37th Motor Rifle Brigade managed to advance all the way to Andryvka before the sunset. A day later, the same unit was ordered to secure

Makariv, then block the E40 highway and continue in a south-eastern direction. Facing only light resistance from scattered groups of ZSU troops and armed Ukrainian volunteers, its T-72s and BMP-2s rapidly drove via Kopyliv to Motyzhyn. An attempt by a pair of Mi-8s of the 16th Brigade ZSU to stop them ended with the helicopter crewed by Colonel Aleksandr Grygoryev, Captain Dmytryy Nesteryuk, and Senior Lieutenant Vasyli Gnatyuk being shot down and the crew killed.

Eventually, it was only on the approaches to Yasnohorodka that the Russians ran into an ambush, set up by regular ZSU units, and suffered losses. While supporting this drive, the VKS lost its second Su-34 bomber when, on 28 February, Bort 05 (registration RF-81259) from the 2nd Guards Mixed Aviation Regiment, was shot down by the Ukrainians south of Buzovava, in the Bucha area. This time, the crew was killed. Eventually, determined Ukrainian resistance forced the 37th Motor Rifle BTG to stop and withdraw into the forests near Severynivka. Similar was true for another Russian attempt in a similar direction: including a BTG of an unknown unit that ran down the western side of Irpin, via Zabiuchchya, towards Kapitanivka on the E40, before losing numerous armoured vehicles to ambushes in the Dmytrivka area and being forced to stop and withdraw.

The PSZSU also regularly attempted to strike the advancing Russians, but at around 18.00hrs a Su-24M of the 7th Brigade was shot down over the Bucha area and its crew – consisting of Major Ruslan Bylyus and Captain Roman Dovgalyuk – killed. Some unofficial Ukrainian sources have reported this loss as caused by friendly air defences. However, it should be kept in mind that the VSRF was now deploying its own ground-based air defences in the area, too. For example, the Buk M2-equipped 297th Anti-Aircraft Regiment was present in the Hostomel area by 28 February and its commander, Colonel Vladimir Nikolaevich Polyakov, was subsequently decorated for shooting down 'five Ukrainian Su-24s and 25 UAVs, including 12 Bayraktars'.[3]

Pieces of the fin of the Su-34 Bort 31 from the 277th Bomber Aviation Regiment, shot down outside Borodyanka on 27 February 2022. This was the first ever combat loss of this type. (courtesy MilitaryAviationInUA)

A still from a video showing the Mi-8MSB-V crewed by Grygoryev, Nesteryuk, and Gnatyuk going down in flames near the E40 highway, south of Makariv, on 28 February 2022. (Ukrainian social media)

Ultimate Failure of the 35th CAA

As mentioned above, in addition to ordering the VKS into close air support operations, the *GenStab* did request sporadic air strikes deeper behind the Line of Control: on 2 and 3 March 2022 Russian air strikes were reported all the way from Zhytomyr in the west to Bila Tserkva and Kyiv. This effort came at a cost and a Su-30SM was shot down and crashed into the town hall of Irpin. Indeed, between 28 February and 1 March 2022, ground-based air defence units of the PSZSU claimed a total of seven Russian jets as shot down. Reacting to the string of losses, the VKS began equipping a growing number of its Su-30SMs and Su-35S with Kh-31P anti-radiation missiles, and they were regularly vectored by A-50s and Il-22s into strikes on any detected Ukrainian SAM unit.

However, by this point in time, the situation of the 35th CAA west of Kyiv began slipping out of the control of its commanders. Certainly enough, the frontline along the Irpin River was well-defined, alone by its geography, and the headquarters of this army even began using its ATMS. However, it lacked intelligence about Ukrainian dispositions. Indeed, on its western flank, numerous mechanised BTGs were forced to advance through a labyrinth of villages and forests while all critically short of infantry, and intermingled with minor Ukrainian units that constantly ambushed

them. Although the GRU could still rely on its well-developed network of informants behind the enemy lines, the intelligence provided in this fashion was nearly useless for following tactical developments in real time. Finally, because the 35th CAA was stretched over 150 kilometres, its units experienced extensive problems with their communications. Putin's telephone calls to commanders of multiple BTGs only increased the chaos, because he was issuing orders for additional assaults in the direction of Kyiv without any consultations with Shoygu, Gerasimov, the *GenStab* or the headquarters of the OSK West. The result was a situation that was anything but as prescribed by the *GenStab* and exercised by most of the involved troops: rather unsurprisingly, the first major Ukrainian counterattack – conducted by the 14th Mechanised and the 95th Airborne Assault brigades – caught the Russians entirely unprepared and pushed them back to Makariv on 1 March 2022, and then all the way to Bucha, two days later. The VKS reacted with attack helicopters and Su-25s and is known to have lost a Ka-52 from the 18th Assault Brigade: this was hit by a MANPAD and made an emergency landing outside Babyntsi in the Hostomel area on 1 March. While the crew escaped to friendly positions, the helicopter was subsequently destroyed by the Russian ground troops.

Ka-52 Bort 14 seen following its emergency landing outside Babyntsi on 1 March 2022. Abandoned, it was destroyed by the Russian ground troops during their withdrawal, sometime between 28 and 31 March of the same year. (Ukrainian social media)

Early on 2 March 2022, the PSZSU announced that in the course of an air combat fought during the previous night, its fighters had shot down a Russian Su-30SM and a Su-35S, while losing one MiG-29. However, no corresponding evidence has ever surfaced. On the ground, heavy fighting continued raging north of and along the E40 highway. Despite worsening weather conditions, the A-50 on station over southern Belarus continued directing pairs of Su-25s into action and one of these was hit by a MANPAD while attacking Ukrainian positions in the village of Motyzhyn. The pilot, Major Ivan Pavlovich Redkokashkin, ejected safely and, two days later, was found by troops of the 64th Guards Motor Rifle Brigade. Another Su-25 was damaged too, but Captain Sergey Cherny managed to return it for an emergency landing in Belarus.[4]

Unimpressed, Putin continued pushing his generals and thus, on 4 March, Sanchik deployed a BTG of 64th Guards Motor Rifle to advance around Makariv and in a western direction. Unaware of the presence of two well-equipped brigades of the ZSU in front of it, the air support for this operation quickly ran into massive problems as the Ukrainians were well-supplied with both SAMs and MANPADs. At least two Mi-8AMTSh were shot down, as were two Su-25s: other than the pilot of one of the latter (who managed to escape to the Russian lines), all the crews were killed. The Russian push on the ground ended in similar fashion. The 64th Guards Motor Rifle lost numerous vehicles while advancing towards the E40, and then withdrew. Further south-east a BTG of the 37th Motor Rifle Brigade advanced from Berezivka along the E40 highway in a western direction: after passing Nevelytsy and shortly before reaching Sytnyaky, it was ambushed, lost several tanks and infantry fighting vehicles, and fell back. With this, the Russian attempts to complete the isolation of Kyiv through advances west and south of the city had reached their high point: it was obvious that even with use of its mechanised units, the 35th CAA lacked the punch for operational-level success.

Battle of Moshchun[5]

Realising that the 35th CAA was unable to isolate Kyiv, but under constant pressure from Putin, the *GenStab* in Moscow then devised a new plan, dependent on the availability of Sanchik's operational reserve: the 98th and 106th VDV divisions, and the 155th Naval Infantry Brigade. General Sanchik's principal problem was time: it took the units in question no fewer than three days to roll through the massive traffic jams down the R02 highway and deploy into starting positions along the Irpin River. Meanwhile, several Spetsnaz teams were searching for a suitable crossing point before, early on 5 March, reporting that river was shallowest in the Moshchun area. On the next morning, the VDV troops began crossing in that area, thus springing a battle that was to last for longer than two weeks.

Actually, this effort came much too late. The Russians had reached Moshchun for the first time on 27 February, when a convoy of BMDs from the 104th VDV Regiment used a minor bridge over the Irpin River. However, their appearance was promptly reported by the local population to the ZSU and the commander of the 72nd Mechanised Brigade, Colonel Oleksandr Vdovychenko ordered a company of troops, supported by several T-72s and UAVs, to counterattack. These quickly scattered the enemy, sending most of the survivors back over the Irpin River, then took care to blow up the bridge, and received reinforcements in the form of a detachment each of the Territorial Defence and the Alpha Group. Perhaps unintentionally, the Ukrainians thus established a blocking position right in the way of the coming Russian offensive.

Due to traffic jams north of Demydiv, Sanchik took almost 24 hours to organise his first major strike: on the morning of 6 March, he sent a BTG of the 155th Naval Infantry Brigade – reinforced by a company of Spetsnaz – over the river. The Ukrainians hit back with artillery and mortars, but the Russians continued sending reinforcements over the Irpin and a long, chaotic firefight ensued in the forests around the north-western side of the village in which the disoriented assailants suffered dozens of casualties before being stopped. Undaunted by this failure, Sanchink prepared a new attack, this time deploying almost all the means available. On the morning of 7 March 2022, two BTGs of the 98th VDV Division – supported by air strikes by the VKS, barrages from the 1065th VDV Artillery Regiment, and massive volumes of electronic countermeasures – initiated a new assault and constructed a pontoon bridge over the Irpin near Moshchun. However, at this point in time, Ukrainian sappers blew up the dam near Kozarovichi, thus exposing the floodplain of the Irpin River to the water from the Kyiv Reservoir. The result was a flooding that washed away the Russian bridge, in turn spoiling the entire attack.

To buy time for organising another, even larger crossing attempt, Sanchik then brought in another artillery regiment, and a brigade of multiple rocket launchers to the scene. Directed by Orlan UAVs, for the next four days they shelled and rocketed ZSU positions in the Moshchun area with such ferocity that it became near-suicidal for the artillery of the 72nd Mechanised to attempt hitting back in fashion. In one instance, the Russians used the live feed from a Ukrainian blogger that showed a Ukrainian artillery unit deploying in the field to shell the bridgehead: they triangulated the position and hit it with an Iskander ballistic missile, killing dozens of artillerymen. Moreover, the Russian ECM was blinding both Ukrainian communications and making the work of their UAVs impossible. Eventually, this is what enabled Sanchik's engineers to construct their second pontoon bridge in this area: to their surprise, the ZSU then used the services of a hacker who penetrated the Andromeda-D ATMS of VDV units of the 35th CAA to download the live feed from the Russian UAVs. With the aid of the resulting intelligence, the 2S9 Pion howitzers of the 43rd Artillery then knocked out the bridge.

Once again, the 35th CAA reacted with vicious air strikes and artillery barrages. These reached their peak on 14 March 2022, by when the third pontoon bridge in the Moshchun area was constructed. Immediately after, a BTG each of the 76th and 106th VDV divisions, supported by a BTG of the 40th Naval Infantry Brigade crossed, and assaulted the village. In the course of bitter, house-to-house fighting that went on four days, the Russians eventually captured the western side of Moshchun, causing such losses to the 72nd Mechanised Brigade that Colonel Vdovychenko requested permission to withdraw. Commander-in-Chief ZSU, General Valerii Fedorovych Zaluzhnyi ordered him to fight to the last solider. That said, the losses on the Russian side were even heavier: not only was the commander of the 331st VDV Regiment, Colonel Sergei Sukharev killed, but nearly all the 600 troops of the II Battalion of that unit, as well as large parts of BTGs from both the 215th and the 217th VDV regiments, were destroyed. The water in the Moshchun area had meanwhile risen to a level such that it not only washed away dozens of Russian fighting vehicles but the third pontoon bridge as well. Finally, on 19 March, the ZSU began deploying reinforcements that had flanked the Russian bridgehead in western Moshchun: demoralised, the surviving VDV troops were withdrawn from the bridgehead on 20 and 21 March 2022. All the time pursued by the Ukrainian artillery, they left behind more than 30 destroyed or damaged armoured fighting vehicles and hundreds of dead. The final Russian attempt to reach Kyiv from the north-west thus collapsed due to stubborn Ukrainian resistance and skilful creation of a major water obstacle.[6]

A still from a video taken by a Ukrainian UAV in the Kozarovichi area, north-west of Kyiv, on 5 March 2022. It shows a direct hit by a Ukrainian MANPAD on Mi-24P Bort 32 (registration RF-95286), crewed by Captain Vyacheslav Baraev and Lieutenant Alexander Khripunov, as it was approaching the Moshchun area at high speed. (Ukrainian Ministry of Defence)

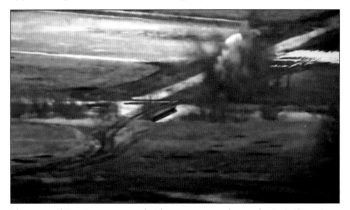

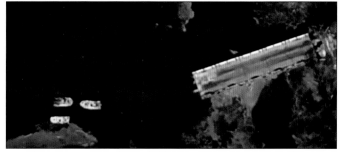

A section of the third Russian pontoon bridge seen while being swept away by floodwater on 18 March 2022. Also visible are several abandoned BMD infantry fighting vehicles of the VDV. (Ukrainian Ministry of Defence)

The second Russian pontoon bridge constructed over the Irpin River in the Moshchun area, seen while under fire from 43rd Artillery Brigade's 203mm howitzers, on 13 March 2022. (Ukrainian Ministry of Defence)

Wreckage of the second Russian pontoon bridge over the Irpin River in the Moshchun area, destroyed by Ukrainian artillery on 13 March 2022. (Ukrainian Ministry of Defence)

5
THE FLYING FIRE BRIGADE

Paradoxically enough, the Russian ground forces arrayed for the invasion of Chernihiv and Sumy Oblasts (pending their further advance on Kyiv and Poltava), all proved to be not only commanded by corrupt and incompetent generals, but also so poorly trained, yet pushed so hard by Putin, that for the first week of the all-out invasion three Russian armies were stumbling from one mishap and major crisis to another, and suffering massive losses, rather than seriously advancing anywhere. As usual, the reasons for such massive failure were many.

As in the case of the onslaught on Kyiv, both the FSB and the GRU proved unable to conduct an objective analysis of Ukrainian defence capabilities: indeed, they seem to have provided the same set of 'best case' assessments, according to which very few Ukrainians were ready to fight and the entire country was likely to roll over – or even to join them – upon merely seeing the advancing Russians.

The involved units were informed about the attack only 24 hours before it was initiated. As a result, they lacked fuel, food, ammunition, communications, up-to-date maps, and even an understanding of their tasks. Once the operation was initiated, the GRU added lots of fuel to the fire by failing to provide reliable battle damage assessment for at least the first week of fighting, while both the *GenStab* in Moscow and headquarters of both the North and South OSKs proved incapable of timely integrating of intelligence with the targeting process. Bad weather over north-eastern and eastern Ukraine hampered VKS operations in the first few days of the war. In addition, the Ukrainian population was non-cooperative: on the contrary, it regularly provided intelligence about Russian movements and positions to the ZSU.

As a result, the invasion of north-eastern Ukraine proved a disastrous failure in which entire armies tasked with marching up to 100 or even 150 kilometres a day, fell apart amid total chaos in the chain of command, breakdown of communications, hopelessly insufficient logistics support, poor (or non-existent) training of their troops, and the poor technical state of their vehicles. The consequence for the war in the air was that after only 48 hours of operations, the Western OSK was forced to cease tasking the VKS with targeting Ukrainian air bases and air defences and redirect it to close air support. For all practical purposes, the air force was to act as a fire brigade. However, due to the bad weather and a breakdown in communications, the crews of Russian fighter-bombers and attack helicopters responsible for operations in the Chernihiv, Konotop, and Sumy areas initially found very few ground troops organised well-enough to be able to request and receive close air support. Indeed, most of the field commanders were out of touch for the first few days of the invasion. This was just as well because, for its part, the PSZSU had next to no units home-based in this part of Ukraine: indeed, late in the evening of 23 February it evacuated about a dozen transport aircraft and helicopters from Pevtsi (Chernihiv), Nizhyn, and Pryluky air bases, towards Kyiv and Poltava. The task of air defence was thus assumed by anti-aircraft defence battalions of the ZSU brigades deployed in this part of the country.

41st CAA in Chernihiv

At 05.00hrs on 22 February 2024, the spearheads of Lieutenant General Sergey Ryzhkov's 41st CAA crossed the border and rushed in the direction of Chernihiv along two highways (the E95 in the west, and the P13 in the east). On paper, the idea of advancing over 70–90km down two good roads in a single day certainly appeared sound. However, in reality, the routes for the 41st CAA were surrounded by dense woods and marshes in the north, and then with numerous villages further south. Because of soft, muddy terrain, this offered many good positions for the Ukrainian defences. Moreover, not only were the officers of Ryzhkov's army informed about the invasion just 24 hours before it was about to start – which left them unable to plan and prescribe their operations in time – but most of their troops had never been informed about what they were about to do, even once they had been ordered to cross the border and drive into Ukraine. Unsurprisingly, poorly-prepared and understaffed units began losing troops and vehicles to all possible reasons while driving down the E95 highway; and then the communication system of the 41st CAA collapsed.

In comparison, Ukrainian defences – centred on the 1st Tank and the 58th Motorised brigades, supported by the 27th Rocket Artillery Brigade (equipped with BM-27 Uragan self-propelled 270mm multiple rocket launchers), and by the 19th Missile Brigade (equipped with OTR-21 Tochka tactical ballistic missiles) – were few, but reasonably well-prepared. Arguably, they could not deploy in time to stop the Russians along the line connecting Ripky with Tupychiv and Pekurivka, as originally planned, but they quickly found a way to do so further south.

Instead of reaching Chernihiv on the afternoon of 24 February, the spearheads of the 41st CAA were stopped by numerous ambushes about 25km north of the city, and then hit by several Tochkas, suffering hundreds of losses in troops and dozens in armoured fighting vehicles. The following morning, one of the BTGs launched a new attempt, but ran into an ambush in the Horodnya area and stopped, only to be demolished by Ukrainian tube artillery. The third BTG then relaunched the advance and attempted to reach the disused Pivtsi AB, outside northern Chernihiv: most of its vehicles became struck in the mud as soon as they left the tarmacked roads and were then shot away by Ukrainian tanks as if they were on a shooting gallery. When the 41st CAA launched its fourth attempt, on the morning of 26 February, one of its BTGs lost the way and drove into the city instead of assaulting the air base: unsurprisingly, it was ambushed, suffered heavy losses, and fell back in disarray. North-east of Chernihiv, the part of the 41st CAA advancing down the P13 highway operated slightly better and, on the same day, reached the Desna River in the Makoshyny area: however, every pontoon bridge they constructed was destroyed by the BM-27s of the 27th Brigade.

As a result of these failures, Ryzhkov's army began falling apart: hundreds of disgruntled troops were streaming back to Belarus while others were surrendering without a fight – and most were out of touch with any of their superior officers. Thus, when the VKS was ordered into action, on 28 February, it found nobody to support. Indeed, Ryzhkov's deputy, Major General Andrey Sukhovetsky was shot by a Ukrainian sniper while trying to restore order and redirect his BTGs to bypass Kynika by circumnavigating to the west of Chernihiv. Eventually, the manoeuvre was successful because of a good bypass road and because the vastly outnumbered Ukrainians preferred to fight from well-concealed positions in the suburbs of the city. The same day, the Russians reached the Desna River in the Shestovytsya area and constructed a pontoon bridge. However, this was knocked out by a Ukrainian Tochka missile. Unable to organise close air support for the 41st CAA, the Western OSK then began tasking tactical bombers of the VSK with striking military bases in the city, but both the intelligence provided and aiming of the Russian crews were poor. For example, on 3 March 2022, at least one Su-34s released four bombs on the residential area between Viacheslava Chornovola and Kruhova streets in south-western Chernihiv, including Schools 18 and 21, massacring 47 civilians.[1]

The air defences of the city were provided by air defence battalions of the 1st Tank and the 58th Motorised brigades, equipped with older Strela-10, Osa-AKM, and also modern 2K22 Tunguska-M1 self-propelled air defence systems. Early on, and due to cloudy weather, they found very few targets operating within their reach. However, this changed as the Russians moved closer to and around Chernihiv, and then began attacking individual Ukrainian tanks on the basis of intelligence provided by their informants inside the city. On 5 March, an Osa-AKM system of the 58th Motorised was successful in downing Su-34 Bort 24 (registration RF-81879) over Chernihiv as it descended below the cloud cover. The crew ejected but, while the pilot, Major Alexander Krasnoyartsev was captured (after attempting to evade and shooting a civilian), his weapons system officer, Major Konstantin Krivopavlov, was killed. A few hours later, shortly before midnight of 5/6 March 2022, the Ukrainians also shot down Su-34 Bort 26 (registration RF-81864) of the 2nd Composite Aviation Regiment over the Hrabivka area, 15km south-east of the city. Both crewmembers – Majors Ravil Romanovich Gattarov and Dimtry S Runov – were killed as the jet, which was diving for its bombing run, flew straight into the ground. After these two losses, the VKS generally avoided operating tactical aircraft over the city.

Ultimately, it took the disorganised Russians several days to bring in and construct a new pontoon bridge in the Shestovytsya area and even then Ryzhkov's next deputy was killed – on 7 March 2022 – while trying to organise a determined assault across the Desna in an eastern direction, aiming to encircle Chernihiv. On the same day, following vicious bombardment from the air and by artillery, a BTG of the 41st CAA then attempted to assault Kolychivka from the south, but was completely destroyed by the defenders. Subsequently, Ryzhkov redirected his remaining BTGs on Lukashivka instead: while securing this village on 9 March, a day later his troops were repelled at Baklanova Muraivka.

With this, the offensive operations of the 41st CAA were over: Chernihiv was almost encircled and was subjected to heavy bombardment from the air and the ground, but the ZSU managed to keep a few field paths south-east of the city under control, and thus the garrison remained supplied. Indeed, not only did the artillery of the 1st Tank and the 58th Motorised remained operational, but in the second half of March they began receiving US-made FIM-92E Stinger RMP Block I MANPADs, the deployment of which forced the Russian airmen to keep their distance and drop their bombs from medium altitudes – usually with negligible military effect but with terrible consequences for the local population. Almost certainly acting on tips from local informants of the GRU or FSB, on 16 March 2022 the Russian air strikes and

Piece of wreckage of Su-34 Bort 26 (registration RF-81864), from the 2nd Composite Aviation Regiment, shot down over the Hrabivka area on 5 March 2022. The aircraft was hit while in a dive for an attack run and went straight into the ground, almost disintegrating on impact. The insignia visible is that of the Akhtubinsk State Flight Test Centre (see colour section for details). (Ukrainian social media)

artillery and rocket barrages killed at least 53 civilians. Only a day later, fighter-bombers also bombed Hospital No. 2, the Children's Regional Hospital, and a dormitory in Chernihiv, killing scores.

A street scene in Chernihiv on 3 March 2022, showing two FAB-500M-62 bombs dropped by a fighter-bomber of the VKS about to hit several family homes. (Ukrainian social media)

2nd GCAA in Konotop and Nizhyn and 1st GTA in Sumy

The operations of the 2nd Guards Combined Arms Army (2nd GCAA), commanded by Major General Vyacheslav Nikolaevich Gurov, were only nominally better. Marred by the same set of problems as the 41st CAA, this at least had a few functional BTGs. However, they proved hopelessly too little to quickly secure Shostka and Konotop, which in turn bought time for the Ukrainians to mobilise. With Putin's plan being based on the expectation that the Russians would be accepted as liberators, and thus allow the VSRF to rapidly advance deep into Ukraine, much of the 2nd GCAA was close to disintegration for the first days of the war. Arguably, its advance down the M02 proceeded very quickly, but then so many of its columns were ambushed, that they ran out of steam by 26 February, when reaching the Altynivka area. The advance in the direction of Nizhyn was thus relaunched only days later. Meanwhile, the Russian hopes for a quick conquest of north-western Ukraine were all refocused to the 1st Guards Tank Army (1st GTA). Nominally consisting of the best trained and equipped units of the Russian army, indeed, some of the most powerful, it was tasked with securing Sumy, Trostianets and Okhtyrrka, before continuing for Kyiv via Romny.

Initially, the spearheads of the 1st GTA progressed very well: essentially, on 24 February 2022 they were more troubled by traffic jams while advancing on, and then through, Sumy and Trostianets, than they were by the Ukrainian defences. However, while there were no Ukrainian troops in the latter town, in the former a company of 50 Ukrainian paratroopers counterattacked the same evening, destroying the better part of one BTG and scattering its survivors. Although the paratroopers were subsequently withdrawn from Sumy, this bought enough time for the local population to arm itself from an abandoned military base and organise the defences of the city. This is what prevented its capture. In Okhtyrka, the war began with a strike by two Su-34s on the base of the 91st Engineering Regiment ZSU, in which thermobaric bombs were deployed to kill up to 70 troops and injure scores. Nevertheless, the survivors reorganised and, together with local volunteers and the Territorial

Defence troops organised the defence of this town, thus preventing its capture.[2]

The detonation of an ammunition dump outside Sumy following a Russian missile attack early on 24 February 2022. (Ukrainian social media)

The failure to seize Sumy and Okhtyrka left the commander of the 1st GTA, Lieutenant General Sergey Kisel, in a predicament. Under pressure from Putin, he was left no option but to order his units to bypass to the north of Sumy and then rush in the direction of Konotop. Constantly supported by attack helicopters of the VKS, they ground along secondary roads for four days, before meeting the 2nd GCAA south of Konotop. Behind them, the defences of Sumy, Trostianets, and Okhtyrka proved effective enough to attract the attention of the PSZU: late on 26 February, one of 1st GTA's battalion tactical groups camping in a forest west of Okhtyrka was hit by two Su-24MRs using FAB-500M-62 bombs and lost numerous vehicles and dozens of killed and wounded. For the first time ever,

A Ka-52 armed with B-8M rocket pods, seen patrolling a road ahead of a convoy of Russian military vehicles, somewhere between Konotop and Sumy, in early March 2022. Generally, VKS operations in this part of Ukraine through late February and early March 2022 were greatly hampered by the chaos amongst the ground forces, poor communications, and bad weather. (Russian Ministry of Defence)

the Ukrainians had pressed their precious reconnaissance fighters into combat and did so with success.[3]

On 1 March 2022, Kisel's troops overcame the resistance in Trostianets: while this enabled them to control most of the H12 highway, in grand total it helped relatively little, because this communication route ran in a north-south direction. Left with no options, the general then ordered his troops into an advance along secondary roads in a western direction: towards Lebedyn, Kamyane and Hadiach. Deep in his left flank, the 93rd Mechanised Brigade of the ZSU remained particularly successful in tying down the 4th Guards Tanks Division in the area between Lebedyn and Okhtyrka – and thus this crucial junction of five highways remained under the control of the defenders even once Kisel had dispatched at least two of his BTGs, supported by Ka-52 and Mi-35M attack helicopters, in that direction. Correspondingly, the VKS increased its pressure and on 3 March a pair of Su-34s bombed the local thermal powerplant, knocking out the electricity and heating supply for most of Sumy Oblast. However, the 93rd Mechanised Brigade held out, leaving Kisel with little choice but to subject both places to artillery barrages and air strikes in frustration – while searching for alternative routes forward. Amid general confusion, growing losses and spreading chaos, by 1 March 2022 the campaign of the 1st GTA – the crucial Russian effort in north-eastern Ukraine – had stalled after achieving less than a third of its aims.

The Battles of Romny, Nizhyn and Brovary

Through 29 February and 1 March 2022, Gurov's 2nd GCAA made a return and rushed one of its BTGs down the P44 highway to take the Ukrainians by surprise and approach Konotop from the south. While the ZSU fell back in good order, on 2 March the Russians entered negotiations for the surrender of the town with the local civilian authorities. Simultaneously, Gurov sent his leading BTG further south-west: via Dubovyazivka to Veryky Sambir. Reinforced

A Su-30 of the VKS passing low over Sumy on 3 March 2022. With the majority of the defenders consisting of poorly armed civilians, local air defences were limited to hand-held firearms and thus the Russians had a relatively free hand to operate over this area. (Ukrainian social media)

by a BTG of the 1st GTA, the Russians then turned south to secure Talalivka, before reaching the H07 highway. This manoeuvre was of crucial importance because although by 3 March the 1st GTA had reached Romny, it proved unable to overcome the Ukrainian defences in this area. However, the possession of Talalivka enabled both Gurov and Kisel to bypass Romny and continue in the direction of Pryluky. The PSZSU is known to have reacted by dispatching a pair of Su-24s and two Su-25s to strike the Russian columns in the Romny area that day but lost one attack aircraft of the 299th Brigade during a take-off from Starokonstyantyniv AB, where Captain Aleksander Bogdanovich Korpan was killed.

Although surrounded by the Russians, and essentially left to their own device by the ZSU, the defenders of Sumy not only prevented the seizure of their city by the Russians, but repeatedly set up ambushes for Russian columns trying to bypass to the north. This Osa-AKM TELAR of the VSRF was knocked out by them on 27 February 2022. (Ukrainian social media)

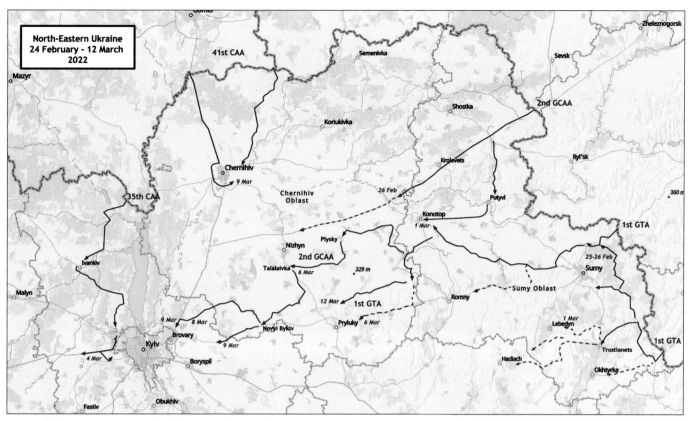

A map of the Russian invasion of north-eastern Ukraine, from 24 February until 12 March 2022. Dotted arrows denote failed Russian attempts to advance. (Map by Tom Cooper)

Next, slowed down by bad weather and continuous ambushing by Ukrainian forces, the 1st GTA and the 2nd GCAA took days to overcome the Ukrainian defences of Nizhyn and Pryluky. Both armies were now experiencing growing problems because neither their flanks nor the supply routes had been secured: they found no respite because while moving they ran into one ambush after another, while if stopping, they would suffer losses to repeated counterattacks by the Ukrainian 58th Motorised Brigade. For example, on 6 March, a BTG of the 2nd Guards Motor Rifle Division – the famed 'Tamanskaya' – ran into an ambush on the approaches to Pryluky and lost dozens of tanks. Indeed, this division then spent the next three days unsuccessfully trying to secure this town.

Eventually, Gurov found a solution by redirecting his efforts to the area between Nizhyn and Pryluky, and, on 6 March, managed to achieve a breakthrough in the Talalaivka area: from there, he first directed his units in the southern direction, before swinging west and reaching Novyi Bykiv. Indeed, on 8 March his spearheads drove all the way to the village of Bohdanivka, near the E95 highway, and only 20km north of Brovary. Alarmed by the sudden Russian appearance in this area, the ZSU scrambled to block this advance, and deployed several minor ground units in its way. Moreover, around 09.00hrs on 8 March, the 11th Brigade of the Ukrainian Army Aviation sent four of its helicopters armed with B-8M pods for unguided rockets to attack the Russians in the Bohdanivka area: in a matter of minutes, the Russian air defences chopped out of the skies the Mi-24 crewed by Lieutenant Colonel Oleksandr Marynyak and Major Igor Bezzub, and the Mi-8MTV crewed by Colonel Oleg Irodievich Gegechkori and Captain Ihor Moroz. Another Mi-8MTV was badly damaged and forced to make an emergency landing: while two crewmembers – Major Ivan Papalyashkin and Captain Ivan Chich – were captured in injured condition, Captain Volodymyr Sklyar was killed. The fourth helicopter – a Mi-24 – returned to base heavily damaged.[4]

The reason the area was so well protected by air defences was that the Russians were in the process of reorganising the remnants of the 6th and 239th Tank regiments of the 90th Tank Division into a new BTG. Reinforced by a few self-propelled artillery pieces and TOS-1 Buratino heavy flamethrower systems, on 9 March, this BTG rolled down the E95 in a southern direction with the aim of entering Brovary. Underway there, it ran into another ambush: the Ukrainian plan to knock out the leading and the last vehicle in the column, forcing it to stop pending an artillery attack, failed, and the Russians continued pressing further south, eventually rolling into the village of Skybyn, immediately north of Brovary. At that point in time, the vehicle carrying Colonel Andrey Zakharov, commander of the 6th Tank Regiment, was destroyed and the officer killed. Amid ensuing confusion, the entire BTG in a four-lane wide column piled into the centre of Skybyn, uncertain what to do next: due to low clouds, snow, and freezing temperatures, it was not supported by helicopters nor UAVs, and then lost contact with its superiors. All the while monitoring the situation with help of their UAVs, the Ukrainian artillery then blew up several of the Russian tanks, collapsing the already shaky morale of the survivors: they turned around and beat a hasty retreat.

Certainly enough, the battle for Brovary was far from over. For example, during the night of 11 to 12 March, Kisel attempted to reinforce his troops in the Pryluky area, but a BTG of the 228th Motor Rifle Regiment was ambushed by the ZSU and largely destroyed.[5] Moreover, elements of Gurov's 2nd GCAA continued to assault the Brovary area for three days longer. By 12 March, reinforcements from the 1st GTA also attempted to cut off the road and the railway connecting Kyiv with Poltava. However, all their attacks remained unsuccessful and, in grand total, the eastern outskirts of the Ukrainian capital remained under the control of the ZSU. Putin's last-ditch attempt to reach downtown Kyiv had failed between 20 and 30 kilometres short of its aim.

A Russian T-72 rolling through eastern Bohdanivka early on 8 March 2022. (Ukrainian social media)

A still from a video taken by a Ukrainian UAV, showing the crucial scene from the village of Skybyn, directly north of Brovary, on 9 March 2022. Clearly visible are numerous main battle tanks, BMP infantry fighting vehicles, BTR-82 armoured personnel carriers, and TOS-1 heavy flamethrower systems of the 6th Tank Regiment. Several vehicles were already afire, and most of the column was in the process of making a 180-degree-turn to run away following the death of Colonel Andrey Zakharov. (Azov Regiment)

The wreckage of one of two Mi-8MTVs of the 11th Brigade Ukrainian Army Aviation, shot down between Bervytsia and Bohdanivka, north of Brovary, while attempting to stop the advancing Russians on 8 March 2022. (Ukrainian social media)

6
BATTLE OF KHARKIV

According to the Russian planning, Kharkiv, the second largest city in Ukraine (and a city with a majority Russian-speaking population), was expected to be free of Ukrainian troops. Correspondingly, in its planning the *GenStab* expected mechanised formations of the 6th and 20th CAA to rapidly encircle the city and cut it off in a matter of 48 hours. Then, on 27 February, the Russian special forces were to enter all the vital facilities and raise Russian flags. The plan was spoiled by several factors: the city was protected by the 92nd Mechanised Brigade ZSU, the rapidly mobilising National Guard, and a few detachments of special forces, all of which resisted stubbornly. Moreover, bad weather – including low clouds and snow – prevented the VKS from providing close air support. Because of bad weather, the onslaught was supported by just missile strikes, most of which

targeted the base of the 164th Radio Technical Brigade and the 302nd Anti-Aircraft Missile Regiment (equipped with S-300PTs). Taken by surprise, the two units were hit simultaneously at 05.00hrs on 24 February 2022 and suffered heavy losses in personnel and equipment.[1]

About 35 kilometres south-east of Kharkiv, Chuhuiv Air Base was targeted by multiple Russian ballistic missiles. On 24 February 2022, it was used as a FOB by a detachment of MiG-29s from the 114th Brigade: these were scrambled in reaction to the attack, but while rolling for take-off one veered to the left and crashed into a recently-constructed fence. Apparently declared a write-off, the jet in question was still there in June 2022. Also destroyed during the initial Russian strikes on Chuhuiv were up to five L-39 training

Right: This is a still from a video taken by a Russian UAV showing two launchers of the S-300PT SAM system of the 302nd Anti-Aircraft Missile Regiment destroyed in the opening Russian missile strike. (Russian Ministry of Defence)

Below: Another still from the same video showing from left to right three launchers and the F5MU mast antenna radar of an S-300 SAM system of the 302nd Anti-Aircraft Missile Regiment, all destroyed by Russian missiles in the first minutes of the invasion on 24 February 2022. (Russian Ministry of Defence)

jets and four Bayraktar TB.2 UAVs and a ground control station for them.[2]

On the ground, and due to the lack of reconnaissance and close air support by helicopters, the Russians were much less successful. Long columns of mechanised units of the 6th CAA were repeatedly ambushed while advancing from the border, and never managed to bypass Kharkiv. When multiple Spetsnaz teams infiltrated the city on 26 February, the authorities imposed a curfew for 24 hours, and then launched a systematic hunt in which most of the infiltrators were arrested or eliminated. On 27 February, a column of the 25th Guards Motor Rifle Brigade and additional Spetsnaz troops then entered Kharkiv from three directions – only to run into ambushes: an entire BTG of the 25th was encircled and largely destroyed, and even very few Spetsnaz came away, leaving the frustrated commander of the 6th CAA no option but to request air strikes and barrages of BM-30 Smerch multiple rocket launchers on the north-western suburbs of the city. According to official Ukrainian sources, nine civilians were killed and nearly 40 wounded. The VKS appeared only during the night, when several Su-34 bombed Ivan Kozhedub National Air Force University.

Spoiled Second Attempt

As in the case of Chernihiv, many of the subsequent Russian air and artillery strikes on Kharkiv were based on 'intelligence' provided by informants of the FSB and the GRU. With these having a financial incentive to provide as much information as possible, and their tips then frequently forwarded straight to the headquarters of the Western OSK without any kind of objective cross-examination by intelligence services, this practice resulted in countless massacres of civilians – and the merciless prosecution of informants by the Ukrainian authorities. On 1 March 2022, the buildings of the Kharkiv Regional State Administration and the Regional Council – both in Svobody Square in the centre of the city – were targeted by two Kalibr cruise missiles that killed 29 people, while the VKS exploited a short improvement in weather to bomb numerous apartment buildings, the Opera House, and the Philharmonics Society, killing at least seven civilians.[3]

When the weather deteriorated on 2 March, the Russians targeted the main police headquarters with a ballistic missile; as soon as the weather cleared sufficiently on 4 and 5 March, the VKS began flying air strikes on Kharkiv again. At least according to the available Ukrainian accounts, the Russian selection of targets appeared rather 'random', indicating a high dose of frustration on the part of the involved commanders. For example, early on 6 March 2022, two fighter-bombers identified as 'Su-25s' bombed out the Lyceum 89 and nearby apartment buildings, killing scores – before one of them was shot down and its pilot captured. Eventually, it turned out that the jet in question was a Su-34 of the 47th Bomber Aviation Regiment (Bort 06, registration RF-95070) felled by an Osa-AKM of the 92nd Mechanised Brigade. The crew ejected: Lieutenant Colonel Maxim Sergyevich Krishtop, deputy commander of the 47th Bomber Aviation Regiment, was captured alive, while his weapons system officer, Captain Artem Norin, was killed. Their jet crashed in between two apartment buildings, further increasing the damage caused by continuous artillery barrages. Later the same day, two other air strikes by Su-34s knocked out the heating supply in the city, and at least one major TV mast. At least according to the Russian planning, these strikes were expected to soften-up the Ukrainian defences pending the second major attempt to assault the city on 7 March. However, this effort collapsed also because five days earlier – under the cover of low clouds and snow – the Ukrainian 92nd Mechanised Brigade launched a local counteroffensive. As first, it defeated a BTG of the 200th Motor Rifle Brigade, destroying and capturing dozens of armoured fighting vehicles. A day later, the 92nd hit the 488th Motor Rifle Regiment (from the 144th Guards Motor Rifle Division), knocking out dozens and capturing more than 30 of its armoured vehicles. Finally, on 6 March, the 92nd smashed a BTG of the 138th Motor Rifle Brigade and forced it away from Chuhuiv, 20km south-east of Kharkiv.

With this, the Russian attempts to quickly surround and seize Kharkiv had all failed: although continuing to rocket and strike the city for weeks and then months longer, the VSRF abandoned all related ideas, and refocused all of its attention to developments further east, which will be covered in the next volume of this mini-series.

On 3 March 2022, the Russians knocked out this Osa-AKM TELAR of the Ukrainian Army deployed in the Korotych area, west of Kharkiv. While most of such strikes were delivered by Russian tactical ballistic missiles, Ukrainian SAM units detected by the enemy often also found themselves on the receiving end of low-altitude attacks by Su-34s deploying free-fall bombs. (Ukrainian social media)

Taken during an exercise in early February 2022, this photograph shows a Su-34 of the VKS with a weapons configuration representative of its operations in Ukraine later the same month and through much of 2022: six FAB-500M-62 general purpose, free-fall bombs. (Russian Ministry of Defence)

A Su-34 thundering low over the Kharkiv area on 28 February 2022. Although lauded as a 'multi-role fighter' before the war, the type was deployed exclusively as a tactical bomber. With the VKS being critically short of targeting intelligence and precision weapons, and their crews lacking training in all-weather operations, the Su-34s were reduced to flying bombing and unguided rocket attacks from below the cloud cover. (Ukrainian social media)

7

THE SIEGE OF MARIUPOL

The scene of bitter fighting between separatists and Ukrainian forces in 2014; home of two of Ukraine's largest iron and steel factories; one of the largest ports in the Black Sea (exporting coal, steel, and grain around the world); and 89 educational facilities (including 15 universities), Mariupol was the third primary target of Putin's invasion in February 2022. Shoygu and Gerasimov planned to overrun the city with a combination of subversion by local sympathisers and a pincer advance on the ground: while the I Army Corps (I AK) was to assault in the direction of Volnovakha and thus cut off Mariupol from the rest of Ukraine, before swinging north and driving into the rear of ZSU units deployed along the Line of Control (LOC) in Donbas, the 8th Combined Arms Army (8th CAA) was to march in from the east. Finally, the 58th Combined Arms Army (58th CAA) was to complete the pincer from the west through an amphibious landing in the Berdyansk area. What came in between was bitter resistance by the Ukrainian garrison, including three battalions of the 36th Naval Infantry Brigade, the 18th Special Forces Regiment (colloquially known as the 'Azov Regiment'; which was in the process of expansion to a brigade of three battalions), the task force of the Azov Military School, paratroopers of Task Force Vedmedi, a squadron of KORD Special Police, a unit of Border Guards, and a miscellany of detachments from the local police and the semi-mobilised 109th Brigade Territorial Defence. Northeast of the city, the defences of the Line of Control with the Russian-controlled parts of Donetsk Oblast were held by the 56th Motorised Infantry Brigade, which developed a major defence complex in the Volnovakha area.

Fog and Rain

At 05.00hrs on the morning of 24 February 2022, the Russians hit Mariupol airport with several cruise and anti-radiation missiles.

Next to no details about the results of this attack are known, but photographs appearing in the Ukrainian social media have revealed that the strike knocked out an old Soviet-era P-14 long-range surveillance radar (ASCC/NATO reporting name 'Tall King'), a PRV-11 Vershina ('Side Net') height-finding radar, and an 1L22 Parol secondary radar (on Ural-375 truck; ASCC/NATO reporting name 'Dog Tail'). At the same time, the I AK and the 8th CAA launched their assaults: supported by the 163rd Tank Regiment of the 150th Motor Rifle Division, VSRF, the former breached the defences of the 56th Motorised in the Bohdanivka area but suffered severe losses in the process and progressed very slowly. East of Mariupol, the 103rd Motor Rifle and the 163rd Tank regiments took two days to breach the lines of the 53rd Motorised Brigade and capture Vodiane, Chernenko and Shyrokyne, before reaching the small town of Sartana in the northern suburbs of Mariupol. However, further south, the lines of the 36th Naval Infantry Brigade and the Azov Regiment held out. Due to the bad weather, the VKS only deployed a few helicopters to support the I AK that morning. However, it did provide reconnaissance and top cover for the amphibious assault near the port of Berdyansk, 70km west of Mariupol. Taking the Ukrainians completely by surprise, this assault landed a BTG from the 58th CAA – followed by a regiment operating Buk M1 SAMs – deep in the rear of the ZSU defences. Because the ZSU units garrisoned in the Berdyansk area – the 501st and 503rd Naval Infantry battalions of the 36th Naval Infantry Brigade – had been mobilised and rushed to Mariupol between 17 and 24 February, the Russians encountered only little opposition. In turn, upon their arrival in Mariupol, around the noon of 24 February, the 501st found the city already under Russian air strikes and near-constant artillery shelling. Indeed, this scattered the unit, with some of its elements taking positions in the village of Myrne, while others pushed through

This PRV-11 Vershina height-finding radar (centre) and 1L22 Parol secondary radar at Mariupol airport, were both knocked out during the opening Russian strike early on 24 February 2022. (Ukrainian social media)

The ruined antenna of the Soviet-era P-14 long-range/surveillance radar at Mariupol airport, knocked out early on 24 February 2022. (Ukrainian social media)

to take positions in the Illich Steel and Iron Works, and – together with the 503rd Naval Infantry Battalion of the 36th Naval Infantry Brigade – the giant Azovmash factory.

As the weather began to improve, through 26 and 27 February, Su-34s of the VKS bombed Mariupol airport again, while Su-25s began flying air strikes in support of ground troops advancing from the east. The 8th CAA managed to breach the Ukrainian frontline and, late in the morning of 27 February, captured Domske, south of Volnovakha, while the 58th CAA secured Berdyansk and then rushed in an eastern direction. Two days later, the elements of the two armies took the villages of Shirokino and Stary Krym, thus effectively cutting off Mariupol from the rest of Ukraine.

The Siege[1]

In the face of stubborn Ukrainian resistance, the advance of the I AK and the 8th CAA then slowed down to a creep. North of Mariupol, separatist units from the self-declared Donetsk People's Republic and the Russians took six days of bitter fighting to secure Volnovakha, and the VKS lost at least one Su-25, and a helicopter sent to recover its downed pilot, in the process. The 150th Motor Rifle Division VSRF took two days to secure Sartana, and then another to move from there to the coast of the Azov Sea. Only then, around 3 March, did the Russians, accompanied by separatists, push into the eastern districts of Mariupol for the first time, forcing the 3,000-strong garrison back into the industrial zone along the city's coastline. Over the following days, the Russians continued bombing Mariupol from the air and the ground: their strikes on Ukrainian positions within the industrial facilities were less effective, but those targeting apartments and other buildings around the city often had terrible consequences. Around 14.50hrs on 9 March 2022, the VKS bombed Maternity Hospital No. 3. Situated in the western part of the city, 400 metres from the nearest military object and 2,000 metres from the historic Donets Academic Regional Drama Theatre (colloquially 'Drama Theatre'), this also functioned as a children's hospital and was painted in bright yellow and green. Underneath the hospital was a large underground bunker where dozens of civilians had taken shelter. Two Russian bombs actually hit the ground nearby, but their detonations were powerful enough to demolish the entire hospital:

A Russian 9A310M-1 TELAR and a transloader of a mobile Russian Buk M2 SAM system on the streets of Berdyansk early on 27 February 2022. (Ukrainian social media)

A still from a video taken by a Ukrainian UAV (probably the locally designed and manufactured PD-2), showing precise hits by the ZSU artillery on Russian vehicles in the village of Stary Krym on 1 March 2022. With the VSRF reaching this place, it cut off the land connection between Mariupol and the rest of the country: thus began the siege of the city where an estimated 450,000 civilians were either unable or unwilling to leave. (ZSU)

at least four people were killed and 16 injured.[2] Immediately after, the Russians also bombed Pryzovsky State Technical University, where hundreds of people were sheltering in basement classrooms and corridors, killing at least two civilians.

While the Russian Ministry of Defence was explaining away this affair by stating that the 'facility was used by the Azov Regiment' – who Moscow declared to be 'Nazis' – the 8th and the 58th CAA, and the VKS continued subjecting Mariupol to relentless bombardment. On 11 March, Su-25s and Su-34s targeted multiple Ukrainian positions around the city, but most of their bombs missed, usually smashing apartment buildings full of civilians instead: on 12 March, they also bombed out the building of the International Committee of the Red Cross and the Ukrainian Branch of the Red Cross. Amid continuous fighting, a temporary ceasefire agreement of 14 March enabled tens of thousands of people to escape Mariupol in cars or on foot for Zaporizhzhya: a voyage of about 30 kilometres to safety often took two or even three days as they passed dozens of Russian checkpoints. The ceasefire was barely over when, on 16 March 2022, the Russians committed an entire series of atrocities. First, fighter-bombers of the VKS completely destroyed Military Hospital 555, forcing the surviving personnel to move their patients to the Illich Steel and Iron Works, although this was under constant shelling. Next, the Russians targeted the 61st Mobile Military Hospital of the ZSU encamped near the Neptune indoor swimming pool, in northern Mariupol, forcing surviving personnel to evacuate injured troops to the Azovstal plant. Finally, just before midday, the VKS then bombed out the historic Drama Theatre: located in the city centre, this was used as a shelter for over 1,000 civilians and clearly marked in large white characters 'Deti' (Children) on the pavement in front and at the rear of the building. The building was completely demolished by several bombs dropped by at least a pair of Su-25s. The official explanation from the Ministry of Defence in Moscow was that 'it was blown up by the Ukrainian Azov Battalion.'

A still from a video showing one of a pair of Russian Su-25s streaking low along the Kalmius River to bomb central Mariupol in early March 2022. (Ukrainian social media)

Above: A residential building in Mytropolytska Street in Mariupol, demolished by a VKS air strike on 11 March 2022. This attack massacred at least 17 civilians taking shelter in the cellar of the building. (via HRW)

Right: The back yard and the building of Maternity Hospital No. 3, wrecked by a VKS air strike on 9 March 2022. (Ukrainian Ministry of Defence)

Ukrainian Resupply Effort[3]

Knowing it could not relieve the garrison, but aware that its survival was of crucial importance through tying down up to a dozen Russian BTGs with around 20,000 troops that could cause bigger problems somewhere else, the High Command ZSU, the Special Operations Forces Command (SSO), and the SBU then took several decisions. On one hand, they permitted female military personnel to leave Mariupol on their own: several dozen managed to do so dressed as civilians. On the other, they decided to attempt resupplying the garrison with the use of Mi-8 helicopters while evacuating the injured. For this purpose, a forward operating base was established somewhere south-east of the Velyka Novosilka area in southern Zaporizhzhya. Moreover, several landing sites were selected in Mariupol, and arranged with the commander of the besieged garrison, Colonel Denis Prokopenko: these sites had to be alternated between flights as whenever they detected activity by Ukrainian helicopters over this part of the city, the Russians began shelling them.

Supported by diversion operations by PSZSU Su-24MRs – which also monitored the work of the Russian air defence systems deployed in the Mariupol area – the first such operation was launched late on 21 March, when two Mi-8s of the 16th Brigade Army Aviation took off from the FOB: flying extremely low and fast (up to 220km/h), they proceeded towards the coast of the Azov Sea before turning east to reach Mariupol. Both helicopters managed to deliver ammunition, medical supplies and StarLink terminals, while flying out about 20 injured troops. On 25 March, the Ukrainians repeated the exercise: while Su-24MRs distracted the attention of the Russian air defences away two Mi-8s flew extremely low over nearly 120km to reach Mariupol. While successfully delivering their cargo, during the return flight one Mi-8 was hit by a MANPAD – which failed to detonate after embedding itself in the right engine. After shutting

the engine off, the crew managed to nurse their helicopter on single engine for one hour and eight minutes over 100km back to the FOB.

Late on 27 March, the Ukrainians initiated their third resupply operation: this included two Mi-8s operating as single-ships, and a Su-24MR of the 7th Brigade piloted by Colonel Yevhen Bulatsyk: as now usual, the latter had both the task of detecting the positions of the Russian air defences and distracting them away from the vulnerable helicopters. By this time, the Russians had become aware of the Ukrainian resupply effort: they deployed additional ground units – including Pantsyr SAMs – along the routes taken by the helicopters on previous occasions. Therefore, the Ukrainians began this mission with the ZSU artillery shelling all the known enemy SAM positions within its range. While this enabled the Mi-8s to penetrate the enemy-controlled territory without problems, once they reached the coast of the Azov Sea, the crews found themselves confronted with an unexpected threat: several warships of the Black Sea Fleet. The latter took the Mi-8s under fire, forcing them into evasive manoeuvring. Indeed, on 28 March both the separatists of the self-declared Donets People's Republic and the Ministry of Defence in Moscow claimed one Mi-8 as 'shot down over the Sea of Azov as it headed to Mariupol to evacuate the commanders of the Azov nationalist battalion'. Actually, all the helicopters involved in this mission returned safely.[4]

The fifth resupply operation was undertaken during the night of 31 March to 1 April: it included four Mi-8s from the 16th Brigade that picked up a bigger group of injured from a point on the coast in Mariupol about two kilometres south-west of the demolished Drama

Theatre. While three helicopters returned safely, the fourth – Bort 64, crewed by Major Yury Tymus and Lieutenants Ivan Vakhovsky and Denis Badika – was shot down in the Rybatskoye area, with the loss of 15 out of 17 crewmembers and passengers.[5]

The sixth resupply operation took place during the night from 4 to 5 April: it not only delivered ammunition and medical supplies, but also another group of veteran Azov troops. Because the Mi-8s involved were now encountering fierce Russian resistance and their crews left all the armament on the ground in order to increase the weight of other cargo they could carry, the decision was taken to henceforth escort them with Mi-24 gunships. The seventh mission was undertaken by crews from 12th Brigade Army Aviation and successful in reaching Mariupol once again. Indeed, both Mi-8s were well on their way back when tragedy struck. Just six kilometres short of the Ukrainian-controlled territory, the lead helicopter – crewed by Major Borys Horoshko, Captain Bohdan Chichura, and Lieutenant Vyacheslav Sindiy – was hit by a Russian missile. It caught fire and made a hard landing within occupied territory. As far

as is known, Horoshko and Sindiy were killed in the crash, together with most of the wounded carried by their helicopter, but Chichura's fate remains unknown. The other Mi-8 returned back to the FOB, where a decision was taken to launch a search and rescue operation. A third helicopter – crewed by Lieutenant Colonel Vyacheslav Voronyi, captains Bogdan Lyshenko and Dmitry Burlakov – thus launched and crossed the Russian lines in a search for signs of life from the downed crew. Eventually, while trying to approach the crash site, it too was shot down by a Russian MANPAD. This time, only Captain Burlakov survived: he was captured by the Russians and subsequently released in a prisoner exchange.[6]

After this loss of two helicopters, it became obvious that such missions were much too dangerous and all further attempts to keep the garrison resupplied were abandoned. Overall, the operation resulted in 18 successful flights to Mariupol, in which a total of 30 tons of cargo and 72 reinforcement soldiers were delivered. Sixteen of those missions ended with the safe return of everybody on board: these evacuated 64 injured. Three Ukrainian Mi-8s were written off.

A still from a video showing two Mi-8s from the 18th Brigade Ukrainian Army Aviation, on arrival at the Azovstal compound, during one of the early resupply operations for the garrison of Mariupol. Eventually, the ZSU managed to insert 72 reinforcement troops into the city in this fashion, together with 30 tons of ammunition and medical equipment. (Yulia Paievska)

A piece of wreckage of the Ukrainian Mi-8 shot down while returning from the resupply run to Mariupol during the night of 31 March to 1 April 2022. (Russian social media)

The End of Mariupol[7]

Meanwhile, through mid-March 2022, the Russians managed to widen the isolation of the garrison through advances north of the city. Despite continuous and vicious bombardment from the air and the ground, their initial assaults into Mariupol were costly – primarily because of massive problems with communications and coordination of their troops. On 15 March, a BTG of the 150th Motor Rifle Division was mauled while attacking along the M14 highway from the east and the Livoberezhnyi District in the south-east, while a day later a BTG of the 810th Naval Infantry Brigade – reinforced by separatist-operated T-64 main battle tanks – was ambushed by elements of the 36th Naval Infantry Brigade while attacking the city centre from the north. In reaction, the command of 8th CAA strengthened the artillery barrage and air strikes and ordered the VKS to start striking the city with Tu-22M3 bombers. As well as carpet bombing with their usual loads of eight FAB-500M-62 bombs, the Russian airmen also deployed a number of ancient but massive 3,000kg FAB-3000M-46 bombs. With the help of this onslaught, the Russians tightened the siege and by 18 March fierce house-to-house fighting was raging in the north-west, north, and east of the city. Two days later, during continuous air strikes, the Russians bombed out the G12 Art School, where hundreds of women, children, and elderly were sheltering.[8]

Through 22 and 23 March, assaults by three Russian BTGs forced the defenders – who claimed a Su-25 of the VKS as shot down during this time – to withdraw from the airport, while a pincer attack by the 810th Naval Infantry Brigade from the north and a BTG of the 150th Motor Rifle Division from the east destroyed part of the 501st Naval Infantry Battalion in the Kalmiusky District, killing up to 30 troops and forcing the rest of this unit to withdraw to the Illich Steel and Iron Works and Azovmash. On 24 and 31 March 2022, the Russian forces managed to enter the centre of Mariupol again, to seize the Church of the Intercession of the Mother of God and to cut off the 36th Brigade's three battalions from the Azov Regiment entrenched in the giant Azovstal works. The position of the garrison now became critical, as all the remaining vehicles were either damaged or non-operational due to the lack of fuel and ammunition, while remaining stocks of water, medicine, and anti-tank weapons were rapidly dwindling. The command of the garrison thus either recommended all the units to launch a joint operation and break out, or to entrench in the Azovstal compound, but the commander of the 36th, Colonel Volodymir Baraniuk, refused. Indeed, without informing his troops or the rest of the garrison, late on 3 April 2022, the commander of the 501st Battalion, Lieutenant Colonel Mykola Biriukov, negotiated the surrender of his unit: early the next morning, 267 Ukrainians went into captivity. On 10 April 2022, Baraniuk decided to break out: the group he led drove out on several armoured personnel carriers but was quickly surrounded by the Russians and captured. Late on 11 April 2022, the remaining 186 troops of the 1st Battalion and the 503rd Battalion, 36th Naval Infantry Brigade, made a dash for Azovstal: although suffering some losses in the process, they joined the Azov Regiment and other units defending the compound. Another group of 76 Ukrainian naval infantry soldiers escaped by infiltrating the Russian lines while it was snowing, early on the morning of 12 April: after a march of more than 100 kilometres behind enemy lines, seven survivors reached ZSU positions in the Zolota Nyva area, during the night of 3–4 May. The garrison held out until 16 May: it surrendered the following morning after receiving official permission from Kyiv to do so. The completely savaged Mariupol thus became only the second major urban centre in Ukraine captured by the Russians in the course of their invasion.

A Tu-22M bomber of the VKS seen over Mariupol sometime in March 2022. (Ukrainian social media)

A 3,000kg FAB-3000M-46 bomb on its transport trolley, shortly before being loading into the bomb bay of a Tu-22M3 bomber (visible in the background, left). (Russian social media)

A Tu-22M3 bomber of the 52nd Guards Heavy Bomber Aviation Regiment seen during an exercise in early February. The unit is known to have flown over 50 combat sorties against targets in the Mariupol area. (Russian Ministry of Defence)

Table 12: VKS and VM-FA Units arrayed around south-east and southern Ukraine, 20–24 February 2022

4th Air and Air Defence Army (attached to OSK South, HQ Rostov-on-Don)
Roughly 200 to 220 combat jet aircraft in total, Naval Aviation included but reinforcement excluded, as those might have come from within OSK South

51st Air Defence Division	Novocherkask	3 regiments (1 S-300PM regiment, 1 Buk regiment, 1 S-400 regiment with Pantsyr S1)
31st Air Defence Division	Crimea	3 regiments (1 radar, 1 with S-400, 1 with S-300PM-2)
30th Transport Aviation Regiment	Rostov-on-Don	miscellaneous transport aircraft
3624th Aviation Base	Erebuni (Armenia)	1 squadron Su-30SM, 1 squadron miscellaneous helicopters
16th Army Aviation Brigade	Zernograd	2 squadrons Mi-8, 2 squadrons Mi-28N and Mi-35M, detachment Mi-26
55th Helicopter Aviation Regiment	Korenovsk	1 squadron Mi-8, 1 squadron Mi-28N and Mi-35M, 1 squadron Ka-52
487th Helicopter Aviation Regiment	Budyonnovsk	1 squadron Mi-8, 2 squadrons Mi-24, Mi-28N and Mi-35M, 1 squadron Forpost UAV
1st Composite Aviation Division	Krymsk	
3rd Composite Aviation Regiment	Krymsk	2 squadrons Su-27M3, a few Su-30M2
31st Composite Aviation Regiment	Millerovo	2 squadrons Su-30SM; reinforced with Su-25, Mi-8, Mi-24 and Ka-52 by 20 February 2022
3661st Aviation Base	Mozdok	detachment of helicopters and Forpost UAV
559th Bomber Aviation Regiment	Morozovsk	3 squadrons Su-34; reinforced with 9 Su-24 by 20 February 2022
4th Composite Aviation Division	Marinovka	
11th Composite Aviation Regiment	Marinovka	2 squadrons Su-24M, 1 squadron Su-24MR
368th Attack Aviation Regiment	Budyonnovsk	2 squadrons Su-25SM
960th Attack Aviation Regiment	Primorsko-Akhtarsk	2 squadrons Su-25SM; reinforced with 10 Su-34 by 20 February 2022
27th Composite Aviation Division	Belbek (Crimea)	
37th Composite Aviation Regiment	Gvardeyskoye (Crimea)	1 squadron Su-24M, 1 squadron Su-25SM; reinforced with 14 Su-25 by 20 February 2022
38th Fighter Aviation Regiment	Belbek	2 squadrons Su-27P/SM; possible Su-30SM; reinforced with 13 Su-34 by 20 February 2022
39th Helicopter Aviation Regiment	Dzhankoy	1 squadron Ka-52, 1 squadron Mi-8, 1 squadron Mi-28N and Mi-35M
Naval Aviation of the Black Sea Fleet (attached to the OSK South, HQ Sevastopol)		
43rd Composite Naval Aviation Regiment	Saki	1 squadron Su-24M and Su-24MR, 1 squadron Su-30SM
318th Composite Aviation Regiment	Kacha	1 squadron An-26 and Mi-8, 1 squadron Ka-27 and Ka-29, detachments Be-12 and Forpost UAV

8
SOUTHERN UKRAINE

While it can be said that the Russian assaults on Kyiv, Sumy and Kharkiv were spoiled by unrealistic expectations and Putin's obsession with security, and that the mechanised onslaughts on Chernihiv, Konotop, Sumy, and Kharkiv collapsed because of poor planning, corrupt and incompetent generals, and poorly trained troops, none of this was true for the Russian invasion of southern Ukraine. Indeed, the advances of the 49th and 58th Combined Arms Armies (49th and 58th CAA) into southern Kherson and southern Zaporizhzhya not only caught the Ukrainians completely by surprise, but rapidly developed from operational-level activities into undertakings with potentially strategic consequences.

Fall of Melitopol

Positioned east of Dnipro, in the southern Zaporizhzhya Oblast, Melitopol is a major road and railway hub, and an economic centre with a population of about 150,000. The town became the primary target of the land component of the 58th CAA, commanded by Major General Mikhail Zusko – which, as mentioned in previous chapter, also had the task of quickly completing the seizure of Mariupol through an amphibious landing in the Berdyansk area, pending a possible similar operation in the Odesa area.

Nominally in preparation for possible action along the Line of Control, a detachment of six Su-25s from the 299th Tactical Aviation Brigade, PSZSU, was forward deployed to the military side of the local airport when the Russian attack came. Alerted only minutes before the onslaught began, at 05.00hrs in the morning, all six aircraft rolled to the runway – only to watch as a Russian missile hit an Il-76 transport nearby (registration UR-76683). As they continued to taxi, the attack pilots found their way blocked by another Il-76MD transport – which then stopped and began loading cargo. As the Russian missiles continued exploding around them, the Su-25s taxied under one of the wings of the transport to reach the runway and take-off. Even once the formation had reached its destination – probably Kryvyi Rih AB – the ordeal was not over: they found the runway blocked by vehicles, and were then fired upon. For a minute, the pilots thought the place had been captured by the Russians: only then did the ground crews recognise them as friendly, ceased fire and began removing the obstacles from the runway. While the Su-25s thus came away, one An-26 transport and four helicopters of the 25th Brigade, PSZU, are known to have survived as well: however, they were all captured by the Russians – just like a total of 21 stored Il-76MD transport aircraft. None had been airworthy for years, but at least one (registration UR-76699) was undergoing overhauls.[1]

Indeed, dramatic scenes would develop in and around Melitopol IAP for the rest of the day. A battalion of the 208th Anti-Aircraft Missile Brigade (equipped with S-300PS and S-300PT SAMs) was on an exercise outside the city and was caught unaware: although not attacked by any missiles, it was subsequently caught by rapidly advancing units of the 58th CAA and cut off: only a few of its officers and other ranks managed to escape with the help of local friends.[2]

A battalion of the 223rd Anti-Aircraft Missile Regiment was deployed in the Askania-Nova area, in the southern Kherson Oblast for an exercise when the Russians invaded. Indeed, during the night of 23 to 24 February, the unit was in the process of exercising redeployment from one position to another and for most of the first day of the war, it was busy rapidly withdrawing. Even then, the

enemy advanced so quickly that its column several times had to stop and search for alternative routes because it was overtaken by the enemy. Eventually, the 223rd managed to not only evacuate all of its equipment, but also to escape – by driving north instead of west. Once in Zaporizhzhya, it was split and reorganised: operational SAM systems were sent to protect ZSU units along the emerging frontline, while those not operational were loaded on a train and sent west for repairs.[3]

After securing Melitopol, late on 25 February, Zusko sent several of his BTGs in the direction of Bilozerka and Tokmak, while in his rear the VKS began converting the local airport into its forward air base. Thanks to local informants, the Ukrainians learned of this and three days later targeted Melitopol IAP with Tochka ballistic missiles equipped with 9N123K submunition warheads. Around the same time, the ZSU also fired two Tochkas at Taganrog AB in south-western Russia. One was shot down by Russian air defences, but the other reportedly damaged an Il-76 transport.

The lightning advance of the 58th CAA on Melitopol was well-supported by attack helicopters of the VKS. Amongst others, these destroyed the only Ukrainian attempt to launch a local counterattack in that area. This Ka-52 equipped with B-8M rocket pods and drop tanks was caught on video while passing low over the city. (Ukrainian social media)

The Race to Dnipro

The Russian all-out invasion of southern Ukraine west of the Dnipro River began in exactly the same fashion as everywhere else: with multiple strikes by ballistic and cruise missiles. Known examples included the port of Ochakiv and the nearby base of the 73rd Special Operations Centre, SSO, which were hit by several missiles, at least one of which caused a large fire. Also hit was a military base in Podlisk, where one missile is known to have killed seven. At Kulbakyne Air Base – a combined civilian and military facility outside Mykolaiv and the home-base of the 299th Tactical Aviation Brigade – the alert was sounded at 04.00hrs. Two BRDM-2 armoured cars and several ZU-23 guns were rapidly brought into position, while pilots and ground personnel of the 299th Brigade were scrambled into action according to pre-war planning. Correspondingly, all the Su-25s still at this base were dispersed to several FOBs, followed by ground personnel that loaded the necessary equipment into trucks. The subsequent Russian missile strike destroyed two stored Su-25s (Borts 12 and 42, neither flown for over a decade), and two operational L-39 training jets. Chornobaivka Air Base – the military side of Kherson International Airport, and one of the FOBs of the 299th Brigade – is known to have been hit by at least two missiles that morning.[4]

Hard on the heels of the missiles came the major Russian coup in this part of Ukraine: at dawn, a formation of about 30 Mi-8, Mi-24, Mi-35M, and Mi-28 helicopters deployed a BTG of the 7th VDV Division commanded by Colonel Denis Shishov, and two detachments of Spetsnaz operators, on either end of the giant Kakhovka dam and the Nova Kakhovka Hydroelectric Power Plant on the Dnipro River. With there being no ZSU troops anywhere nearby, this strategically important facility was secured in a matter of minutes.

A Ka-52 of the 55th Regiment passing low over the town of Armiansk, early on 24 February 2022. Combat air patrols by such attack helicopters not only proceeded the spearheads of the 49th CAA during its advance on Kherson and Mykolaiv, but also supported a heliborne landing of the VDV in the Nova Khakovka area. (Ukrainian social media)

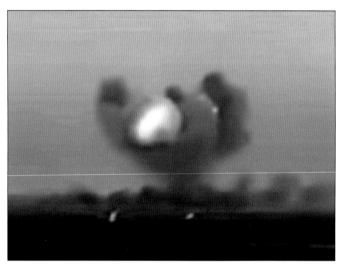

The detonation of one of the Russian missiles that hit Kulbakyne AB early on 24 February 2022. (Ukrainian social media)

Indeed, once there, the Russian airborne assault troops experienced no problems in holding out until the arrival of the first of two BTGs of the 126th Coastal Defence Brigade, which advanced over 100 kilometres from their starting point in Armiansk and then via Chaplynka along the T2202 highway within fewer than 12 hours. With this, the 49th Combined Arms Army (49th CAA), commanded by Major General Yakov Rezantsev had a bridgehead on the western side of the Dnipro. Rezantsev's task was challenging: he was not only to secure Kakhovka and Nova Kakhovka – and with them the entry to the North Crimean Canal, the principal sweet water source for Crimea – but also to raid further west, to Mykolaiv with its huge port, cross the Buh River and reach Odesa. Rezantsev was in a hurry also because his 49th CAA had to make the way free for the troops of XXII AK. Commanded by Major General Denis Lyamin, this corps

was advancing along the M17 highway, with the task of crossing the Dnipro, and securing Kherson. As far as is known, although multiple units of the ZSU were garrisoned in their way, mainly in Nova Kakhovka and Radensk, only one had mobilised and deployed in Donbas. A few battalions of the Ukrainian army and ground-based units of the PSZSU were on exercise in the southern Kherson Oblast, but not one was in a position to offer serious resistance.

Therefore, it was up to the PSZSU to be the first to react to the Russian advance on Nova Kakhovka. Early in the afternoon of 24 February, the 299th Brigade scrambled a pair of Su-25s to attack a Russian column underway in the Chorna Dolyna area. Leading the pair was Lieutenant Colonel Oleksandr Zhybrov. His wingman later recalled that they first attacked with bombs, before turning around to attack with unguided rockets. As Zhybrov's Number 2 was busy dodging a Russian missile, he noticed a flash to his right: bursting into a ball of flame the lead Su-25 crashed only 20 metres away from the Russian column. The body of Lieutenant Colonel Zhybrov was later found by the locals and buried nearby.[5]

The fin of the Su-25M1 '19', piloted by Lieutenant Colonel Zhybrov during his strike on the Russian column outside Chorna Dolina, on the afternoon of 24 February 2022. (Red Cross)

THE FATEFUL PMP BRIDGE

Based on experience from the Second World War, in the early 1950s, a group of Soviet Army engineers developed the PMP floating bridge as a means to quickly cross major water obstacles. The bridge consisted of numerous folding sections – or 'links' – each carried on the back of a truck. When released into the water, each would unfold to create a barge capable of carrying 20 tons, with a carriageway of 6.5m width. When connected, the links created a bridge: a complete PMP – or 'Pontoon Park' in the Russian military parlance – consisted of 32 folding sections, 12 bridging boats, and three shore pontoons. It could span 382 metres and had a capacity of 20 tons. Alternatively, if only a section of 227–268m was deployed, it could carry 90 or 60 tons, respectively. The standard within engineering units of the Soviet Army in the 1960s and 1970s was to have the bridge assembled in a matter of 30 minutes, regardless the width of the obstacle: the actual average time achieved during exercises was about 2–3 hours. However, in 1979, the 1257th Separate Pontoon-Bridge Battalion managed to span a section of the Elbe River in Czechoslovakia in a matter of 14 minutes.

The original PMP was superseded by the slightly improved PPS-85, and then the PP-91, but all variants used the same principle and very similar links and other parts with only minor modifications. Originally, major elements were mounted on KrAZ-214 trucks, and later on the KrAZ-255 and KamAZ 63501 trucks: these could bring them directly to the edge of a body of water, and then release them to unfold automatically.

As became clear only days later, whether by accident or design, during their air strike on the afternoon of 24 February 2022, Lieutenant Colonel Zhybrov and his wingman had demolished almost a complete column carrying a PMP floating bridge: a piece of equipment the 49th CAA badly needed if it was to cross the Buh River at a place of its choice – probably somewhere north of Mykolaiv – and continue for Odesa. However, with two Ukrainian Su-25s destroying most of the PMP park underway in Chorna Dolyna, Rezantsev was left with little choice but to find alternatives in the form of existing bridges. This is what led to the showdowns in Bashtanka and then in Voznesensk in particular.

Wreckage of KrAZ-255 trucks and sections of the PMP pontoon bridge hit by Lieutenant Colonel Zhybrov and his wingman outside Chorna Dolyna on the afternoon of 24 February 2024. As subsequent developments were to show, the loss of this equipment was to prove fatal for the outcome of 49th CAA's mission. (Red Cross)

The Race to Kherson

Not only the 49th CAA, but also the spearheads of the XX AK encountered little resistance – at least until they reached the area of Pishchanivka (about 120km from Armiansk), when a pair of Ukrainian Mi-24s (probably scrambled from Chornobaivka AB), attacked a column including MT-LB armoured personnel carriers and a battery of Tor M1 mobile SAMs, and destroyed a number of vehicles. Meanwhile, attack helicopters of the VKS were roaming the roads ahead and knocking out dozens of vehicles belonging to several ZSU units that were trying to reach the 10-kilometre-long Antonovski Bridge that spanned the Dnipro east of Kherson. Following a short clash with a Ukrainian reconnaissance company mounted on BRDM-2s, by the next morning the Russians had crossed the Antonovski Bridge and established their second bridgehead on the western side of the Dnipro, in the Antonivka

area. Amid the resulting chaos, a company of Ukrainian T-64s then followed them, early on 25 February, shooting up BMP-2s, several T-72s and other Russian vehicles while crossing the bridge, but losing four of their own vehicles in return. As far as is known, these were the last elements of the Ukrainian armed forces to cross this bridge. What was left of the ZSU units garrisoned in between Armiansk, the Antonovsky Bridge and Nova Kakhovka either quickly surrendered or scattered in all possible directions, attempting to evacuate and avoid capture, while coming under repeated strikes from Russian attack helicopters.

That said, the charge of the lonesome T-64 company over the Antonovsky Bridge proved its worth, because it stopped the XXII AK for more than 24 hours. Therefore, early on 25 February, Rezantsev swung his leading BTG – an element of the 7th VDV Division – in a southern direction and ordered it into advance along the M14 on Kherson. Much to the surprise of the Ukrainians, the unit in question not only bypassed Kherson but then drove for another 50 kilometres: late in the afternoon, it approached Kulbakyne AB, south of Mykolaiv. The home-base of the 299th Tactical Aviation Brigade, thus became the first active air base of the PSZSU to come under direct attack by the Russian ground forces. By then though, the Ukrainian defences had been strengthened through the troops of the 73rd Special Forces Centre, National Police, and Territorial Defence, and the assailants were quickly repelled.[6]

Due to the surprise and the breakdown of their strategic communications, the ZSU and the PSZSU were slow to react to this manoeuvre. Early on 26 February, Ukrainian ground troops attempted to counterattack the VDV at Nova Kakhovka. This action came too late because Shishov's troops were significantly reinforced and held out, although their commander was wounded in action.[7]

Around the same time, the 'Melitopol Detachment' of the 299th Brigade evacuated to Kryvyi Rih AB had received an order to attack another of the Russian units travelling along the road from Chaplynka to Nova Kakhovka. To its leader – Lieutenant Colonel Rostyslav Lazarenko – the target was described as 'large column' and 'escorted by Ka-52 helicopters'. Followed by his wingman, Alexander Shcherbakov, Lazarenko took a course down the road from Nova Kakhovka and found the target when almost out of fuel: a line of vehicles was parked around a petrol station and refuelling from several fuel bowsers. Any doubts the two Ukrainian pilots initially had about the nationality of the troops on the ground were forgotten as soon as the enemy opened fire at them with all means available. Losing the moment of surprise, Lazarenko led his wingman away from the scene, pretending the vicious anti-aircraft fire had scared them away. The two Su-25s continued south before, about 15 seconds later, turning around to attack. Ignoring at least one MANPAD fired in their direction, the two Ukrainians unleashed salvoes of S-8 80mm unguided rockets, causing massive explosions of several vehicles. These threw so much debris into the sky, that both Su-25s were damaged: Lazarenko's jet was then hit by another MANPAD, which knocked out one of the two hydraulics systems. The pilot returned to the FOB and landed safely, despite severe damage to the fin and wings of his jet: indeed, the damage proved so heavy that his Su-25 was irreparable. Even more tragic was the fact that Shcherbakov was no more: he was shot down and killed during this attack.

The Race to Mykolaiv

Rezantsev was too busy to be impressed by the courage of Ukrainian Su-25 pilots: meanwhile, he deployed a BTG of the 20th Guards Motor Rifle Division to secure Molodizhne, north-east of Kherson, and then ordered another one to follow the VDV along the M14 to Mykolaiv. By the morning of 27 February, this unit briefly probed the defences of Voskresenske and eastern Mykolaiv, before fanning out along the H11, H14, and P06 in a northern direction,

in a search for a free route: eventually, it found out that there was a Ukrainian position blocking the southern approach to Nova Odesa, but that the way around the H11 – in the direction of Bashtanka – was free. Meanwhile, another of Rezantsev's BTGs quickly overran Chornobaivka AB/Kherson IAP: this happened so quickly that about 20 stored helicopters of the 11th Brigade of the Ukrainian Army Aviation – including three Mi-2MSBs, two Mi-9s (a rare command post variant of the Mi-8 series), one Mi-8MT, two Mi-24Rs, and 12 Mi-24Ps (amongst them several examples that had served with the Ukrainian missions in Africa) – were captured intact.

A still from a video showing a missile hit on the Su-25 piloted by Lieutenant Colonel Rostyslav Lazarenko during the strike on a Russian column in the Chaplynka area, early on 26 February 2022. (Ukrainian social media)

A still from a video showing Su-30M1 Bort 30, piloted by Captain Aleksander Shcherbakov of the 'Melitopol Detachment', 299th Brigade, during the air strike on a Russian column south of Chaplynka. Notable is the weapons configuration, including a drop tank and two B-8M1 rocket pods under each wing. About a minute later, the jet was shot down by Russian air defences. (Ukrainian social media)

A rare Mi-9 (a command post variant of the Mi-8 series) (left) and a Mi-2MSB of the Ukrainian Army Aviation captured by the Russians at Chornobaivka AB/Kherson IAP. The VKS eventually towed away a few of the 20 Ukrainian helicopters that were stored there, but most were stripped of any useful parts and left where they were found. (Russian social media)

Not only did such a rapid advance of the 49th CAA take the ZSU completely by surprise, but the appearance of VDV and VSRF units at different spots 20, 55, and 75 kilometres west of the Dnipro spread chaos and insecurity amongst the Ukrainians: just three days into the war, the Russians had already bypassed Kherson, captured the local airport and then bypassed Mykolaiv too. Moreover, Rezantsev's logistic tail worked flawlessly and regardless of all the chaos along the highways from Armiansk and Chaplynka to the Antonovsky Bridge and Nova Kakhovka, and delays experienced by the XXII AK, it rapidly brought fuel and ammunition forward. On the contrary, the Southern Command ZSU was not only suffering from communication problems caused by cyberwarfare, and the chaos in its chain of command, but took time to mobilise and bring its units into position. Eventually, its only elements that were mobilised successfully and in time were parts of the 35th Naval Infantry Brigade, the 36th Naval Infantry Brigade, the 59th Motorised Brigade, and the 123rd Territorial Defence Brigade, which established a defence perimeter around Mykolaiv, along the H14 highway. On the contrary, the PSZSU still had rather poor situational awareness about what was going on in the Kherson area, while the diminutive Ukrainian Navy scuttled its flagship in the port of Mykolaiv, before deploying its TB.2 Bayraktar attack drones to attack the Russians at Chornobaivka AB/ Kherson IAP during the night of 26 to 27 February. Amongst others, these found a column of VSRF Buk mobile SAMs neatly parked along the runway and knocked out several with hits from MAM lightweight precision-guided munitions. Obviously, the air force was not informed about this development, because early on 27 February, it ordered a pair of Su-25s into another attack on VSRF columns moving in the direction of Nova Kakhovka. This time, the jet flown

by Lieutenant Andriy Maximov was shot down, but the pilot ejected in time and was captured by the Russians. Of course, this was the proverbial 'too little, too late': early on 28 February, Rezantsev's 49th CAA completed the isolation of Kherson, and then began probing into the western outskirts of the city: after bringing additional units into position, supported by an artillery barrage, on 1 March 2022, the 49th CAA – led by the 247th VDV Regiment – advanced deep into the city from the north and west, while the XXII AK moved in from the east. The next day the Kherson surrendered, becoming the only capital of any Ukrainian oblast captured by the Russians in this war.

Last Minute Reinforcement

On the Ukrainian side, it was only the realisation that the Russians might drive all the way to Odesa that prompted Kyiv into action. Early on 29 February 2022, the *GenStab* in Kyiv ordered a battalion of the 80th Airborne Assault Brigade from Lviv to Voznesensk in the Mykolaiv Oblast. Moving in a great hurry, the unit arrived without most of its heavy weapons. However, it brought with it a large number of FGM-148 Javelin anti-tank guided missiles and M72 light anti-tank weapons of US origin, and Polish-made PPZR Piorun MANPADs. One of the latest weapons systems of this kind, Javelin was a fire-and-forget missile with lock-on before launch and automatic guidance employing a top-attack profile, to strike the usually thinner top armour. The Piorun was a major upgrade of the Soviet-made 9K310 Igla-1 (ASCC/NATO reporting name 'SA-16 Gimlet'), with an improved seeker head and a proximity fuse, developed in the second half of 2010s. Like much similar Western-made light equipment, both systems were delivered to Ukraine only days – if not literally hours – before the 80th Airborne was sent to the Mykolaiv Oblast.

Indeed, this brigade arrived just in time, because next Rezantsev rushed a BTG each of the 20th Guards Motor Rifle Division and the 126th Coastal Defence Brigade, with a total of more than 30 tanks, 200 other vehicles, and 50 artillery pieces, from Mykolaiv towards the north. The first of these travelled along the H11 highway to reach Bashtanka on 1 March. The town was defended by local volunteers and parts of the 190th Battalion of the 123rd Territorial Defence, many of whom were armed with hunting rifles and Molotov cocktails only. However, due to low clouds and rain, the long Russian column received no support from attack helicopters. Therefore, the Ukrainians found it easy to set up an ambush: while the armoured elements of the two BTGs turned west before entering Bashtanka, the following column of a few BTR-80s and dozens of KamAZ 6x6 trucks and Ural-4320 tankers drew into the town: the Ukrainians destroyed scores of them and captured two BTR-80s and 28 enemy troops. When the Russians then deployed a few D-30 howitzers and BM-21 multiple rocket launchers to shell the town, these were silenced by another strike by two Su-25s from the 299th Brigade.[8]

Probably under pressure from Putin, Rezantsev was forced to ignore the Ukrainians in Bashtanka. Leaving them for follow-up troops from the XXII Corps, he ordered his two BTGs to traverse along field paths from H11 to H14 and then to P06

A still from a video geolocated to the runway of Kherson IAP, where Ukrainian TB.2s destroyed a number of vehicles of the Russian 56th VDV Regiment early on 27 February. Presumably, the UAV deployed its MAM lightweight PGMs. (ZSU)

in a western direction and press at maximum possible speed to Voznesensk. By the evening of 1 March, they reached the P06 north of Nova Odesa, and were thus well-positioned for an onslaught on the town that had three bridges over the Buh River, and the nearby air base, north of them. This attack began with a heliborne landing by VDV troops deployed from several Mi-8AMTShs onto a low height south of the town (and thus west of the Buh), while the BTGs of the 20th Guards Motor Rifle Division and the 126th Coastal Defence Brigade advanced along the P06 via Rakove from the south. However, the 80th Airborne and the 187th Battalion of the 123rd Territorial Defence Brigade had already been informed about the enemy approach and were in position and ready: the heliborne assault was tackled by a barrage by 123rd Brigade's artillery, which scattered the survivors. Moreover, the columns of Russian tanks, armoured personnel carriers and other vehicles were allowed to enter southern Voznesensk but then hit hard at short range. The result was another disaster in which the Russians lost over 100 killed, 30 out of 43 armoured fighting vehicles destroyed, and about 20 other vehicles captured.

A scene from the streets of Bashtanka, on 1 March 2022, where the determined resistance by the local population smashed the better part of a BTG of the 49th CAA, preventing the first Russian attempt to either reach Voznesensk from the east, or push in a northern direction and quickly seize Kryvyi Rih. (Rubryka.com)

Assaults on Kulbakyne and Mykolaiv

With hindsight, it is clear that Putin remained unmoved by the heavy losses of the 49th CAA: on the contrary, he continued pushing Shoygu, Gerasimov, and Rezantsev to not only effect a breakthrough at Voznesensk, but also to seize Mykolaiv. Considering the urgency, the geographic distances and resulting communication problems, and also how few troops he actually had on hand, it is unsurprising that the commander of the 49th CAA took three days to organise both operations and then conduct them in quick succession, one after the other. In the south, he regrouped his assets, deploying two BTGs of the 7th VDV and one of the 20th Guards Motor Rifle Division for renewed assaults on Mykolaiv. His first target was logical: Kulbakyne AB, east of Mykolaiv. This was assaulted at 11.30hrs on 4 March 2022 by about 400 VDV troops supported by BMD armoured fighting vehicles. With the Ukrainian defenders having only two BRDM-2s and a few ZU-23 automatic twin 23mm guns in terms of heavy weapons, the Russians found it rather easy to penetrate the defence perimeter, destroy most of the Ukrainian vehicles and secure the runway. However, they failed to secure the fortified western side of the base. Moreover, the commander of the 299th Brigade PSZSU, Colonel Serhiy Samoilov, requested help – and the powerful garrison of Mykolaiv was in a position to react positively. A battalion of the 35th Naval Infantry Brigade was rushed in this direction, supported by several main battle tanks. Counterattacking around 13.20hrs, this quickly drove the Russians out and several kilometres away from the base.[9]

The other two of Rezantsev's BTGs in the Mykolaiv area assaulted a day later. One consisted of the 247th VDV Regiment, which was tasked with the seizure of Mykolaiv IAP: initially, the Russian airborne assault troops secured most of the airport, but when the Ukrainians deployed their naval infantry supported by artillery, main battle tanks, and advanced US-made light weapons, the 247th suffered heavy losses and, late on 6 March, was forced to withdraw. According to a social media post by one of the survivors, in two days of fighting for Mykolaiv IAP, the regiment lost 76 officers and other ranks killed (including its commander, Colonel Konstantin Zizevsky), while another 140 were wounded. Similarly, an attempt by a BTG of the 20th Guards Motor Rifle Division to drive into the centre of Mykolaiv on 5 March ended in yet another fiasco. The Russians reacted in their now usual fashion: having failed to secure the city, they subjected it to a vicious artillery barrage, including several volleys from BM-27 Uragan multiple rocket launchers deploying cluster munitions.

Taken early on 2 March 2022, this still from a video shows one of the Mi-8AMTSh involved in the assault on Voznesensk. (Ukrainian social media)

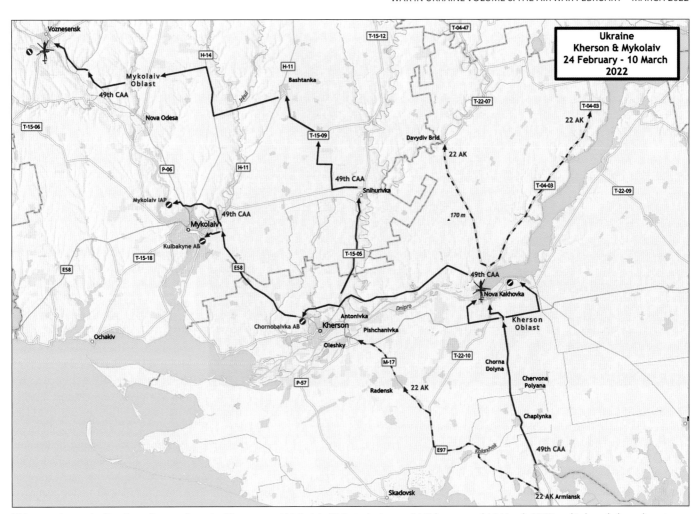

This map shows the Russian advances into the Kherson and Mykolaiv Oblasts, between 24 February and 10 March 2022 and is largely based on a captured Russian map. Full lines denote the march routes of the 49th CAA, dotted lines those of the XX AK. Notably, by 10 March, the 49th CAA had its headquarters set up in Nova Kakhovka, while the headquarters of the XX AK was established at Chornobaivka AB. (Map by Tom Cooper)

Special forces operators of the 73rd Centre SSO seen on the roof of Mykolaiv Airport, about to fire an ATGM at the assaulting Russian VDV, on 4 March 2022. (Ukrainian social media)

A view of the area outside Kulbakyne AB, late in the afternoon of 4 April 2022. Clearly visible are multiple fires, marking VDV vehicles knocked out when ambushed while assaulting this crucial facility. (Ukrainian social media)

The Second Battle of Voznesensk

The other prong of Rezantsev's final push was to again try to secure Voznesensk. Exactly why this operation was undertaken remains unclear: not only everybody in the headquarters of the 49th CAA, but especially everybody in Ministry of Defence and the *GenStab* in Moscow must have known that: the Ukrainians had blown up all the three bridges the Russians wanted to secure; due to earlier strikes by Su-25s on its engineering units, the 49th CAA had no pontoon bridges to replace them; and that Voznesensk was now defended by a crack unit of the Ukrainian army.

Above all, the top brains of the *GenStab* must have known that there was no point in reinforcing failure. The conclusion to be drawn is that it must have been Putin who overruled everybody – and that both Shoygu and Gerasimov let him do so. Therefore, early on 5 March a large formation of helicopters from the 39th Helicopter Regiment took off from Chornobaivka AB, with the aim of deploying a BTG of the 7th VDV Division in the Voznesensk area. This assault was supported by one A-50, one Il-20M airborne command post, two Mi-8MTPRI electronic warfare helicopters, and several pairs of Su-30SMs and Su-25s. However, while all of this was now usual, the planning for this action was obviously very poor: instead of following a circuitous route, so as to confuse the opponent (as when assaulting Antonov IAP outside Hostomel, or during the first attack on Voznesensk), on 5 March the Russians went straight in. Their helicopters flew north along the P06 highway.

Unknown to the Russians, the 80th Airborne had meanwhile secured several forward positions in the villages of Troitske and Yastrubynove, north of Nova Odesa, and deployed at least two MANPAD teams there equipped with Pioruns. Therefore, as soon as the low-flying Russian helicopters appeared from the south, they found themselves confronted by weapons their Vitebsk L370 directional infrared countermeasures systems were unable to match. The first section of the Russian formation included a Mi-24VM and Mi-35M each, followed by two Mi-8AMTShs. The Mi-24V was piloted by Lieutenant Colonel Yuri Orichak, commander of one of the squadrons of the 39th Regiment: his helicopter – the Mi-24VM registration RF-13017 – was shot down first and the crew

killed. Flying the Mi-35M Bort 22 (registration RF-13017), Lieutenant Eldar Faridovich Timushev never had a chance to figure out what happened to his formation leader before his helicopter was hit by another Piorun and crashed. The same befell the two Mi-8AMTShs that followed: the Bort 58 (registration RF-91165) was hit by a MANPAD and crashed directly outside Troitske, killing all five on board. The last Mi-8AMTSh (probably the example with registration RF-91164) is known to have been crewed by Captain Andrius Kyatvirtis and lieutenants German Zakharov and Dmitry Taranets: all three were killed. With Ukrainian MANPAD operators in Troitske having spent most of their ready-to-use rounds, the second Russian formation managed to reach Rakove before it ran into a similar ambush: there, the Mi-24P Bort 24 (registration RF-94966) was felled by two MANPADs, and crashed, killing the crew. The rest of the helicopter formation beat a hasty retreat.

As several Russian fighter-bombers appeared to strike Ukrainian positions in support of the heliborne assault and were then diverted to search for and support the downed crews, they came within range of Ukrainian MANPADs as well. Major Sergey Volynets was killed when his Su-25 of the 368th Attack Aviation Regiment was hit and then crashed south of Nova Odesa. Moreover, two Su-30SMs of the 43rd Composite Naval Aviation Regiment were hit as well. One, Bort 45 (registration RF-33787), managed to distance before crashing in a field outside Shchaslyve, 45 kilometres west of Mykolaiv, and its crew – consisting of Major Alexey Golovensky and Captain Andrey Kozlov – was captured. The crew of the other – consisting of Lieutenant Colonel A. N. Khasanov and Captain Vasily Valentinovich Gorgulenke – was killed.

Despite such heavy losses of the VKS and embarked VDV troops, the ground component – involving a BTG each from the 20th Guards Motor Rifle Division and the 126th Coastal Defence Brigade – attacked with vigour. After three days of bitter fighting, on 9 March it managed to grind itself all the way into Voznesensk again. However, by then, the Russians were facing impossible odds: due to losses, both of their BTGs were in tatters, and because the Ukrainians retained control over Bashtanka, their supply columns could not reach them and they were short of ammunition. With no reinforcements in sight, it took only a counterattack of the 80th Airborne launched on 13 March to quickly enthuse the Russians into abandoning the town and withdrawing for more than 50 kilometres south-east of it. With this, the 49th CAA's advance on Odesa was checked once and forever.

A Mi-8AMTSh of the 39th Helicopter Regiment: this was the most advanced assault/attack version of this venerable type in service in 2022. (Russian Ministry of Defence)

Wreckage of the Mi-24P Bort 24, registration RF-94966, found outside Rakove, south of Voznesensk, on 6 March 2022. It was one of five helicopters and three fighter-bombers shot down in a matter of minutes by Piorun MANPADs of the 80th Airborne Assault Brigade, ZSU. (Ukrainian social media)

The smouldering wreckage of Su-30SM Bort 45 (registration RF-33787) of the 43rd Composite Naval Aviation Regiment, found in a field outside Shchaslyve on 5 March 2022. The two crewmembers – Major Golovensky and Captain Kozlov – were captured nearby. (Ukrainian social media)

Chornobaivka under Pressure

As if a failed heliborne assault and heavy losses of the 39th Helicopter Aviation Regiment from 5 March were not enough, late that evening, the ZSU plastered Chornobaivka AB with an artillery barrage, in which it claimed the destruction of 30 Russian helicopters. This was certainly an exaggeration, because as much as the VKS already had a sizeable contingent deployed there, no evidence surfaced confirming the destruction of as many machines. That said, by this time Rezantsev's 49th CAA was in tatters: not only badly overstretched but suffering losses and facing odds that made not only an advance on Odesa impossible but prevented it even from continuing to besiege Mykolaiv. Therefore – and although at 05.15hrs on the morning of 7 March, a Russian missile hit the barracks of the 79th Airborne Assault Brigade in Mykolaiv, killing 10 Ukrainian soldiers and wounding 19 – the 49th CAA began retreating towards Kherson. By 11 March, it was 15–20 kilometres east of Mykolaiv when hit by the first of several counterattacks by the 28th Mechanised and the 59th Motorised brigades, which drove the Russians out of Prybuzke, Ukrainka, Luch, Posad-Pokrovske, and Stepova Dolyna over the following four days. Moreover, late on 11 March, ZSU artillery shelled Chornobaivka AB/Kherson IAP again: this time, a video captured by a Ukrainian TB.2 confirmed the destruction of at least six or seven Russian helicopters. The VKS attempted to strike back, and its Su-34s are known to have bombed not only Kulbakyne and Voznesensk in retaliation, but they also did their best to strike targets in the Odesa area. However, Ukrainian air defences were now in much better condition than at the start of the invasion. When two Su-34s of the 559th Bomber Aviation Regiment bombed a school in Zelenyi Hay, outside Mykolaiv, on 13 March, killing seven, one of them – Bort 35 (registration RF-95010) – was hit by a SAM and crashed while limping back in the direction of Kherson.

Two days later, on 15 March, the Ukrainians unleashed their third artillery barrage upon Chornobaivka AB and this time definitely caused massive losses to the 39th Helicopter Aviation Regiment, VKS. Subsequently released videos and satellite photographs confirmed the destruction of at least nine helicopters – including two Ka-52s, one Mi-28, and six Mi-8s and Mi-24s – while during the following days the Russians are known to have towed away a total of four badly damaged Mi-28s, two Mi-8s, three Mi-24s, and two Ka-52s.

A still from a video showing one of four Mi-28s damaged during Ukrainian artillery barrages on Chornobaivka AB being towed by a truck in the direction of Kherson. (Ukrainian social media)

XXII Army Korps and Kryvyi Rih

While assaults by the hard-pushing – and hard-pressed – 49th CAA on Bashtanka, Voznesensk, and Mykolaiv thus ended with a series of bloody disasters and a withdrawal, behind it the XXII Army Corps secured Kherson before turning north. What happened next is hard to explain because there are no Russian accounts available: the only conclusion currently possible is based on the deduction that the following operation was another one planned and conducted 'against the rules' – indeed, against the very basics of Russian military doctrine – and thus, probably, on Putin's personal initiative. Instead of following in the wake of the 49th CAA along the T1505 road to Snihurivka and then further north on the next actual Russian aim – Kryvyi Rih – Major General Lyamin dispersed his effort into three columns. Arguably, the westernmost one did follow the 49th CAA, but it spent days securing bridges over the Inhulets River. This operation also attracted most of the Ukrainian attention and the PSZSU reacted by tasking the 7th Brigade with targeting the Russian column in question. Correspondingly, between 1 and 4 March, Ukrainian Su-24Ms are known to have bombed columns of the XXII AK near Snihurivka, Davydiv Brid and Bila Krynytsia on the Inhulets. Indeed, a pair of Su-24MRs equipped with FAB-500M-62 bombs hit a battalion of 18 precious MSTA-S self-propelled 152mm howitzers as it was approaching Davydiv Brid and destroyed a number of vehicles. The column was then finished off by a pair each of Ukrainian Mi-8s, Mi-24s, and Su-25s.[10]

Meanwhile, Lyamin's two other columns marched from Kherson to Nova Kakhovka and then along the T2207 in the direction of Davydiv Brid, and on the T0403 in direction of Nikopol. The latter column is known to have also attracted some Ukrainian attention and was attacked by a pair of Su-24Ms while underway in the Mylove area. While these Ukrainian air strikes were relatively successful and the involved aircraft and helicopters came away without any losses, another one resulted in yet another tragedy. On 6 March 2022, two Mi-8s of the 18th Brigade Army Aviation tasked with striking Russian units advancing along the T1505 in the direction of Bashtanka were both shot down and their crews – consisting of Major Konstantin Zebnytsky, Major Ihor Turevich and a third, unknown crewmember, and Captain Vladislav Horban, Captain Ihor Ivanovich Pazich, and Captain Sergei Bondarenko – were killed.

Whether due to their own incompetence, communications or logistics-related problems, or whatever other reason, Lyamin launched the assault on Kryvyi Rih from the Arkhanhelske area only on 11 March 2022. This was supported by a missile strike on the local air base, which caused quite some damage to the facilities, including the local fuel dump. However, this left the ZSU troops defending the city unimpressed and, when the XXII AK then pushed forward, it ran into several ambushes and suffered heavy losses. Realising that the enemy was well-entrenched, well-armed, and ready to fight, under repeated air strikes of the PSZSU's fighter-bombers and helicopters, and with the battered 49th CAA under heavy pressure and falling back towards Kherson in his deep flank, Lyamin was left with no choice but to withdraw. His units fell back to the Mala Shestirnya area, around 50 kilometres south of Kryvyi Rih. The only positive achievement the XXII AK was able to report in these days was the downing of a Su-24 of the 7th Brigade in the Belyaevka area (Berislav District), on 12 March 2022. The crew, comprising Lieutenant Colonel Valery Oskhalo and Major Roman Chehun, was killed.

In turn, the VKS continued to suffer losses to Ukrainian MANPADs: on the same day, while supporting ground troops sent to mop-up scattered Ukrainian forces in the Oleshky area, it lost

A Mi-24MV damaged by shrapnel from Ukrainian artillery at Chornobaivka on 22 March 2022. (Russian social media)

two helicopters. A Mi-35Ms was shot down outside this town and its crew killed. The Ka-52 Bort 74 (registration RF-13409) fared only slightly better: it remained airborne for a while after being hit by a MANPAD but then crashed, badly injuring the pilot, Captain Andrey Lyulkin, and killing his gunner.

For the rest of the month of March, both the 49th CAA and the XXII AK were preoccupied with withdrawing into positions favourable for defence and fortifying these. Meanwhile, the headquarters of the Southern OSK was busy trying to keep the Ukrainians under pressure with ballistic and cruise missile strikes.

On 18 March 2022, two Kalibr cruise missiles launched by warships of the Black Sea Fleet hit the barracks of the 36th Naval Infantry Brigade in Mykolaiv, killing at least 10 and wounding more than 50 troops. A day later, two cruise missiles hit Martynivske – a disused air base from Soviet times, reactivated as a FOB for the PSZSU, about 90km north-west of Mykolaiv – and the Ministry of Defence in Moscow claimed the destruction of two Ukrainian Su-24s.

Unknown to everybody involved was that the times of rapid Russian advances and manoeuvring warfare deep into Ukraine were over.

The wreckage of one of two Mi-8s of the 18th Brigade shot down by Russian air defences in the Bashtanka district on 6 March 2022. (Ukrainian social media)

BIBLIOGRAPHY

Beehner, L., *Analyzing the Russian Way of War; Evidence from the 2008 Conflict with Georgia* (West Point, Modern War Institute, 2018)

Benedek W., Bilkova V., Sassoli M., *Report on Violations of International Humanitarian and Human Rights Law, War Crimes, and Crimes Against Humanity committed in Ukraine since 24 February 2022* (OSCE, 13 April 2022)

Boyd, A., *The Soviet Air Force since 1918* (London: Macdonald and Jane's Ltd., 1977)

Butowski, P., *Flashpoint Russia; Russia's Air Power: Capabilities and Structure* (Wien: Harpia Publishing, 2019)

Chung, W., J., *War in Ukraine, Volume 4: Main Battle Tanks of Russia and Ukraine, 2014–2015; Post-Soviet Ukrainian MBTs and Combat Experience* (Warwick: Helion & Company, 2023)

Chung, W., J., *War in Ukraine, Volume 5: Main Battle Tanks of Russia and Ukraine, 2014–2015; Soviet Legacy and Post-Soviet Russian MBTs* (Warwick: Helion & Company, 2023)

Collins, L., 'In 2014, the "decrepit" Ukrainian army hit the refresh button. Eight years later, it's paying off', *The Conversation* (online), 8 March 2022

Cooper, T., *Moscow's Game of Poker: Russian Military Intervention in Syria, 2015–2017* (Warwick: Helion & Company, 2018)

Cooper, T., Fontanellaz, A., Crowther, E., Sipos, M., *War in Ukraine, Volume 2: Russian Invasion, February 2022* (Warwick: Helion & Company, 2023)

Crowther, E., *War in Ukraine, Volume 1: Armed Formations of the Donetsk People's Republic, 2014–2022* (Warwick: Helion & Company, 2022)

Crowther, E., *War in Ukraine, Volume 3: Armed Formations of the Luhansk People's Republic, 2014–2022* (Warwick: Helion & Company, 2023)

Dabrowski, K., *Defending Rodinu, Volume 1: Build-up and Operational History of the Soviet Air Defence Force, 1945–1960* (Warwick: Helion & Company, 2022)

Dabrowski, K., *Defending Rodinu, Volume 2: Development and Operational History of the Soviet Air Defence Force, 1961–1991* (Warwick: Helion & Company, 2023)

Defense Intelligence Agency, *Russian Military Power; Building a Military to support Great Power Aspirations* (DIA, 2017)

Elfving, J., *An Assessment of the Russian Airborne Troops and their Role on Tomorrow's Battlefield* (Washington D.C., The Jamestown Foundation, 2021)

Facon, I., *La nouvelle armée russe* (Paris, L'Observatoire franco-russe, 2021)

Fiore, N. J., 'Defeating the Russian Battalion Tactical Group', *Armour*, No. CXXVIII, Spring 2017

Francois, D., *Operation Danube: Soviet and Warsaw Pact Intervention in Czechoslovakia, 1968* (Warwick: Helion & Company, 2020)

Grau, L. W. & Bartles, C. K., *The Russian Way of War; Force Structure, Tactics, and Modernization of the Russian Ground Forces* (Fort Leavenworth, Foreign Military Studies Office, 2017).

Grau, L. W. & Bartles, C. K., 'Getting to Know the Russian Battalion Tactical Group', *The Royal United Services Institute* (online), 14 April 2022

Gressel, G., 'Waves of Ambition: Russia's Military Build-up in Crimea and the Black Sea' (European Council on Foreign Relations, 2021)

Gunston, B. & Spick, M., *Modern Air Combat: The Aircraft, Tactics and Weapons employed in Aerial Warfare Today* (London: Salamander Books Ltd., 1983)

Gunston, B. & Spick, M., *Modern Fighting Helicopters* (London: Salamander Books Ltd., 1986)

Harris, C., Kagan F. W., *Russia's Military Posture: Ground Forces Order of Battle* (Washington, Institute for the Study of War, 2018)

Holcomb, F., *The Order of Battle of the Ukrainian Armed Forces: A key component in European Security* (Washington, Institute for the Study of War, 2016)

Lambeth, B. S., *Russia's Air Power in Crisis* (Washington D.C.: Smithsonian Institution, 1999)

McDermott, R., N., Bartless, C., K., *The Russian Military Decision-Making Process & Automated Command and Control* (German Institute for Defence and Strategic Studies, October 2020)

Milyukov, I., *The Soviet War in Afghanistan, 1979–1989* (Warwick: Helion & Company, 2023)

Ministry of Defence of Ukraine, *White Book 2013*; The Armed Forces of Ukraine (Kyiv, 2014)

Ministry of Defence of Ukraine, *White Book 2014*; The Armed Forces of Ukraine (Kyiv, 2015)

Ministry of Defence of Ukraine, *White Book 2015*; The Armed Forces of Ukraine (Kyiv, 2016)

Ministry of Defence of Ukraine, *White Book 2016*; The Armed Forces of Ukraine (Kyiv, 2017)

Ministry of Defence of Ukraine, *White Book 2017*; The Armed Forces of Ukraine (Kyiv, 2018)

Ministry of Defence of Ukraine, *White Book 2019–2020*; The Armed Forces of Ukraine (Kyiv, 2021)

Mladenov, A., 'Tough Days for Ukraine's military Helicopter Community', *Kiakaha Medias*, 23 August 2020

Muzyka, K., *Russian Forces in the Western Military District* (Arlington, CNA, 2021)

Sandler, E., *Battle For Grozny, Volume 1: Prelude and the Way to the City, 1994* (Warwick: Helion & Company, 2023)

Zhirokhov, M., *Airwar in Ukraine, February-May 2022* (Kyiv: Vizitochka, 2023)

Zhirokhov, M., *Hot Skies over Ukraine: Aerial Warfare, June-December 2022* (Kyiv: Vizitochka, 2023)

Zhirokhov, M., *Fire in the Sky: Airwar over Ukraine, January-August 2023* (Kyiv: Vizitochka, 2023)

Zhirokhov, M., *Sukhoi Su-24 in Service* (in Ukrainian) (Chernihiv: Knizhni Bal, 2023)

Zhirokhov, M.., *Sukhoi Su-25 Frogfoot* (in Ukrainian) (Chernihiv: Knizhni Bal, 2023)

Zhirokhov, M., *Su-27 Guardians of the Ukrrainian Sky* (in Ukrainian) (Chernihiv: Knizhni Bal, 2023)

Chapter 1

1. Bary G Royden, *Tolkachev, A Worthy Successor to Penkovsky: An Exceptional Espionage Operation*, CIA Center for the Study of Intelligence, Studies in Intelligence Vol 47, No. 3, 14 April 2007.
2. Unless stated otherwise, based on Dr Eugene Kogan, 'Under the Cloak of the OAK', *Military Technology*, 4/2007 & Dr. Eugene Kogan, 'Restructuring the Russian Aerospace Industry', *Military Technology*, 8/2009
3. Unless stated otherwise, based on V. J. (veteran VVS/VKS officer), interviews, 02/2022 & 03/2022; L. M. (veteran VVS/VKS officer), interviews, 02/2022, 03/2022, 08/2022, 01/2023; I. D. (veteran PVO/VKS officer), interviews, 01/2022, 02/2022, 03/2022, 09/2023.
4. Alexander Mladenov, 'Reforming a Formidable Foe', *AirForces Monthly*, 9/2010 & Alexander Mladenov, 'Back on the Beat', *AirForces Monthly*, 4/2012.
5. Even some top Russian military commanders have publicly concluded that what the Russian defence sector was delivering to them in the 2010s was not only below Western quality standards but below those of the People's Republic of China, while also much more expensive. For example, while commenting on the production of the T-14 Armata main battle tank, Chief-of-Staff Ground Forces, Colonel General Posnikov observed, 'It would be easier for us to buy three Leopards (German-made main battle tank) with this money', see Dr Gary K Busch, 'The Delusion of Russian Power', *ocnus.net*, 25 November 2016.
6. For details see Roger N McDermott and Charles K Bartles, *The Russian Military Decision-Making Process & Automated Command and Control*, German Institute for Defence and Strategic Studies, October 2020.
7. V. J. (veteran VVS/VKS officer), interviews, 02/2022 & 03/2022.
8. V. J. (veteran VVS/VKS officer), interview, 04/2024.
9. 'How Kyiv fended off a Russian missile Blitz in May', *The Economist*, 13 June 2023. Notably, as in the case of Kh-555 and Kh-101 cruise missiles, Kinzhals also experienced a number of malfunctions. For example, on 14 September 2022, one crashed about 200km northeast of Stavropol, in the northern Caucasus.
10. According to the Russian Ministry of Defence's release from 29 June 2021, the first eight Su-34Ms were handed over to the 21st Composite Aviation Regiment, to replace old Su-24MRs.
11. Unless stated otherwise, this content is based on zakupki.gov.ru (published in November 2015 and retrieved on 6 Mar 2019), 'Single Day of Acceptance of military Products, 24.03.2017', foto-i-mir-ru, 24 March 2017;
12. Circular Error Probable (CEP) being the area around the target within which 50 percent of missiles could be expected to land.
13. Additionally, the Ministry of Defence in Moscow planned to add to the Black Sea Fleet a total of six Project 22800 Karakurt-class corvettes that have vertical launch cells compatible with the 3M54 by 2030. However, as of 2022, none of these was in service.
14. Sam Cranny-Evans and Dr Sidharth Kaushal, 'The Iskander-M and Iskander-K: A Technical Profile', *RUSI.org*, 8 August 2022.

Chapter 2

1. 'Ukraine's Air Force rebuilds amid War', *KyivPost*, 15 March 2019.
2. Vladyslav Nazarkevych, 'Ukraine Pilot on Combat Duty and Russian Missile Attacks', *ArmyInform.com.ua*, 11 December 2023.
3. Unless stated otherwise, based on Zhirokhov, *Sukhoi Su-25*.
4. In the 2000s, Artem did develop the Gran short-range, infrared homing air-to-air missile, but this never entered series production.
5. Illia Ponomarenko, 'Jet Pilots leave Ukraine's Air Force en masse, threatening Security', Kyiv Post, 31 July 2021.

Chapter 3

1. Christian Vasquez and Elias Groll, 'Satellite Hack on Eve of Ukraine War was a coordinated, multi-pronged Assault', *Cyberscoop.com*, 10 August 2023.
2. PSZSU, 'Thanks to modern Aircraft and Western Technology, 2023 could be a Turning Point in Ukraine's War with the Global Aggressor' (in Ukrainian), *Facebook.com*, 8 April 2023.

3. Vladislav Nazarkevich, 'Ukrainian Armed Forces Officer tells about combat work of Radio Technical Troops' (in Ukrainian), ArmyInform.com.ua, 30 November 2022.
4. PSZSU, 'Hero of Ukraine, Captain Andriy Herus' (in Ukrainian), *Facebook.com*, 23 February 2023.
5. Vladyslav Nazarkevych, 'Ukraine Pilot on Combat Duty and Russian Missile Attacks', *ArmyInform.com.ua*, 11 December 2023.
6. Oleksiy Trigub, 'Since 24 February, the Air Force's Radio Technical Troops have detected over 240,000 Aerial Targets' (in Ukrainian), *ArmyInform.com.ua*, 30 November 2022.
7. PSZSU, 'Sergeant Serhii Churaiev, Anti-Aircraft Gunner' (in Ukrainian), *Facebook.com*, 18 November 2022.
8. PSZSU, 'Hero of Ukraine, Serhiy Poberezhets' (in Ukrainian), *Facebook.com*, 25 October 2022.
9. Natalia Zadvernyak, 'Andry's Unit destroyed 6 Enemy Aircraft, 8 Helicopters, 4 Cruise Missiles, and Dozens of UAVs', *ArmyInform.com.ua*, 25 November 2022.
10. PSZSU, 'Hero of Ukraine, Volodymyr Vesnin of Bukyvet', *Facebook.com*, 3 January 2023.
11. In both Prague in 1968 and Kabul in 1979, small advance parties landed in civilian aircraft and secured the airport facilities before the main force followed-on in larger fixed-wing aircraft.
12. Vladyslav Demyanenko & Oksana Uretiy, 'How an Anti-Aircraft Gunner with MANPADs destroyed a Racist Helicopter over the Kyiv Sea' (in Ukrainian), *ArmyInform.com.ua*, 21 December 2022.
13. Violetta Orlova, 'Died in a fierce Air Battle' (in Ukrainian), *Unian.ua*, 4 September 2022.
14. 'Pilots Major Viktor Dudin and Senior Lieutenant Ivan Porepelkin' (in Russian), Russian MOD, 19 March 2022; 'Major Dudin became the first Pilot to receive the Title of Hero of Russia for his exploits in "Operation Z"', *life.ru*, 20 March 2022 & 'Sizov Ilya Andreyevich' (in Russian), warheroes.ru, 4 August 2022. On the contrary, unofficial Russian sources (V. J., veteran VKS officer, interview, 02/2022), reported that Dudin claimed one Su-27 on 26 February, one Buk SAM system on 28 February, and two Su-27s on 1 March 2022.
15. Elena Pocelueva, 'Heroes Z: Denis Litvinov', Kontingent.press, 27 May 2022.
16. Elena Pocelueva, 'Heroes Z: Ivan Boldyrev', kontingent.press, 14 April 2022.
17. Unless stated otherwise, based on V. J., (veteran VKS officer), interviews, 02/2022, 03/2022, & 02/2024.
18. Oleksii Trygub, 'The Air Force has withstood and is effectively destroying the Occupiers' (in Ukrainian), *ArmyInform.com.ua*, 25 February 2023; 'Sizov Ilya Andreyevich' (in Russian), warheroes.ru, 4 August 2022. An alternative version indicates that Kolomiets was shot down while evacuating an L-39 from Ozerne AB.
19. V. J. (veteran VKS officer), interviews, 02/2024.
20. 'A Feat on the First Day of the War' (in Ukrainian), *Strakon.City*, 26 February 2024.
21. Based on PSZSU release, Facebook.com, 26 February 2022; AP, 'The latest on the Russia-Ukraine Crisis', 26 February 2022', and press releases by mayor of Vasylkiv, Natalya Balasinovich. General Zaluzhny claimed an Il-76 shot down over Vasylkiv via his Telegram account early on 26 February, and this claim was repeated by the Associated Press. Both claims for shoot-downs of Il-76s were repeated by 'Juice' (MiG-29 pilot of the PSZSU) in an interview with Thomas Newdick, published as 'Ukrainian MiG-29 Pilot's Front-Line Account of the Air War against Russia', *The War Zone/twz.com*, 2 April 2022. The Pentagon 'confirmed' the downing of two Il-76s on 26 February 2022, while Colonel Alexander Vladimirovich Mostovoy was subsequently decorated for courage for his feats of that night. That said, even as of spring 2024, and contrary to their usual practice, the Ukrainians have never provided any kind of evidence for any of these intercepts or at least for a major Russian ground attack on Vasylkiv AB. This is extremely unusual because thousands of civilians in the Kyiv area were taking videos of whatever action, and especially the Russian troops, they could see, and then forwarding these to the civilian and military authorities. However, in this case, nothing similar appears to have happened.
22. S. P., (local eyewitness), interview provided on condition of anonymity, 04/2024.

Chapter 4

1. V. J., (veteran VKS officer), interviews, 03/2022.
2. 'In the Kyiv region, a downed Russian Su-34 was identified', Militarnyi/mil.in.ua, 18 April 2022.

3. Elena Pocuelueva, 'Heroes Z: Vladimir Polyakov', kontingent.press, 8 June 2022. According to the same source, over the following months the 297th went on to claim 14 additional kills.
4. Maxim Sreletsky, 'Heroes Z: Ivan Redkokashin', *kontingent.press*, 28 September 2023 & Elena Poceluevа, 'Heroes Z: Sergey Cherny', *kontingent-press*, 2 June 2022.
5. Unless stated otherwise, this sub-chapter is based on 'The Battle for Kyiv', *Radio Svoboda/YouTube.com*, 25 February 2023; President of Ukraine, 'The Fate of Ukraine and the Capital was decided in the Battles for the towns and villages of Kyiv Region', *president.ua*, March 2023 & Dan Rice, 'The Untold Story of the Battle for Kyiv', *Small Wars Journal*, 31 May 2022. Notably, throughout this battle – and contrary to the Russian expectations – the local population supported the ZSU by all means available: in addition to reporting the movements of the Russian troops early on, they helped by digging trenches, cooking food and feeding troops, and using their own cars and trucks to haul ammunition to forward positions and evacuate casualties.
6. Subsequent investigation by journalists of *Radio Free Europe* revealed that the 155th Naval Infantry Brigade alone suffered at least 30 officers and other ranks confirmed as killed in this battle, while the 331st VDV Regiment had at least 45 confirmed fatalities (see: Anna Myroniuk and Alexander Kherbet, 'Journalists identify 100 Russian soldiers killed trying to seize Kyiv last March', *The Kyiv Independent*, 7 March 2023). According to Zelensky, 118 Ukrainian soldiers were killed in the course of the Battle of Moshchun (see President of Ukraine, 'The Fate of Ukraine and the Capital was decided in the Battles for the towns and villages of Kyiv Region', *president.gov.ua*, March 2023).

Chapter 5

1. Amnesty International, 'Ukraine: Russian "Dumb Bomb" Air Strike killed Civilians in Chernihiv – new Investigation and Testimony'. 9 March 2022.
2. Yuriy Butusov, 'The Feat of the 91st Regiment of Operational Support', *Facebook.com*, 1 March 2022.
3. Vladyslav Nazarkevych, 'Ukraine Pilot on Combat Duty and Russian Missile Attacks', *ArmyInform.com.ua*, 11 December 2023.
4. 'Memorial to Military Pilot Volodymyr Sklyar', *Chernihiv.today*, 11 February 2023 & Memorial Platform, victims.memorial (entries for Oleg Gegechkori, Aleksandar Marinyak, and Ivan Bezzub).
5. Valentina Mereshchuk, 'In two Days, up to 80 Units of Enemy Equipment were destroyed in Chernihiv Oblast', lb.ua, 13 March 2022.

Chapter 6

1. Oleksiy Trigub, 'Since 24 February, the Air Force's Radio Technical Troops have detected over 240,000 Aerial Targets' (in Ukrainian), *ArmyInform.com.ua*, 30 November 2022.
2. Ukrainian Ministry of Justice, 'Resolved, in the Name of Ukraine' (in Ukrainian), Case No. 642/1618/22, *reyestr.court.gov.ua*, 8 December 2022.
3. Human Rights Watch, 'Ukraine: Cluster Munitions launched into Kharkiv Neighbourhoods', *hrw.org*, 4 March 2022 & Elsa Court, 'Man who aided Russian strikes on central Kharkiv sentenced to life in Prison', *The Kyiv Independent*, 13 November 2023.

Chapter 7

1. Based on Professors Wolfgang Benedek, Veronick Bilkova, and Marco Sassoli, *Report on Violations of International Humanitarian and Human Rights Law, War Crimes, and Crimes Against Humanity committed in Ukraine since 24 February 2022* (OSCE, 13 April 2022), p. 48 & Denys Volokha, 'The Helicopter skimmed the Treetops', Human Rights in Ukraine/khpg.org, 19 June 2022.
2. Professors Wolfgang Benedek, Veronick Bilkova, and Marco Sassoli, *Report on Violations of International Humanitarian and Human Rights Law, War Crimes, and Crimes Against Humanity committed in Ukraine since 24 February 2022* (OSCE, 13 April 2022), p. 46.
3. Unless stated otherwise, based on 'Video of Ukrainian Helicopter breakthrough to Azovstal shared online', *LB.ua*, 31 May 2022; Valius Venckunas, 'Ukrainian Pilots details daring Mi-8 Rescue Flight to Russian-occupied Mariupol', *Aerotime Hub/Aerotime. aero*, 7 June 2022; Roman Petrenko, 'Journalists discover number of Helicopters Ukraine lost during supply deliveries to Azovstal and how they were lost', *Ukrainska Pravda*, 9 June 2022; Denys Volokha, 'The Helicopter skimmed the Treetops', *Human Rights in Ukraine/khpg.org*, 19 June 2022; 'Ukraine's secret, deadly rescue Missions in the besieged City of Mariupol', *abc.net.au*, 22 June 2022.
4. 'Russia says Helicopter downed near Mariupol was headed to evacuate Azov Unit Leaders', TASS, 28 March 2022.
5. 'Ukrainian Mi-8 Helicopter shot down near Mariupol', *CCTV*, 1 April 2022. Eduard Basurin, Deputy Commander of the 'Donetsk People's Republic People's Militia' claimed the helicopter was shot down by a captured US-made FIM-92 Stinger MANPAD. According to him, this was a second Ukrainian helicopter shot down while involved in such operations (the first was claimed on 28 March), and out of 17 crewmembers and passengers, 'two gunmen survived' (see 'Ukrainian Helicopter flying to Mariupol was downed by captured Stinger – Basurin', *Donetsk News Agency/dan-news.ru*, 31 March 2022).
6. Notably, months later, the Russian Ministry of Defence decorated Senior Sergeant Andrey Lebedev for 'protecting Russian military personnel from enemy air attacks and shooting down an enemy Mi-8 helicopter' (see Elena Pocelueva, 'Heroes Z: Andrey Lebedev', kontingent.press, 9 August 2022). As usual, the feat in question was not dated, but Lebedev is known to have commanded a Pantsyr S1 SAM system, and it is possible that he was involved in the interception of the final, seventh Ukrainian attempt to resupply the garrison of Mariupol and evacuate the injured from there.
7. 'Disappearance of the 501st Naval Infantry Battalion: Unknown Circumstances of Captivity', *MediaInitiative/mipl.org.ua*, 25 April 2023 & Olha Kyrylenko, 'Escaping the besieged City by Foot: The untold Story of a Marine's Escape from Mariupol', *Ukrainska Pravda*, 4 August 2022.
8. According to Benedek et al (p. 36), by 22 March 2022, the OSCE has verified 74 Russian attacks on healthcare facilities in Ukraine. Amongst these were 46 hospitals, seven psycho-neurological facilities, and 21 other facilities – mainly in Mariupol, Ovruch, Volnovakha, Vuhledar, and Chernihiv.

Chapter 8

1. Oleksandr Shulman, 'The first Missiles hit the Russian convoy and detonated' (in Ukrainian), *ArmyInform.com.ua*, 29 March 2023.
2. 'How our Anti-Aircraft Warriors ground dozens of Enemy Targets' (in Ukrainian), *ArmyInform.com.ua*, 13 March 2023.
3. Vladislav Nazarkevich, 'They accounted for 34 destroyed Aerial Targets and 3 Enemy hits on their Buk' (in Ukrainian), *ArmyInform.com.ua*, 22 December 2022.
4. Oleksandr Shulman, 'How the Attempt to seize the Airfield in Mykolaiv at the beginning of the large-scale Invasion by Russia was foiled' (in Ukrainian), *ArmyInform.com.ua*, 10 April 2023 & Oleksandr Shulman, 'Our Su-25s take off to hit the Enemy in a matter of Minutes, and we haven't lost a single one of them to Missile Attacks yet', *ArmyInform.com.ua*, 23 March 2023.
5. Anna Myshyshyn, 'Father of Oleksandr Zhybrov, who died on 24 February: Do not write about his Heroism. This is the Job of a Military Pilot' (in Ukrainian), *kp.ua* (Korotko pro), 6 June 2022.
6. Oleksandr Shulman, 'How the Attempt to seize the Airfield in Mykolaiv at the beginning of the large-scale Invasion by Russia was foiled' (in Ukrainian), *ArmyInform.com.ua*, 10 April 2023 & Oleksandr Shulman, 'Our Su-25s take off to hit the Enemy in a matter of Minutes, and we haven't lost a single one of them to Missile Attacks yet', *ArmyInform.com.ua*, 23 March 2023.
7. Elena Pocelueva, 'Heroes Z: Denis Shishov', 12 April 2022.
8. 'Ukrainian Armed Forces destroyed a Column of Russian military moving from Mykolaiv to Bashtanka', rubryka.com, 1 March 2022; '28 Russian occupants were detained in Mykolaiv Region', frontnews.eu, 2 March 2022; 'The Story of Defence of Bashtanka Community, Mykolaiv Region', uacrisis.org, 19 March 2022. For known details on the First Battle of Voznesensk, see Volume 2, pp. 58–60.
9. Oleksandr Shulman, 'How the Attempt to seize the Airfield in Mykolaiv at the beginning of the large-scale Invasion by Russia was foiled' (in Ukrainian), *ArmyInform.com.ua*, 10 April 2023.
10. Vladyslav Nazarkevych, 'Ukraine Pilot on Combat Duty and Russian Missile Attacks', *ArmyInform.com.ua*, 11 December 2023.

ABOUT THE AUTHORS

Tom Cooper is an Austrian aerial warfare analyst and historian. Following a career in the worldwide transportation business – during which he established a network of contacts in the Middle East and Africa – he moved into narrow-focus analysis and writing on small, little-known air forces and conflicts, about which he has collected extensive archives. This has resulted in specialisation in such Middle Eastern air forces as of those of Egypt, Iran, Iraq, and Syria, and various African and Asian air forces. In addition to authoring and co-authoring more than 50 books – including an in-depth analysis of major Arab air forces during the wars with Israel in 1955-1973 – and over 1,000 articles, Cooper is a co-editor of Helion's @War book series.

Adrien Fontanellaz, from Switzerland, is a military history researcher and author. He is a member of the Scientific Committee of the Pully-based *Centre d'histoire et de prospective militaries* (Military History and Prospectives Centre), and regularly contributes to the *Revue Militaire Suisse* and various French military history magazines such as *Défence & Sécurité Internationale*.

Milos Sipos is a Slovakian military historian. While pursuing a career in law he has collected extensive documentation on interconnected political, industrial, human resources and military-related affairs in Iran, Iraq, and Syria. His core interest is a systematic approach to studies of their deep impacts upon combat efficiency and the general performance of local militaries. After more than 10 years of related work on the ACIG.info forum, he specialised in research about the Iraqi Air Force and the Syrian Air Force, and about losses of the Russian Aerospace Forces in Ukraine.